Hannah Arendt and Martin Heidegger

Hannah Arendt and Martin Heidegger

Philosophy, Modernity, and Education

Paulina Sosnowska

LEXINGTON BOOKS
Lanham • Boulder • New York • London

Published by Lexington Books
An imprint of The Rowman & Littlefield Publishing Group, Inc.
4501 Forbes Boulevard, Suite 200, Lanham, Maryland 20706
www.rowman.com

6 Tinworth Street, London SE11 5AL, United Kingdom

Originally published in Polish as *Arendt i Heidegger. Pedagogiczna obietnica filozofii*.
© Paulina Sosnowska and Towarzystwo Autorów i Wydawców Prac Naukowych UNIVERSITAS. English translation © 2019 by The Rowman & Littlefield Publishing Group, Inc.

All rights reserved. No part of this book may be reproduced in any form or by any electronic or mechanical means, including information storage and retrieval systems, without written permission from the publisher, except by a reviewer who may quote passages in a review.

British Library Cataloguing in Publication Information Available

The hardback edition of this book was previously catalogued by the Library of Congress as follows:

Library of Congress Cataloging-in-Publication Data Is Available

ISBN 978-1-4985-8241-4 (cloth)
ISBN 978-1-4985-8243-8 (pbk)
ISBN 978-1-4985-8242-1 (electronic)

Contents

Preface vii

Acknowledgments xv

PART I: PHILOSOPHICAL TRADITION AND EDUCATION   1

1   The *Paideia* of Plato's Cave 3

2   The German Idea of *Bildung* 29

3   Authenticity: The Pedagogical Promise of Heidegger 55

PART II: PHILOSOPHY AND EDUCATION AT A CROSSROADS   79

4   The Broken Thread of Tradition and Heidegger's Breaks 81

5   Reading Aristotle 109

6   Freedom and the World 131

PART III: THE PEDAGOGICAL PROMISE OF PHILOSOPHY   153

7   "The Educational Principle": The Human Condition and the Power of Precedence 155

8   The Promise of Thinking 185

Afterword 211

Bibliography 215

Index 225

About the Author 233

Preface

I.

On October 28, 1960, shortly after the publication of the German translation of *The Human Condition* (as *Vita activa*), completed by Hannah Arendt herself, she wrote to Martin Heidegger, interrupting his almost yearlong silence. In this letter she informed Heidegger that she had asked the publisher to send him a copy of the book, and commented: "You will see that the book does not contain a dedication. If things had ever worked out properly between us— and I mean *between*, that is, neither you nor me—I would have asked you if I might dedicate it to you; it came directly out of the first Freiburg days and hence owes practically everything to you in every respect. As things are, I did not think this was possible, but I wanted at least to mention the bare fact to you in one way or another."[1] The copy of this letter, found posthumously in Arendt's papers, also contains a verse, the text of the planned dedication, which succinctly reflects not only the biographical, but also the philosophical relationship between the two thinkers:

> *Re vita activa:*
> *The dedication of this book is omitted.*
> *How could I dedicate it to you,*
> *trusted one,*
> *whom I was faithful,*
> *and not faithful to,*
> *And both with love.*[2]

This declaration of loving faithfulness and unfaithfulness is, such is the thesis of this book, the key to understanding the tensions in the intellectual relations between Hannah Arendt and Martin Heidegger. This relationship has also been treated as the paradigm of a more universal problem: the question of the educational role of philosophy. The basic idea of my endeavor focuses on the philosophical relationship between Arendt and Heidegger and on its educational relevance. Arendt's philosophical answer to Heidegger's philosophy, seen in the wider context of the struggles of both thinkers with the philosophical tradition of the West, is relevant also in the context of the question of the educational sense of philosophy.

The philosophical relationship between the two thinkers was largely unilateral. The reasons for this state of affairs were basically of a non-philosophical nature: psychological, historical, and biographical. While Arendt's thought crystallized itself in a constant dispute with Heidegger, the latter mostly remained indifferent to her works and did not undertake a dialogue with them. Instead, he read the mature Arendt's writings as a "declaration of independence from central aspects of his philosophy."[3] He ignored *The Origins of Totalitarianism*, officially because the book was in English which he did not understand; *The Human Condition* he dismissed with a cool silence, which lasted five years. He was disturbed by the public regard for Arendt, for he wanted to have a muse and a disciple in her, and not a philosophical partner, even less a shrewd critic of his own philosophy. He wanted Arendt to continue to play the role he had assigned to her when she was a young student: "listen and try to *follow along*."[4] Arendt usually accepted this role, although later she was well aware of its inadequacy.[5]

Apart from this unilateralism, I believe that the clash of these two worlds, the world of thinking being and the world of thinking action created a tension, which can be interesting as a context for the question of the connections between philosophy and education. This belief is also one of the most important premises of this book.

II.

When we read Arendt, most of the time we can hear her silent struggle with Heidegger, hidden below the surface of the text. Nonetheless, finding the main motifs of this dialogue is not the simplest task. In the books and essays Arendt wrote with the intention of publication, references to Heidegger are scarce. If we do not take into consideration the last philosophical writings comprised in *The Life of the Mind*, we have basically two exceptions, functioning at the margins of their postwar history: *What Is Existential Philosophy?* (1946)[6] and *Martin Heidegger at Eighty* (1969).[7]

In *What Is Existential Philosophy?* Arendt compared the Heideggerian description of the human ways of being with Hobbesian realism and disavowed this description as functionalistic. Being-in-the-world is here equated with survival.⁸ Jaspers' philosophy "remains much more modern, whereby 'modern' means simply that it continues to provide direct impulses for contemporary philosophical thought."⁹ On the contrary, in the laudation for his eightieth birthday, Heidegger appears in a completely different light: not as a nihilistic epigone of Hobbes and Nietzsche, but as a true teacher through whom "thinking has come to life again," one who "made to speak the cultural treasures of the past, believed to be dead."¹⁰

But, alas, these two "exoteric" texts, where Arendt expressly addresses Heidegger, cannot be taken into consideration without reservations. The text on existential philosophy was written thirteen years after Arendt's flight from Germany, while she was still a stateless and displaced person (she received American citizenship only in 1951). Heidegger's controversy, which was just about to come out, reached her as a collection of appalling, though incomplete, pieces of information. We can faintly feel what was happening in Arendt's mind when we notice that the text was composed in the same year in which Arendt wrote to Jaspers: "I can't but regard Heidegger as a potential murderer,"¹¹ so it is difficult to consider this piece of writing a reliable account of her understanding of *Being and Time*. It is so evidently fueled by bitterness, the result of Heidegger's alliance with Nazism (the bitterness retreated just after their first post-war meeting in 1950), that it cannot be equated with Arendt's other writings, even less so seeing that she herself recoiled from it. In one of her letters she wrote: "I must warn you about my essay on existentialism, especially about the part on Heidegger, which is not just entirely inadequate, but in part simply false. Please just forget about it."¹²

The second text is, so to say, the exact opposite of the first one and because of this it has to be considered with the same reservations. *Martin Heidegger at Eighty* was a birthday present, a public homage to the old master and cannot be treated as a reliable source either. Therefore, both writings have been regarded here very carefully. As more reliable sources of knowledge about the factual intellectual tension between Arendt and Heidegger, I have taken (1) the writings published by Arendt, which rarely undertake an open dialogue with Heidegger (one of the more relevant exceptions is *Concern with Politics in Recent European Philosophical Thought*, 1954), but which I propose to read as the result of her constant struggle with his thought, foremostly of the 1920s; (2) the works completed toward the end of Arendt's life, where Arendt for the first time undertook an open critique of Heidegger's later thought; (3) the documents of the *Nachlass* of both thinkers, mostly correspondence and Arendt's *Denktagebuch* ("The Diary of Thought"), published only in 2002.

Although in this book I have tried to maintain a certain balance in description, the essential perspective is informed by Arendt's position. The reason is the asymmetry of this dialogue: The tension between Arendt and Heidegger is tangible in Arendt's work, while in Heidegger this struggle is practically nonexistent. Thus, the status of the chosen sources is also different: Heidegger's writings do not function in this book entirely self-sufficiently, for they have been selected either as factual fields of the discussion between the two thinkers (*Being and Time* is the most important source of this type), or as sources which enabled an outline of the fuller background of this discussion. Therefore, they have been chosen and analyzed according to these criteria. Hannah Arendt's oeuvre, instead, has been considered in a much more complex way, since it serves as the initial perspective of the analyses. Thus, my goal was to fairly reconstruct the meanderings of Arendt's thought without slavishly clinging to her premises and conclusions.

What on the level of intellectual biography can be presented as a feud between the master and student, full of tensions and not stripped of the taste of revolt on Arendt's part, when put in the wider context of the Western intellectual tradition, provides a conceptual framework for the relation between philosophy and education, which has been reflected in the structure of this book.

When we turn our attention to the *pedagogical* relation between the two philosophers, one problem is unavoidable: Many previous books undertaking the problem of the intellectual relationship between Arendt and Heidegger were written from a specifically American perspective, within which Heidegger's work (and German thought of the first half of the twentieth century in general) was assessed according to heterogeneous and anachronous criteria (such as pragmatism or "democratic thinking") and on the basis of a firm premise (that the thought of the fascist has to be fascistic from the very beginning and to the core). As a result, some interpreters were unable to fairly reckon with the Heideggerian role in Arendt's thought in an objective, neutral way. They accepted the false, in my opinion, assumption that the intellectual influence of Heidegger on Arendt could have been only harmful. Moreover, such authors have had a tendency to explain any theoretical difficulties, of which Arendt's thought is far from free, as a result of a spell cast by the magician of Messkirch.[13] From this perspective, Arendt appears as a more or less masked representative of "German exceptionalism" (a title additionally shared with Carl Schmitt, according to Wolin), anti-modernism (Wolin and Benhabib), the thesis of the decline of the West (Wolin), political existentialism (Wolin and Jay) and other sins of German *Bildung* and *Kultur*. Such an approach is responsible for misinterpretations of the complexity and profundity of Heidegger's influence and for obliviousness in seeing the authentic originality of Arendt's thought and presenting her intellectual achievement in a false light. Among the authors, who have undertaken attempts at decent and unbiased analysis of the work of both thinkers, are foremostly Jacques Taminiaux and Dana Richard Villa.[14]

Although this is not the main idea of this book, it is also a dialogue with these ways of reading the intellectual relationship between Arendt and Heidegger. I have attempted to describe both the Heideggerian motifs in Arendt's thought and Arendt's fundamental corrections of the basic Heideggerian premises in a way free from the a priori negative assessment of Heidegger's influence on Arendt. Contrarily, I raise the contention that apart from any allegations one can have against Heidegger as a human being and a thinker, his influence on Arendt was mostly positive. In combination with Arendt's genius, her intellectual independence, and other non-Heideggerian inspirations, this influence was the catalyst for the eruption of her truly original thought, going against the tide of both the typical tendencies of German intellectuals and the American mainstream. Arendt, when in contact with Heidegger, was not always completely honest, but in her above-cited unsent letter she was incisive: She was, indeed, faithful and unfaithful to Heidegger. Regardless of what Heidegger himself could wish in this matter, Arendt was not an obsequious and humble student, blindly following the teachings of the master. She was conscious of her intellectual debt, yet an original author and insightful critic of the Heideggerian intellectual heritage.

III.

Therefore, this book has been written on two levels: firstly, it is an interpretation of Arendt's thought in the context of Heidegger's philosophy. Secondly, such an interpretative axis serves as an ordering structure that enables a conceptual presentation of some aspects of the history of the relationship between philosophy and education, and to draw some conclusions from this history. In other words, the plane of the history of philosophy intersects with the plane of the philosophy of education. The idea of the book was to present the dispute between Arendt and Heidegger in a wider context. This means that the analyses of their works have had to be presented in a complex historical and cultural background.

The book contains three main parts: Part I, *Philosophical Tradition and Education,* is devoted to a description of the traditional relationship between philosophy and education in the dual context of Heidegger's and Arendt's struggles with the metaphysical tradition of the West. This relationship I capture as a promise given by philosophy to education, a promise reflected in concepts such as *paideia,* *Bildung,* and *authenticity,* and by searching how and to what extent this promise was fulfilled. In Part II, *Philosophy and Education at a Crossroads,* I have questioned the traditional relationship between philosophy and education and the classical promise of philosophy for education; this part is an interpretation of Arendt's thesis of the broken thread of tradition, put in the context of Heidegger's philosophy as well as his entanglement in Nazism. In this part I also undertake the problem of the Heidegger-originated limitations in Arendt's philosophy. Part III, *The Pedagogical Promise of Philosophy*, reopens the question of the relationship between philosophy, thinking, pedagogy, and education in times whose political and ethical framework is no longer designed by the continuity of tradition, but by the caesura of twentieth-century totalitarianism. Here arises a question of the educational role of thinking in post-metaphysical times.

NOTES

1. Hannah Arendt and Martin Heidegger, *Letters 1925–1975*, ed. Ursula Ludz, trans. Andrew Shields (New York: Harcourt, 2004). Hannah Arendt made a mistake here. It is about the first Marburg (not Freiburg) days, when as an 18-year-old student, she listened to Heidegger's lecture for the first time.
2. Arendt and Heidegger, *Letters*, 261.
3. Mark Lilla, *The Reckless Mind: Intellectuals in Politics* (New York: The New York Review of Books, 2001), 40.
4. Heidegger to Arendt, May 8, 1925. Arendt and Heidegger, *Letters*, 20.
5. In 1961 she wrote to Jaspers: "I know that he finds it intolerable that my name appears in public, that I write books, etc. All my life I've pulled the wool over his eyes, so to speak, always acted as if none of that existed and as if I couldn't count to three, unless it was the interpretation of his own works. Then he was always very pleased when it turned out that I could count to three and sometimes even to four," Hannah Arendt to Gertrud and Karl Jaspers, November 1, 1961. Hannah Arendt and Karl Jaspers, *Correspondence 1926–1969*, ed. Lotte Kohler and Hans Saner, trans. Robert and Rita Kimber (New York: A Harvest Book, 1992), 457.
6. Hannah Arendt, "What Is Existential Philosophy?" in Hannah Arendt, *Essays in Understanding 1930–1954. Formation, Exile and Totalitarianism* (New York: Schocken Books, 2005).
7. Hannah Arendt, "Martin Heidegger at Eighty," trans. Albert Hofstadter, *The New York Review of Books*, 17, no. 6 (1971).
8. See Arendt, "What Is Existential Philosophy?" 178–79.
9. Arendt, "What Is Existential Philosophy?" 182.
10. Arendt, "Martin Heidegger at Eighty," 50.
11. Hannah Arendt to Karl Jaspers, July 9, 1946. *Correspondence*, 48.
12. Arendt to Calvin Schraig, December 31, 1955, Archiv des HAZ, as quoted in Antonia Grunenberg, *Martin Heidegger and Hannah Arendt: History of a Love*, trans. Peg Birmingham, Kristina Lebedeva, and Elisabeth von Witzke Birmingham (Bloomington: Indiana University Press, 2017), 192. Schraig was a doctoral student of Paul Tillich, at that time writing his thesis on Heidegger, among others.

13. For instance, Richard Wolin, Martin Jay, to a lesser extent Seyla Benhabib or Michael Jones (see Michael T. Jones, "Heidegger the Fox: Hannah Arendt's Hidden Dialogue," *New German Critique*, 73 (1998): 164–92). References and discussion with the other three authors come later in this book.

14. And also, although their research was on a smaller scale, Richard Bernstein ("Provocation and Appropriation: Hannah Arendt's Response to Martin Heidegger," *Constellations*, 2, no. 4 (1997): 153–71) and Ernst Vollrath ("Hannah Arendt und Martin Heidegger," in *Heidegger und die praktische Philosophie*, ed. Annemarie Gethmann-Siefert and Otto Pöggeler (Frankfurt am Main: Suhrkamp, 1998), 357–72). See also L. P. Hinchmann and S. K. Hinchmann, "In Heidegger's Shadow: Hannah Arendt's Phenomenological Humanism," *The Review of Politics*, 2, no. 46 (1984): 183–211.

Acknowledgments

The presented book is a reformulation and translation of a book published in Polish as *Arendt i Heidegger. Pedagogiczna obietnica filozofii* ("Arendt and Heidegger: The Pedagogical Promise of Philosophy"). I am sincerely grateful to my colleague and friend, Professor Andrew Wiercinski, for all the support I received.

In the English version I have tried to present certain problems more clearly by simplifying the labyrinthine descriptions of German philosophy, where they were inessential for the whole structure. In their place I need to express my deep thankfulness to Professor Andrea Folkierska, who was a source of invaluable advice concerning the abridgments.

My goal was to achieve the clarity characteristic for philosophical works written in English. Insofar as this has been successful, it is owed to my friend Allan Neuvonen, who had the patience to minutely proofread the manuscript, before it was presented to professional editors.

Last, but not least, I need to thank the editors from Rowman & Littlefield (Lexington Books) for their hard work in preparing the book for publication, particularly Jana Hodges-Kluck and Trevor F. Crowell.

Part I

PHILOSOPHICAL TRADITION AND EDUCATION

Within the Western philosophical tradition, the positive relationship between philosophy and education seems seldom to have been undermined. The great philosophers were often the great pedagogues[1] as well, or, at least served as inspirations for them. The most important and compelling pedagogical concepts, describing the essence of education in relation to culture (*paideia*, *Bildung*), were at the same time philosophical concepts with immense cultural impact. On the other hand, concepts "purely" philosophical, like the Heideggerian *Entschlossenheit* ("resoluteness"), embodied a more or less explicit educational potential. Behind this relationship we can find a sort of philosophical promise for education. I will describe this promise in three most relevant episodes: the promise of Plato's *paideia* (chapter 1), the promise of the neohumanistic idea of *Bildung* (chapter 2), and that inscribed in the fundamental ontology of Martin Heidegger (chapter 3).

As we will see, the kinship between pedagogy and philosophy can be interpreted as an attempt to overcome the conflict between philosophy and politics, the abyss between thinking and acting. Philosophy seems to have conquered pedagogy and harnessed it at the service of mollifying this conflict in manifold ways, the common denominator being the promise of freedom from non-philosophically conceived politics.

NOTE

1. The terms "pedagogical" and "pedagogy" are used to indicate a theoretical approach to education.

Chapter 1

The *Paideia* of Plato's Cave

Plato's philosophy is, at each of its many levels, a philosophy of education. A reconstruction of Plato's *paideia* in all its complexity would require critical, philological, and historical analysis of the written legacy of Plato. This requirement was to some extent fulfilled by Werner Jeager in his monumental work on the Greek *paideia*.[1] The great merit of Jaeger was his interpretation of *paideia* as the central theme of Plato's thought. That is why he, naturally, put at the center of his consideration the programmatic pedagogical work of Plato: *The Republic*. Jaeger not only resented ignoring the pedagogical aspect of this dialogue, but also legitimized education as the fundamental problem of *The Republic*, having recognized other themes of the dialogue as ancillary. According to his reading, it is not education that serves the idea of the ideal city, but the other way round. The political dimension is, so to say, a background for education. The structural identity of the city and the human soul enables a magnified display of *paideia* and at the same time the establishing of the fundamental sense of politics in education: "an artificial society in which all interests are subordinated to the education of the moral and intellectual personality, which is *paideia*."[2] Thus, *paideia* becomes the pivotal interpretative category, reaching far beyond pedagogy: It becomes the essential prism for understanding Plato's philosophy.

I am not aiming at a comprehensive analysis of Plato's philosophy of education. Instead, I will concentrate on one image that has had the most powerful impact on the pedagogical imagination of Western philosophy: Plato's allegory of the cave (irrespective of the multiplicity of its possible interpretations) was just the first image of the unquestionable and positive relationship between pedagogy and philosophy. It is also a powerful metaphor of their reconciliation: a metaphor, whose message was sometimes undermined, but which nevertheless imposed on the tradition the paradigm of understanding this relationship up to the twentieth century.

Thus, I will begin this presentation of the traditional relationships between philosophy and education with an outline of the great pedagogical promise of Plato's *paideia*. The allegory of the cave will be analyzed not per se, but as a point of reference for the hidden dispute between the two main figures of this book: *Hannah Arendt and Martin Heidegger*. The Arendtian interpretation of Plato can be read on two levels: first, straightforwardly as an interpretation of Plato, and second, as an interpretation of the Heideggerian interpretation of Plato. This means that Arendt's dispute with Plato is, at the same time, an implicit dispute with Heidegger.

To begin with, I will consider the Heideggerian reading of the cave in the spirit of his fundamental ontology, and subsequently, the reading of Plato in Arendt, in the spirit of her political thought. Both interpretations refer to Jaeger's monumental work.

HEIDEGGER: THE ONTOLOGICAL INTERPRETATION OF PLATO'S CAVE

The Heideggerian interpretation of Plato's allegory of the cave emerges mostly from the lecture of the 1931–1932 winter term in Freiburg[3] as well as the essay *Plato's Doctrine of Truth* (1942).[4] In order to outline the Heideggerian interpretation of Plato, I will concentrate foremostly on the lecture, referring to the essay occasionally when it differs from the lecture or complements it. Nevertheless, it must be noted that while Arendt certainly was acquainted with the essay,[5] it is as well certain that the content of the lecture from the year preceding her forced immigration from Germany, and which was published only in 1980, was unknown to her.

The leitmotif of this interpretation will be the core sentence of Heidegger's lecture, most succinctly rendering his interpretation of Plato:

> Παιδεία is not education (*Bildung*), but ἡ ἡμετέρα φύσις: that which prevails as our ownmost being, both in respect of that to which it empowers itself, and also of what, in its powerlessness, it loses, of that into which it degenerates. It is not a matter just of παιδεία, but παιδείας τε πέρι και ἀπαιδευσίας, of the one as well of the other, i.e., of their confrontation or setting-apart, of what is between both and out of which they both arise, so that they may assert themselves against each other.[6]

The next steps will be devoted to the thoughts of this excerpt.

I

The first thought is "*Paideia* is our nature (*he hemetera physis*), that which prevails as our ownmost being." Plato's allegory of the cave serves as a metaphor of a double phenomenon: the history of human struggles with the concept of truth and individual educational experience. Both aspects are connected to a complex connotation with the word *paideia*. When Heidegger claims that *paideia* is our nature, our *physis*, he, of course, means neither our biological disposition, nor the set of established human features. What he means is the specifically understood essence of man (*das Wesen des Menschen*), that is, essence in the verbal meaning, as happening. This essence is closely connected with the essence of truth, *aletheia*. The problem of truth, kin of the question of being and freedom, is one of the main motifs of Heidegger's thought. The problem of truth is first systematically undertaken in *Being and Time* (1927). But only in the discussed lecture of 1931–1932, Heidegger undertakes this question anew: He searches for the high point of the Greek understanding of *aletheia* and the beginning of its transition in the Western concept of truth in *The Republic* and the famous allegory.

The Heideggerian interpretation of Plato is a deconstruction of both the Western concept of truth and human self-understanding. Heidegger begins his analysis by demonstrating the appearance of self-evident nature and the insufficiency of the classic concept of truth and by connecting the question of truth with the question of the essence of man. Both questions he relates to the question of being. Heidegger is trying to reinstate the problematic character of these questions: In the history of the concept of truth, he looks for distance to our understanding of truth as well as to our self-understanding. Truth as *a-letheia*, unhiddenness, reveals a completely different connotation to our concept of truth. It is not an attribute of sentences, but that of being. It is being that can be concealed or unfolded in front of man. This time Heidegger is not trying to recover the original concept of truth in Pre-Socratics, but where there comes, in his view, a turn in its original understanding: in the allegory of the cave, where truth as *a-letheia* transforms into truth as correspondence or correctness. Let us, following Heidegger, examine the stages of the allegory.

The first stage (514b–514c) Plato describes as the standard human situation. Humans are prisoners chained to the wall at the bottom of a cave who can see only shadows projected on this wall. They are shadows of objects carried over the parapet outside the cave. The dim light, which enables seeing, stems from a fire outside. In Heidegger's interpretation this means that even in this situation, the prisoners have access to a certain kind of *a-letheia*. Unhidden are the shadows, although the prisoners do not know that they are shadows:

For them it is the only sort of being they know. Heidegger emphasizes the human value of this precarious situation: "Here, therefore, being human *also* means, among other things: to stand within the *hidden*, to be surrounded by the hidden."[7] Even at this stage the human being is not completely deprived of an access to truth: "However strange this situation remains, and however peculiar these people—Heidegger refers directly to the puzzlement of Glaucon (515a)—in this situation too man already has τὸ ἀληθές, the unhidden. [. . .] It belongs to being human—this is already indicated at the beginning of the allegory—to stand in the unhidden, or as we say, in the true, in the truth."[8] Shadows are true as shadows. What is hidden from the inhabitants of the cave is their shadowy nature, that they are only shadows. They treat them as beings. They also perceive themselves and other people in a similar way: They see only the shadows of human figures and think they are real humans.

At the second stage, one of the prisoners is released from his shackles, and compelled to turn toward the light and ascend in this direction (515c–e). However, he cannot understand why what he had watched so far (the shadows) is supposed to be less true than the blinding light. Were he allowed to, he would come back to his old place and stare at the wall again. He would never leave the cave on his own accord. The shadows seem to him more real than the things in the light, and more true. Heidegger underscores this gradual nature of truth—things can be unconcealed more, or less: "Unhiddenness, therefore, has gradations and levels. 'Truth' and 'true' is not something in itself, such that for everyone it is in every aspect unchangeable and common. It is not the case that everyone, without further ado, has the same right and same strength to every truth. And every truth has its *time*."[9] This, of course, does not mean that truth is subjective or relative. Analogously to the graduality of truth, being is also gradual—more uhiddenness means more being: "*Closeness* to beings, i.e., the being-with what is there [*das Da-bei-sein des Da-seins*], the inner proximity or distance of being-human to beings, the degree of the unhiddenness of beings, and the *heightening* of beings themselves as beings—these three are intertwined."[10]

At the third stage (516a–e), the prisoner is—with the use of violence—dragged out of the cave and made to stay there. Only then does he begin to get used to the new world, to the things as they are. To begin with he learns to discern the shadows of things, their reflections in water. The skies he watches only in the night in the dim light of the stars. Only after a long preparation is he able to look at the sun. He remembers now his old situation in the cave and his perspective turns upside down (or "downside up"): Now he recognizes it as a deplorable state of unreality. He acquires now a new sight and only at this stage recognizes the shadows as shadows, as things that conceal. For Heidegger this means that the prisoner recognizes them *as* a certain kind of entities, which at the same time means that he begins to understand their way of being.

The Heideggerian interpretation of the third stage of Plato's cave is focused on the fundamental category of Heidegger's philosophy: the ontological difference. In his oeuvre it appeared for the first time explicitly in the time preceding the publication of *Being and Time*. To put it simply, the difference between entities and being is the difference between the entity and the way it appears, or, beings and (their way of) being (*Seiende* and *Sein*). In the context of our metaphor, the ontological difference gains a vertical dimension: If the sun over the cave symbolizes the idea of Good and the shadows in the cave are a certain kind of entities, the sun-idea enables both perception of the shadows and the things that cast these shadows. This means that the idea cannot be an entity of any sort: It is its condition of possibility. Heidegger explains to his students the essence of such a difference with the basic meaning of *idea*: We never can see a book with our sight only. In order to be able to recognize a book as a book, we have to understand *what* a book *is*. To understand what a book is means at the same time to have an *idea* of the book. Without it we can see only an indefinite shape. "We never see beings with our bodily eyes unless we are also seeing 'ideas'. The prisoners in the cave see only shadow-beings and think that these are all *there are*; they know nothing of being, of the understanding of being."[11] The idea is the ability to see things as what they are (there is, of course, nothing accidental in the etymological proximity of *idein*, "to see" and *idea*): "In the idea we see *what* every being is and *how* it is, in short the being of beings [*das Sein des Seienden*]";[12] "The idea allows us to see a being as what it is [. . .]. We see first of all from being, through the understanding of what a particular thing is. Through its what-being the being shows itself as this and this. Only where being, the what-being of things, is understood, is there a letting-through of beings."[13] The affinity between the idea and the light now also becomes clear: The idea, like light, enables seeing, so to say, "lets us through to beings."

Were there in the cave no light at all, the chained could not even see shadows. Had they no ideas at all, they would not be able to even recognize the shadows of things. They see dim light, they have obscure ideas. But they know nothing of light, as they do not know that they have ideas: They see things but they do not know that they perceive more than their eyes tell them. The idea is not a higher entity, but the being of entities. That is why ascending toward light, going through different types of unhiddenness is at the same time a transition from ignorance to knowledge, from *apaideusia* to *paideia*. *Paideia* does not mean instruction on different types of entities we have never known before, but *periagoge holes tes psyches* (518c),[14] the conversion of the whole soul, so that we begin to see the same things *in a different way*. A few years earlier, in the Marburg lectures of the summer term of 1927, Heidegger was bold enough to make the ontological difference a criterion of humanity: "Only a soul that can make this distinction has the aptitude, going beyond the animal's soul, to become a soul of a human being."[15] According to the true sense of *paideia*, education has to help us to become what we are, what in Heidegger's interpretation of Plato means: to become aware of the ontological dimension of our being and of being of the world, which also means to gain distance from our animal nature. The history of truth as unhiddenness is also a history of man: "This allegory gives precisely the history in which man comes to himself as a being in the midst of beings. [. . .] the essence of truth is what first allows the essence of man to be grasped."[16] Plato tells the story about setting man free toward the unhiddenness of beings, which at the same time means toward his own essence. Man as a being who relates to himself and other beings has to somehow understand being. Otherwise this relation, which Heidegger calls existence, would be impossible. For Heidegger the essence of truth, the essence of being, and the essence of man are different names for the same.

II

The second of Heidegger's thoughts, "It is not a matter just of *paideia*, but of confrontation or setting-apart *paideia* and *apaideusia*," stems directly from Plato's opening sentence of the allegory, suggesting that the image of the cave is an image of our nature in relation to *paideia* and its opposite, *apaideusia* (*ten hemeteran physin paideias te peri kai apaideusias*).[17] None of the above aspects of being human, neither *paideia*, nor *aletheia*, become independent from their opposites, hiddenness and ignorance; both opposites belong to the history of being: "At the same time, however, we likewise know from the cave allegory that the question of the essence of truth is the question of the essence of man. Thus the question of the essence of un-truth, as the fundamental question of the essence of truth, will also become a question specifically oriented to the essence of man."[18] At the fourth stage (516e–517e), the prisoner, who has just become a philosopher, comes back to the cave. Accustomed to the bright light he again becomes blind, this time because of the sudden darkness. Philosophy does not release him from his own condition: He who came out of the cave does not become a divine creature, independent, who can continue the contemplation of truth. He has to descend and stand face to face with the other prisoners, and to take the risk that his speech will be incomprehensible for those who have never left the cave, and that they might attack him as an answer to his attempts to release them and may even want to kill him.

In Heidegger's interpretation, this confrontation means the necessity to face one's own mortality: "It is not a matter of death in general, but of death as the fate of him who seeks to release the prisoners, the death of the *liberator*."[19] As shadows become shadows only in contrast to reality, it is only the relation to eternity that confronts the philosopher with his own finitude. Truth as *aletheia* is not something man can possess (unlike the correctness of sentences). The history of human essence, *paideia*, is identical with the history of truth as *aletheia*. Only if we understand that "being" and "beings" are not the same, are we able to discover the original meaning of *aletheia*, partly—according to Heidegger—forgotten by Plato himself. Even in Plato, says Heidegger, *aletheia* refers not to the unhiddenness of being anymore, but to the highest entity, which prevents Plato from positing a clear question of truth as unhiddenness. Since this problem is also a relevant point for Arendt's interpretation of Plato (and Heidegger), we have to pause here for a moment.

Having identified *aletheia* with idea, with sheer visibility, Plato abandons the question of hiddenness. Truth becomes identified with unhiddenness or disclosure, at only one pole of this dialectics. Plato does not posit the question of hiddenness as a moment of truth. Truth as idea becomes truth identified with the highest being, or, rather, with the presence of the highest being (*An-wesenheit*). In this way truth loses its primordial connection with *Lethe* (the river of forgetfulness), and its opposite is not hiddenness anymore, but falsehood (*pseudos*). Thereby truth becomes a feature of seeing and appearing and its counterconcept becomes distortion (*pseudos*). "By this remarkable juxtaposition ἀληθεύειν loses its fundamental meaning and is uprooted from the fundamental experience of unhiddenness."[20] By the same token, in Plato, for the first time, truth becomes correctness, the congruency of seeing (if not, yet, a feature of sentences), opposite to falsehood and distortion. In the later essay Heidegger puts it succinctly: "'Ἀλήθεια comes under the yoke of the ἰδέα [. . .]. The movement of passage from one place to the other consists in the process whereby the gaze becomes more correct. Everything depends on the ὀρθότης, the correctness of the gaze. Through this correctness, seeing or knowing becomes something correct so that in the end it looks directly at the highest idea and fixes itself in this 'direct alignment.'"[21] And thus: "What results from this conforming of apprehension, as an ἰδεῖν, to the ἰδέα is the ὁμοίωσις, an agreement of the act of knowing with the thing itself."[22] In Plato's allegory of the cave, the two understandings of truth, unhiddenness and correctness, coincide: Plato still says "unhiddenness" but now and again already has "correctness" in mind.[23] This is—according to Heidegger—the beginning of Western metaphysics.

When we still have to deal with truth as unhiddenness, it has to be drawn out from the hiddenness, so that an understanding of hiddenness is a condition of the understanding of unhiddenness, *aletheia*. This clarifies the affinity between *aletheia* and *paideia*. Understanding *paideia* is also conditioned by an understanding of its opposite—*apaideusia*. *Apaideusia* as an opposite is not a state we can escape once and for all (by going out of the cave or graduating from university). It is a state we come back to every time we come back to the cave of our everyday, non-philosophical activities. Were we compelled to see things all the time in the brightest light of idea, we would be unable to live our own lives. For that reason even the prisoner, who escaped the cave, has to descend again and face those who never left it. He has to see the shadows and his own finitude again. He also faces his own *apaideusia*, but, unlike his fellow-prisoners, understands this state precisely as *apaideusia*, so he understands that he is seeing the shadows. He already knows that he knows nothing and will desire to come out to the light again, this time not alone. He remembers *paideia* and longs for sharing it with the others: He will be their teacher and liberator.

It is impossible not to associate Heidegger's reading of Plato's allegory of the cave with the ambivalence of authenticity and inauthenticity from *Being and Time*. The analysis of this work as a great pedagogical promise has to wait until the third chapter. Nevertheless, the possible parallel has to be noted: Both *paideia-apaideusia* versus authenticity-inauthenticity describe the ambiguity of human existence. According to Heidegger, human being (*Dasein*) is existence, and to exist means to exceed beings. To exceed beings toward being means then to live in the ontological difference. Each human being exists in this way, but not each is aware of the fact and not every human being understands his ownmost way of being. To the readers of *Being and Time*, both authenticity and inauthenticity appear as the necessary moments of the structure of human being. One is unable to simply decide to be authentic and never relapse into inauthenticity, the way the philosopher is unable to stay outside the cave. One is but able to be resolute, open to one's own finitude, so that everydayness appears in a different light. This means also seeing oneself in a different light, understanding oneself as existence, not as a thing or material-spiritual reality. Analogously, we are—once having ascended the steep path of *paideia*—not able to avoid descending to *apaideusia*, but if we touched *paideia* once, also *apaideusia* changes its meaning: We are no longer in the vicious circle, this ascending and descending corresponds with the structural dimensions of our existence.

ARENDT: THE POLITICAL INTERPRETATION OF PLATO'S CAVE

Hannah Arendt—as indicated above—worked out her interpretation of Plato's allegory of the cave in dialogue with Heidegger.[24] For her, Plato is an important point of reference for reasons partly convergent and partly divergent from Heidegger's. For both of them, Plato's thought is a very important caesura in the tradition of the West. While in Heidegger, as we already know, Plato initiated a turn in the Western understanding of truth (and being), and, by the same token, the history of Western metaphysics, for Arendt, Plato initiated the tradition of political philosophy. We have a parallel here, which Arendt referred to: "Heidegger demonstrates how Plato transformed the concept of truth (ἀλήθεια) until it became identical with correct statements (ὀρθότης). Correctness indeed, and not truth, would be required if the philosopher's knowledge is the ability to measure."[25] Heidegger's reading, though, remains incomplete according to Arendt. Arendt strives to supplement it with her own interpretation. The transformation of the concept of truth is, namely, not of a purely ontological character. Truth becomes correctness for political reasons—ideas are to become measures of human action:[26] "Although he explicitly mentions the risks the philosopher runs when he is forced to return to the cave, Heidegger is not aware of the political context in which the parable appears."[27] This lack of political context turns out to be fundamental not only for Arendt's understanding of Plato, but also, if in a less explicit way, for her understanding of Heidegger. In her interpretation of Plato, the gradual nature of truth, so important for Heidegger, disappears. The chiaroscuro game, the subtle dynamics of ontological difference, will have to be polarized and immobilized. Only then—within the framework of stable opposition—will we be able to see the antinomies emerging from the clash of philosophy and politics, unveiled with the subtlety of philosophical analyses.

I

First, in Arendt, the expressions "the Western philosophical tradition" and "the Western tradition of political thought" are almost synonymous[28] (and they chronologically correspond with Heidegger's "metaphysics of the West"). The beginning of the philosophical tradition is not identical with Greek thought, but with the launch of the conflict between politics and philosophy: the criminal conviction of Socrates. Secondly, for Arendt, "political philosophy" is not simply philosophical reflection on politics, but a name for an attempt to reconcile two things essentially impossible to reconcile: the viewpoint of politics, which is always a viewpoint of action, with a viewpoint of philosophy, which is always a viewpoint of contemplation. Such an attempt always favors philosophy over politics, always leads to the subordination of the immanent rules of politics to the heterogeneous interests of the life of the mind. The first who tried to solve the conflict between philosophy and politics by imposing philosophical rules on the *polis* was Plato.

The turning point in the history of the relationship between philosophy and politics was the trial and conviction of Socrates. It came as a shock to Plato, and resulted in his "despair of *polis* life."[29] And it was he who had enormous impact on the development of Western philosophy. Thus, the trial was the moment of the emergence of the conflict between thought and action that started with Plato and has haunted Western philosophy up to the present times. Arendt juxtaposed Socrates' and Plato's views. She not only accepted Plato's dialogues as a source of knowledge about Socrates, but also followed the mainstream interpretative tendency to look for the testimony of Socrates' thoughts and actions in Plato's early dialogues. Socrates, the hero of the mature and later dialogues, was for her, rather, a medium of Plato's thought. Nevertheless, the historical adequacy of the testimony of the early "Socratic" dialogues was for her of secondary importance. Both "Socrateses" served in her thought as figures, certain "ideal types,"[30] symbolizing two different epochs in Western thought.

The Socrates of the early dialogues, while he surely is not a rhetorician, is neither a philosopher in the Platonic sense of the term. He is a living example of such a mode of speech, which for Socrates-a-medium-of-Plato would be insufficient. Of relevance for Arendt is the aporetic character of the early dialogues; they do not give answers to questions such as nature, justice, friendship, or courage. Socrates does not know the answer to the questions he asks and it seems that it is not answers that are at stake. What is at stake is putting thoughts in motion, realization, what we actually mean when using nouns such as "justice." It is not the ultimate definition of justice we expect, but the confrontation of the concept with its applications in different situations. Arendt compared nouns to *"frozen thoughts which thinking must unfreeze*, defrost as it were, whenever it wants to find out its original meaning."[31] This "Socratic Socrates" (as opposed to Socrates-Plato or "Platonic Socrates") "seems indeed to have held that talking and thinking about piety, justice, courage, and the rest were liable to make men more pious, more just, more courageous, even though they were not given either definitions or 'values' to direct their further conduct."[32] That is why those early dialogues never end with ultimate, tangible results. Nevertheless, already in *Gorgias*, the dialogue preceding the foundation of the Academy, we have a non-Socratic and very Platonic ending, a myth of afterlife (*Gorgias* 523a–527a): "We may not know whether Socrates believed that ignorance causes evil and that virtue can be taught; but we do know that Plato thought it wiser to rely on threads."[33]

In order to underline the differences between the two figures, Arendt juxtaposes *Apology* with *Phaedo*. In *Apology*, Socrates makes a stipulation that he will speak as "in the marketplace" (17c).[34] His speech is a philosophical argumentation based on the art of conversation (*dialegesthai*), but it is free from the elitist, specialist character of the later dialogues. The predominance of Socrates relies solely on his awareness of his own ignorance. His knowledge of ignorance lacks a divine feature, it is purely human knowledge. Socrates denies vehemently to have been a teacher of anybody and has doubts in the possibility of education (20e, 23c, 33a). He addresses people in court as a fellow-citizen anxious about the city, not as a mentor. The philosophical thinking of Socrates has nothing to do with the motionless contemplation of Being; just the contrary is the case, the motion of thought does not let him or his interlocutors rest and consumes time for political life (23b). Arendt's attention is focused on *Phaedo* being a "revised," more successful *Apology*,[35] "more convincing than it was to the jury" (63b).[36] Both *Apology* and *Phaedo* demonstrate a philosophical attitude toward death by answering the question of why death is not to be dreaded. But while the demonstration of *Apology* refers to ignorance of the nature of death, the argumentation in *Phaedo* is based on evidence for the immortality of the soul, dedicated to professional philosophers and supported with a version of the afterlife myth (resp. *Apology* 40b–42a, *Phaedo* 107d–115a).

In Plato, his aversion to politics and the political dimension of rhetoric crystallized into the opposition of truth and opinion (*episteme* and *doxa*)[37]: "Platonic truth, even if *doxa* is not mentioned, is always understood as the very opposite of opinion"[38] (we can see an analogy to Heidegger's interpretation, according to which only in Plato truth became the opposite of falsity). The "failure" of Socrates in the Athens court resulted in Plato's contempt toward the political way of speech, which the Greeks identified with the power of persuasion (*peithein*). The "defeat" of the apology induced Plato to attempt a neutralization of the uncertainty of persuasion and discussion with "absolute measures" (as Arendt often addressed ideas in political application), by introducing absolute criteria into the human world. "The opposition of truth and opinion was certainly the most anti-Socratic conclusion that Plato drew from Socrates' trial."[39]

We face two problems here. First, we have a problem with Socrates. What kind of speech did Socrates use? On the one hand, he surely was not an orator. He almost never delivered speeches, he simply conversed with people. Here lay, according to Arendt, his tragedy: He addressed the judges as a dialectician, although still not as a philosopher in Plato's sense of the term. That is why, although his speech was not political, he observed the rules of political speech in his dialectics. This means that the dialogue he led was a persuasive method based on argumentation, whose purpose was to convince the judges. Nevertheless, in the court he was not surrounded by philosophical interlocutors, but by a crowd of simple listeners: the accusers, the defenders, the witnesses. They were not prepared for Socrates' new, dialectic way of speech. Therefore, as Arendt puts it, "His truth [. . .], since he respected the limitations inherent in persuasion, became an opinion among opinions, not worth a bit more than the non-truths of the judges."[40] Socrates did not yet discern, let alone juxtapose, truth and opinion. If we assume with Arendt, that "the chief distinction between persuasion and dialectic is that the former always addresses a multitude (*peithein ta plethe*) whereas dialectic is possible only as a dialogue between two,"[41] we can draw the conclusion that the tragic "mistake" of Socrates was to deliver a speech incompatible with the circumstances.

Second, we have a problem with Plato. Since Plato tried to correct Socrates' "mistake" by juxtaposing dialectics and persuasion, and developed the first one to a mastery, the question arises: In what way can philosophical dialogue between two become—and precisely this Arendt imputes to Plato—tyranny[42]? Even if we do not mean tyranny in the standard meaning of arbitrary violence, but a "tyranny" of the power of philosophical truth, dialectics is incompatible with it. Plato—I am following the spirit of Arendt's thought here—tried to correct Socrates' "mistake" in a twofold way.

On the one hand, in the dimension of the relationship between a philosopher and the rest of the people, Plato, so to say, allowed double standards. He reserved dialectics for philosophers: serving to think of the highest principles of being. At the same time, where a philosopher has to deal with many people, a new phenomenon emerges, alien to philosophy as well as politics in the Greek understanding: "To Plato persuading the multitude means forcing upon its multitude opinions one's own opinion; thus persuasion is not the opposite of rule by violence, it is only another form of it."[43] Indeed, dialectics, which appears as an element of scholarship of philosophers, has, so to say, an internal influence and crowns decades of didactic processes designed for the elites of the elites.

On the other hand, Plato, in a way, also corrects and rectifies dialectics within the *paideia* of philosophers. The art of wise conversation garlands the cycle of the education of a philosopher and is the pinnacle of Platonic philosophical schooling (see 534e). It is the most abstract of all the sciences, which allows to a higher degree than mathematical subjects the development of abstract thinking and argumentation; thus, it perfectly suits education of those who have to be able to see the essence of things without the support of concrete and sensual objects (see 534c). In the next moment, however, Plato changes his attitude toward dialectics. He draws our attention to the dangers of the art of conversation: the desire to show off in discussion, but also disdain for customs and anarchy that loom over those who have access to independent thought (see 538c). It seems as if Plato started to fear the accusations, faced by Socrates, of spoiling the youth. As Arendt notes, this fear is justified if in the group of Socrates' highly talented pupils we find people like Alcibiades and Critias: "They had not been content with being taught how to think without being taught a doctrine, and they changed the non-results of the Socratic thinking examination into negative results: if we cannot define what piety is let us be impious—which is pretty much the opposite of what Socrates had hoped to achieve by talking about piety."[44] Plato's remedy for the danger of nihilism, inherent in every thinking, is the correction we find toward the end of Book 7: Dialectic education is supplemented with a period of acquiring political experience. At the age of fifty, those who pass the next selection "must be led to the goal and compelled to lift up the radiant light of their souls to what itself provides light for everything" (540b).[45] Thus, dialectics yields to contemplation of idea. This is a detail of great importance for Arendt. Conversation, even highly specialized philosophical conversation, still has something to do with the nature of politics; it is still based on speech and dialogue between two, even if it is a silent dialogue between me and myself. Contemplation, on the contrary, is speechless seeing, requiring absolute loneliness, and it resembles a relationship with God. In this way it is a phenomenon outside the political realm and alien to its nature. And yet, Plato makes it political activity *par excellence* in the very next sentence: "And when they have seen the Good itself, take it as a pattern for the right ordering of the state and of the individual" (540b).

According to Arendt, Plato wanted to undermine the typical Greek opinion that a philosopher by nature is not fit for politics.[46] In *The Republic*, Plato endeavors to demonstrate the opposite. He transforms his own theory of ideas in order to bestow the philosophical text with political meaning. For Arendt, this was the meaning of Plato's acknowledgment of the priority of Good over Beauty, primary in other dialogues. This shift has important consequences. Unlike the idea of Beauty, Good is eligible to connect the world of ideas with the human world in a relationship that is not only the ontological dependence of the second on the first, but has also a pragmatic relevance—Good, unlike Beauty, comprises an element of utility: "Only if the realm of ideas is illuminated by the idea of the good could Plato use the ideas for political purposes."[47] Already Heidegger stressed the connotation of the Greek *agathon*, which, unlike our "good," lacks an ethical dimension and, instead, comprises a pragmatic strain as "fitness for something." Good is something we can use.[48] Arendt emphasizes the idea of beauty as an object of useless contemplation in the dialogues (like *Symposion*), where a philosopher is not obliged to be a political leader: "It is only when he returns to the dark cave of human affairs to live once more with his fellow men that he needs the ideas for guidance as standards and rules by which to measure and under which to subsume the varied multitude of human deeds and words with the same absolute 'objective' certainty with which the craftsman can be guided."[49] The idea of good, as we will see, is responsible for the instrumentalization of politics.

II

In trying to heal the strife between philosophy and politics, Plato sees education playing the role of mediator. Plato's education is different from Socrates' negative education: "The difference with Plato is decisive: Socrates did not want to educate the citizens so much as he wanted to improve their *doxai*, which continued the political life in which he took part. To Socrates, maieutic was a political activity, a give-and-take, fundamentally on a basis of strict equality, the fruits of which could not be measured by the result of arriving at this or that general truth."[50] The allegory of the cave is a pedagogical metaphor, but it is no longer Socratic pedagogy: Here education emerges as a sphere of domination by the one who knows, based on an essential inequality; education understood as upbringing rather than as a sphere of free and mutual education. This kind of education cannot be reconciled with politics, because it excludes equality, the essence of politics by Arendt's definition.[51]

Therefore, the great pedagogical metaphor of Plato at the same time is a record of struggles of the philosopher with politics and his endeavors to dominate politics. "Our tradition of political thought had its definite beginning [. . .] when, in *The Republic*'s allegory of the cave, Plato described the sphere of human affairs—all that belongs to the living together of men in a common world—in terms of darkness, confusion, deception which those aspiring to true being must turn away from and abandon if they want to discover the clear sky of eternal ideas."[52] In the political interpretation of Plato's allegory of the cave, which remains much less systematic than the ontological interpretation of Heidegger, completely different aspects of the metaphor come to the fore.

For Arendt, of utmost relevance are two intertwined themes: First, the metaphor of prisoners chained to the rock is not simply a philosophic image, describing an individual state of human ignorance and is not simply a metaphor of a state of the human soul. Were it the case, Plato would not be the initiator of the tradition of political philosophy, but a philosopher remote to politics and human affairs. The cave is not only a symbol of a state of mind, it is a political symbol as well, describing Plato's assessment of Athens. Secondly, we have the pedagogical power of this metaphor—Plato takes advantage of Homer's language, suggesting an analogy between life in the city and the most pitiable form of human existence: as a shadow in Hades.[53] That is why Arendt, in her remarks on the cave, focuses—unlike Heidegger—foremostly on the cave's interior, on the first and on the last moments of Plato's story.

Arendt is perturbed by Plato's metaphoric image of the *polis*. The image of prisoners in shackles, unable to move their heads, unable to speak, cannot be a metaphor adequately describing political life: "Indeed, the two politically most significant words designating human activity, talk and action (*lexis* and *praxis*), are conspicuously absent from the whole story."[54] The life of the prisoners consists of basically the same as that of a philosopher: in merely watching. Arendt does not interpret the cave in the context of the ontological difference, which for Heidegger was decisive for affinities and differences between the situation of the prisoners and the liberated philosopher. From her point of view, it is not so important that the chained cannot recognize the way of being of the shadows perceived by them, but that they can see them from one perspective only. The fundamental problem of the Platonic description of the cave would be that the prisoners all see the same. That is why the world of the cave does not resemble what Arendt called the world of "human affairs," it is not even a caricature of this world. Plato, rather, constructs "a world of immobile puppets, of men who live one next to the other, without looking into each other's faces and without any relation."[55] For Arendt it means that in the cave there is no place for opinion, for *doxa*, for speaking of what appears to whom. In the cave there is no place for the plurality of people, unless in the numeric sense.

The philosopher who faces things impossible to be rendered in words is situated outside the sphere of politics, and outside the inner Socratic dialogue. The elusive philosophical experience, irreconcilable with conversation, becomes his usual attitude (*bios theoretikos*), "bases his whole existence on that singularity [. . .]. And by this he destroys the plurality of the human condition within himself."[56] According to Arendt, here is also the tragedy of returning to the cave. The philosopher is alienated from political life, exactly because he transformed his own essence (*periagoge holes tes psyches*), he as a king becomes someone strange. He is not able to command a language understandable for his former fellow-prisoners. He cannot convince them to leave the cave; for that reason he would have to become one of them again. The only thing he can do is to impose absolute measures on them, whose sources he is unable to demonstrate to them. That is why he is endangered by a violent reaction on their part.

The philosophical perspective of seeing the world of action is distorted in one more way. The conflict between philosophy and politics results in a sort of insensitivity about different forms of human plurality and different models of the public sphere. From the point of view of philosophy as *bios theoreticos*, human plurality appears as a threatening mass, not to say a mob. Rhetoric is always sophistic. Plato compares people in a democracy to a sick organism or to a giant animal to be subjugated and not to be spoiled or pleased (like Sophists do, see *The Republic*, 493b–494b). As we will see (in chapter 3), a similar distortion of perspective happened to Heidegger.

The description of the *polis*-cave in the moment preceding the return of the philosopher is politically more adequate, although it still relies on seeing: "They may have had practice of honouring and commending one another, with prizes for the man who had the keenest eye on the passing shadows and the best memory for the order in which they followed or accompanied one another, so that he could make a good guess as to which was going to come next" (516d). Nevertheless, a new aspect emerges here. Plato compares the *polis*-cave to the land of the dead from Homeric beliefs, described in the eleventh song of *The Odyssey*: "Would our released prisoner be likely to covet those prizes or to envy the men exalted to honour and power in the Cave? Would he not feel like Homer's Achilles that he would far sooner 'be on earth as a hired servant in the house of a landless man' or endure anything rather than go back to his old beliefs and live in the old way?" (516d).[57] Plato refers to the dialogue between Odysseus and the soul of Achilles in order to make a very significant shift in the traditional hierarchy of ways of being. Achilles does not find consolation in the power he possesses among the dead, because it is only the existence of shadows, just a semblance of true existence. In the *Odyssey*'s perspective (in this respect, different from that of *The Iliad*), it is better to be a poor farmer on the earth, even if it means exclusion from the public world, than to be a master in Hades. Even the most flimsy reality is better than a phantom. There is no connection between the real world and the world of shadows. Nevertheless, Plato identifies the two. Hades is not under the earth, or at the end of the ocean, and it is not the land of souls. The existence of shadows, as described by Homer, is our own existence in the *polis*. In lifting Hades to the level of the earth, comparing life in the *polis* to non-existence, and placing real existence somewhere higher, Plato makes an extraordinary identification. It is as if he were saying to the Greeks: Everything you believe the most, politics, conversations, disputes, are only shadows of true existence, it is not real. What seems to be most real, your bodies, is illusory. Real life, the real world, is somewhere above all this.

For Arendt this shift, being at the same time a reversal (what is bodiless becomes more real than tangible human existence), bears not only a philosophical meaning for Western metaphysics up to Nietzsche, but also a pedagogical and political meaning.[58] The identification of Hades and public affairs is designed to make the Greeks aware of the futility of what they loved most and convince them to radically change their attitude. Having realized the precariousness of their situation, they will more easily yield to a leader, who not only will show them a better world, but also will build an earthly world according to the external norms of a better world.

We face another difficulty here. Plato does not say why the future philosopher is released from the shackles. But we get informed about the way the liberation proceeds: "And suppose someone were to drag him away forcibly up the steep and rugged ascent and not let him go until he had hauled him out into the sunlight" (515e). Since the whole description functions as a thought experiment, an intellectual hypothesis, Plato did not have to philosophically justify the genesis of this ascent. What is important here is that the incentive to leave the cave is an external power, metaphorically reflected by physical violence (*bia*). The situation gets more complicated the moment the king-philosopher comes back to the cave. We have a sort of symmetrical situation here: people chained to the rock and someone who is trying to drag them out. He is violent toward them and they respond with violence. Violence is inherent in the turning points of the story: the initial moment of ascent and the philosopher's final moment of descent. In Heidegger's ontological interpretation, this symmetry is conspicuous: "Liberation must happen βία, with violence. [. . .] the liberator must be a violent person."[59] Of course, it is not about arbitrary physical violence, but violence as a condition of liberation and which is rendered as physical violence only as a metaphorical representation.

In Arendt's interpretation, which is a political interpretation, this symmetry cannot be preserved. By extension, questions arise as to how the philosopher liberates his fellow-prisoners, and what the principle of his rule is. We know he cannot refer to the classical political rules, that he cannot persuade or convince someone to his own point of view. On the other hand, the philosophical argumentation he could use, the dialectic leading to unconditional philosophical truths, could only be directed to the few: "The problem arises of how to assure that the many, the people who in their very multitude compose the body politic, can be submitted to the same truth."[60]

In her essay on authority, Arendt attempts to answer this question. Plato was the first to have established the initial form of what later became authority: a certain instance of coercion that is neither persuasion or argumentation, nor simple violence. The power of this early form of authority has been guaranteed in different ways, mostly by the threat of punishment in future life,[61] directed to the ears of the many, oblivious to philosophical argument. This kind of authority has nothing to do with sheer violence, although it is "an attempt to use violence by words only."[62] The examples of power-relations originate in Plato in the private sphere of natural or acquired inequalities (master-slave, shepherd-flock, pilot-passengers, doctor-patient[63]). "What he was looking for was a relationship in which the compelling element lies in the relationship itself and is prior to the actual issuance of commands; the patient became subject to the physician's authority when he fell ill, and the slave came under the command of his master when he became a slave."[64] These metaphors are imperfect insofar as the philosopher derives the coercive power of his authority from contemplated ideas. But ideas can again be understood only by the few. Thus, in order to address the many, these ideas have to become earthly—they have to become norms of conduct. Here emerges another turnabout in the Western tradition of political thought: Ideas become models of creation of earthly things, including such things as political communities, which derive their measures from the idea of Good. Politics loses its autonomy and is subdued to an external criterion of fabrication.

Arendt is not much interested in the purely philosophical content of the theory of ideas, but in its overwhelming impact on our political thinking. That is why she stresses the reasons for which, in *The Republic*, Plato replaced the idea of beauty with the idea of good. While the first can be exclusively an object of contemplation, and, as such, be apolitical,[65] the second contains a reference to utility and allows the connection of two worlds: philosophy and politics. The idea of good did not emerge from political experience, but from experience of fabrication, *poiesis*, which is of a completely different nature to action.[66] In this way *praxis* was reduced to *poiesis*,[67] which established a standard in Western philosophy (as we will see in chapter 5).

The "authority," which in Plato replaced persuasion in order to avoid violence, was not the same type of authority that later emerged in Rome.[68] In Rome, the awareness of authority emerged from political experience: from the foundation act of the city and derived from that act the political superiority of ancestors over coevals. "Wherever the model of education through authority, without this fundamental conviction, was superimposed on the realm of politics [. . .], it served primarily to obscure real or coveted claims to rule and pretend to educate while in reality it wanted to dominate."[69] Therefore, in Arendt's view, the Roman model is the only legitimate example of a combination of political and pedagogical authority. The Greek models of authority are completely apolitical. Thus, the attempt to introduce authority to politics had to fail by replacing political legitimization with the element of violence. The introduction of authoritarian rule, which has nothing to do with the rule of authority, spoiled the political. That is why in the political interpretation of Plato's cave, *paideia* has a different meaning than in the purely philosophical interpretation: It is not read as the radically understood education and self-education of the individual, but as a mechanism of political domination, based on seemingly natural relations.

The basic features of Plato's political philosophy, that is, seeing action from the point of view of philosophical contemplation, the attempt to replace rhetoric and persuasion with authority, introducing absolute philosophical norms into politics and, last but not least, inscribing action into instrumental categories, have one more implication of great historical import. It is the elimination of a fundamental ontological dimension of politics: the plurality of people. As we have seen above, even the initial image of the cave, which was to serve as a description of the actual situation of people on the earth, allows for human plurality only in a numeric sense. Plato, of course, acknowledges the fact of the *polis* being inhabited by the many, but he does not recognize this plurality as an ontological condition of politics. Instead, he understands this plurality as a dangerous drawback to be removed by the philosopher. That is why the republic structurally reflects the human soul with its principle of unity: reason. In this way the model of the state becomes one man. Subsequently, and contrary to standard views, the private sphere, based on domination, is in Plato not marginalized, but proliferates at the expense of the political.[70]

Socrates initiated the conflict between philosophy and politics by trying to bestow philosophy with political meaning and, in a sense, to reconcile thinking and action. Political philosophy, which emerged from this conflict, can, theoretically, take the point of view of political experience, but mostly at the expense of philosophical depth.[71] Insofar as political philosophy takes the point of view of philosophical experience, which was mostly the case, it had to favor philosophy over politics. It was exactly the reaction of Plato to the conflict started by Socrates and the form was most radical: "Only Plato of all philosophers ever dared to design a commonwealth exclusively from the viewpoint of the philosopher";[72]

> The whole realm of human affairs is seen from the viewpoint of a philosophy which assumes that even those who inhabit the cave of human affairs are human only insofar as they too want to see [. . .]. And the rule of the philosopher-king, that is, the domination of human affairs by something outside its own realm, is justified only by an absolute priority of seeing over doing, of contemplation over speaking and acting, but also by the assumption that what makes men human is the urge to see. Hence, the interest of the philosopher and the interest of man *qua* man coincide; both demand that human affairs, the results of speech and action, must not acquire a dignity of their own but be subjected to the domination of something outside their realm.[73]

The inability to grasp the specific nature of action has been characteristic of Western philosophy since Plato. No less an important feature is the experience of solitude, the fundamental philosophical experience, which, after the descent of the philosopher to the cave, is reshaped into the measure for action. Solitude, in Plato, also means freedom from relations with other people and their opinions: "In the traditional sense, truth is possible only in solitude [. . .]. From the very beginning truth was defined in opposition to δόξα as something non-spectral. Hence, the thinker of truth understands himself as one man."[74] This opposition is still preserved in Heidegger's distinction between authentic speech (which is actually silence) and hearsay. What in the philosophical perspective makes a human being human, from the point of view of human affairs, means sacrificing a certain aspect of humanity (*vita activa*) for another (*vita contemplativa*).

We can obviously see that Arendt's interpretation of Plato is not unproblematic. Commentators of Plato often emphasize the futility of political interpretations of *The Republic*.[75] It is, of course, a justified reaction to Popperian-like ideas, which reduce Plato's masterpiece to a description of proto-totalitarian rule. Against such naïve political interpretations, we have *par excellence* philosophical readings, which understand the political motives in Plato as metaphors for considerations of not political, but ethical or ontological meaning. Arendt's interpretation cannot be completely freed from the allegation of literalism. It is true, in many places she takes Plato's analogies and myths at face value, as if not seeing the distance and irony that often accompanied them. As we have seen, her interpretation does not achieve the level of philosophical subtlety as purely philosophical readings (Heidegger's being a good example). At the same time, while reading Arendt, we have a feeling that she pays the price with full awareness, for the sake of something more important to her than philosophical subtlety: a perspective closed to philosophical depth. Philosophical interpretations, treating the political dimension of Plato metaphorically, bear a certain danger: Philosophical subtlety can, so to say, mask the ideological component of his work. Therefore, Arendt, not accusing Plato of totalitarianism and not taking altogether seriously his positive proposals, takes his political metaphors as expressions of political presuppositions she seeks to draw out.

Both discussed interpretations of Plato's *paideia* are founded on strong premises and overwhelming ideas. Apart from all the differences, one conviction is common to them: Both considered Plato to be the initiator of a great tradition, which, nevertheless, needs to be deconstructed. As Heidegger sought testimonies of true, non-metaphysical thinking in pre-Socratic sources, Arendt tried to find traces of authentic political thought in authors who either were not philosophers, but poets or historians, or philosophers who did not follow the standard path of description of action in terms of fabrication, that is, who practiced political philosophy from the point of view of politics, not philosophy (many such examples we can find in modernity). In Arendt's view, Heidegger's philosophy is basically a continuation, or even a crowning, of the tradition of political philosophy initiated by Plato. As we will see in the following chapters, Arendt's struggles with the Western philosophical tradition is a silent dispute with Heidegger's thought. On the one hand, Heidegger overcame the metaphysical tradition, but on the other, affirmed the philosophical prejudices against action. While it is true that Arendt's debt to Heidegger "is perhaps more important than she is prepared to admit,"[76] one has to bear in mind all the time that Arendt does not simply add political philosophy to Heidegger's deconstruction, but turns his deconstruction against his own premises.

GATEWAY: *PAIDEIA* IS NOT *BILDUNG*

At the very end of this chapter we need to very briefly come back to the third thought present in Heidegger's reading of *paideia*: "*paideia* is not *Bildung*."

Similar to the way in paragraph 44 of *Being and Time*, where Heidegger demonstrates that our understanding of truth as correspondence is derivative of the primordial understanding of truth as *aletheia*, so he does, if in a less systematic way, with the concept of *paideia*. The fundamental thesis of Heidegger, against those who, like Jaeger,[77] would think of a continuity between the Greek *paideia* and the German idea of *Bildung* is this: "paideia is not *Bildung*."[78] The philosophical conceptualization of *paideia* in *The Republic* concerns, as we remember, the whole essence of human *Dasein* as the possibility of discovering truth. The question of the essence of man was at the same time the question of the essence of truth and the question of the essence of being. This close connection of humanity, being, and truth was, according to Heidegger, torn up in modernity.

The German idea of *Bildung* is a derivative phenomenon, since it focuses on the development of the self more than examination of being. *Bildung* is inscribed in the modern relationship between subject and object and the modern way of being-in-the-world. The core of this relationship is not being, but "I," "self." Understanding of being yields to self-development and culture that are at the service of this self-development. Thereby, Heidegger writes on Greek *paideia*: "But at the same time we now know that this questioning concerning the essence of man *precedes* all pedagogy, psychology, anthropology, as well as every humanism,"[79] and continues on modern times, "And we today! Plato's doctrine of ideas has its essence ripped out and made accessible for the superficiality of today's *Dasein*: ideas as values and παιδεία as culture and education, i.e., what is most pernicious from the nineteenth century, but nothing from 'antiquity.'"[80] Heidegger is foremostly worried about the transformation of philosophy, the most fundamental way of being, into the element of education: which means subjectification, egocentrization and relativization of philosophy.

One does not need to share Heidegger's convictions and assumptions to acknowledge that *Bildung* is not a simple continuation of the ancient traditions, but a phenomenon characteristic to a different place and time. Nevertheless, we need to remember that *Bildung* shows at least one important affinity with *paideia*: It turns out to be at the service of mollifying the conflict between philosophy and education. But it will be a different philosophy and different education.

We need, hence, to analyze the idea of *Bildung* separately, and independently from Heidegger's negative assessment of modernity. The next two chapters of this book will be devoted, respectively, to analysis of the *German* idea of *Bildung* (chapter 2) and examining the pedagogical promise of Heidegger's own philosophy (chapter 3).

NOTES

1. Werner Jaeger, *Paideia: The Ideals of Greek Culture*, vol. 2, trans. Gilbert Highet (Oxford: Blackwell, 1946). Jaeger, however, omitted the dialogues relating to education in an unobvious way, like *Timaeus, Parmenides*, or *The Sophist*.
2. Jaeger, *Paideia*, p. 366.
3. Martin Heidegger, *Vom Wesen der Wahrheit. Zu Platons Höhlengleichnis und Theätet*, Gesamtausgabe II Abt., Band 34 (Frankfurt am Main: Vittorio Klostermann, 1997); English: Martin Heidegger, *The Essence of Truth: On Plato's Cave Allegory and Theaetetus*, trans. Ted Sadler (New York: Continuum, 2002). Further quoted as HGA 34 with reference to both the original (G) and the translation (E).
4. Martin Heidegger, "Plato's Doctrine of Truth," trans. Thomas Sheehan, in Martin Heidegger, *Pathmarks*, ed. William Mc Neill (New York: Cambridge University Press, 1998).
5. In her essay on authority, Arendt referred to the Heideggerian interpretation of the cave from the essay "Plato's Doctrine of Truth." See Hannah Arendt, "What Is Authority?" in Hannah Arendt, *Between Past and Future: Eight Exercises in Political Thought* (New York: Penguin Books, 2006), 284, footnote 16. See also *Anmerkungen zu Heft I* in Hannah Arendt, *Denktagebuch 1950–1973* (München-Zürich: Piper, 2003), 1044–45.
6. HGA 34, 114G; 83E. In the quotation from the authors, who use the original Greek spelling, I maintain it. In the other places I use the Latin transcription.
7. HGA 34, 26–27G; 21E.
8. HGA 34, 26G; 20E.
9. HGA 34, 32G; 25E.
10. HGA 34, 33G; 26E.
11. HGA 34, 52G; 39E.
12. HGA 34, 52G; 38E.
13. HGA 34, 57G; 42E.
14. "Just as one might have to turn the whole body round in order that the eye should see the light instead of darkness, so the entire soul must be turned away from this changing world, until its eye can bear to contemplate reality." [*The Republic of Plato*, trans. Francis Macdonald Cornford (Oxford: Clarendon Press, 1944)]. All the English quotations from *The Republic*, if not indicated otherwise, refer to Cornford's translation, as it was relevant for both the translator of Heidegger's lecture, Ted Sadler, and Hannah Arendt.
15. Martin Heidegger, *Die Grundprobleme der Phänomenologie*, II Abt., Band 24 (Frankfurt am Main: Vittorio Klostermann, 1997), 454; English: Martin Heidegger, *The Basic Problems of Phenomenology*, trans. Albert Hofstadter (Bloomington: Indiana University Press, 1982), 319. Further quoted as HGA 24 with reference to both the original (G) and the translation (E).
16. HGA 34, 75G; 55E.
17. In the translation of Friedrich Schleiermacher which Heidegger referred to himself: "Vergleiche dir unsere Natur in bezug auf *Bildung* und *Unbildung* folgendem Zustande," see Platon, *Werke in Acht Bänden. Griechisch und Deutsch*, t. 4,

Πολτεία. *Der Staat*, trans. Friedrich Schleieremacher (Darmstadt: Wissenschaftliche Buchgesellschaft, 1971). In English: "Here is a parable to illustrate the degrees in which our nature may be enlightened or unenlightened"; "Compare the effect of education and of the lack of it on our nature to an experience like this." (trans. G. M. A. Grube and C. D. C. Reeve, in *Plato's Complete Works*, ed. J. M. Cooper, [Indianapolis/Cambridge: Hackett, 1997]).

18. HGA 34, 128G; 92–93E.
19. HGA 34, 81G; 59E.
20. HGA 34, 138G; 100E.
21. Heidegger, "Plato's Doctrine of Truth," 176.
22. Heidegger, "Plato's Doctrine of Truth," 177.
23. See, for instance: πρὸς μᾶλλον ὄντα τετραμμένος ὀρθότερον βλέποι (515d): "being someone nearer to reality and turned towards more real objects, he was getting a truer view" (Cornford); "now—because he is a bit closer to the things that are more—he sees more correctly (Grube and Reeve); "jetzt aber, dem Seienden näher und zu dem mehr Seienden gewendet, sähe er richtiger"(Schleiermacher).
24. Hannah Arendt to Martin Heidegger, May 8, 1954: She informs Heidegger about what she is actually working on: "Starting with the parable of the cave (and your interpretation of it), a representation of the traditional relationship between philosophy and politics" (*Letters*, 120). Two years later she writes to Jaspers: "Heidegger, it seems to me, is particularly off base in using the cave simile to interpret and 'criticize' Plato's theory of ideas, but he is right when he says that in the presentation of the cave simile, truth is transformed on the sly into correctness and, consequently, ideas into standards" (Hannah Arendt to Karl Jaspers, July 1, 1956. *Correspondence*, 288).
25. Arendt, "What Is Authority?" 284.
26. Arendt, *Denktagebuch*, 503.
27. Arendt, "What Is Authority?" 284.
28. Let's compare two statements: "Our tradition of political thought had its definite beginning in the teachings of Plato and Aristotle" (Hannah Arendt, "Tradition and the Modern Age," in *Between Past and Future*, 17) and "Plato as well as Aristotle became the beginning of the occidental philosophic tradition" (Hannah Arendt, "Socrates," in Hannah Arendt, *The Promise of Politics* [New York: Schocken, 2005], 5).
29. Arendt, "Socrates," 6.
30. Hannah Arendt, "Thinking and Moral Considerations," in Hannah Arendt, *Responsibility and Judgment* (New York: Schocken, 2003), 169.
31. Arendt, "Thinking and Moral Considerations," 172–73.
32. Arendt, "Thinking and Moral Considerations," 173.
33. Arendt, "Thinking and Moral Considerations," 181.
34. Plato, *Apology*, trans. G. M. A. Grube, in *Plato's Complete Works*.
35. Arendt, "Socrates," 7. See also, Arendt, *Denktagebuch*, 362, 585–89.
36. Plato, *Pheado*, trans. G. M. A. Grube, in *Plato's Complete Works*.
37. Although the contradistinction itself stems from Parmenides (see Hermann Diels, *Die Fragmente der Vorsokratiker*, v. 1 (Dublin-Zürich: Weidmann, 1966), 28B 1,25; 28B 8,50: beautifully rounded truth and the mortal's opinions [ἀληθείη εὐκυκλής/βροτῶν δόξαι]).

38. Arendt, "Socrates," 7–8.
39. Arendt, "Socrates," 8.
40. Arendt, "Socrates," 13.
41. Arendt, "Socrates," 13.
42. Arendt, "Socrates," 12.
43. Arendt, "Socrates," 13.
44. Arendt, "Thinking and Moral Considerations," 177.
45. Trans. Grube and Reeve, in *Plato's Complete Works*.
46. See the anecdote on Thales in Plato, *Theaetetus*, 174a–b.
47. Arendt, "Socrates," 11.
48. See HGA 34, 106G; 77E.
49. Hannah Arendt, *The Human Condition* (Chicago/London: The University of Chicago Press, 1998), 226 (further quoted as HC). In the essay on authority Arendt refers to a footnote in Jaeger, and corrects him: "The idea that there is a supreme art of measurement and that the philosopher's knowledge of values (*phronesis*) is the ability to measure, runs through all Plato's work right down to the end" (Jaeger, *Paideia*, 416, f. 45)—"is true only for Plato's political philosophy"—adds Arendt ("What Is Authority?" 283).
50. Arendt, "Socrates," 15.
51. See the remarks Arendt made on the relationship between politics and education: "Education can play no part in politics, because in politics we always have to deal with those who are already educated. Whoever wants to educate adults really wants to act as their guardian and prevent them from political activity. Since one cannot educate adults, the word education has an evil sound in politics" (Hannah Arendt, "The Crisis in Education," in *Between Past and Future*, 173), or: "Nothing is more questionable than the political relevance of examples drawn from the field of education" (Arendt, "What Is Authority?" 118).
52. Arendt, "Tradition and the Modern Age," 17.
53. See Homer, *Odyssey*, XI, 500.
54. Arendt, "Socrates," 31.
55. Adriana Cavarero, "Regarding the Cave," trans. Paul Kottman, *Qui Parle*, 1, no. 10 (1996): 10.
56. Arendt, "Socrates," 37.
57. I would rather be a paid servant in a poor man's house and be above ground than king of kings among the dead, *The Odyssey* by Homer, trans. Samuel Butler, XI, p. 194. It is interesting that in the third book of *The Republic* Plato advocated censorship for this particular fragment, for the gloomy description of Hades is injurious for the courage and spirit of the warriors (386b–d).
58. See Arendt, "Tradition and the Modern Age," 36–37; HC, 292.
59. HGA 34, 81G; 59E.
60. Arendt, "What Is Authority?" 107.
61. Mature Plato completes many of his dialogues with such a story, including *The Republic*. The exceptions are *The Laws*, where law becomes the medium of authority. It does not mean that *The Laws* do not follow this tendency: Here Plato can do

without final myths, because he delivers a detailed catalogue of punishments which make them redundant (see Arendt, "Socrates," 13).

62. Arendt, "Socrates," 13.
63. See, respectively: *The Statesman* 289c, 268a–d, *The Republic* 488a–489a, *Gorgias* 521e–522b.
64. Arendt, "What Is Authority?" 109.
65. In *The Human Condition* Arendt finds affinities between contemplation and fabrication. See HC, 301–3.
66. Indeed, in Book 7 we have the idea of Good *tou agatou idea* (517b, 527b), the good *to agathon* (520c) the Good itself *to agathon auto* (540a). Nevertheless, at the same time, idea becomes *paradeigma*, a pattern or model for public affairs (540a–b).
67. See Arendt, *Denktagebuch*, 373.
68. In her *Denktagebuch* Arendt enlisted three forms of authority: the Platonic measure, the Roman beginning of the foundation of the city, and a personified God (see Arendt, *Denktagebuch*, 381).
69. Arendt, "What Is Authority?" 119.
70. HC, 223.
71. For Arendt, the only exception to this rule was Kant. See Hannah Arendt, "'What Remains? The Language Remains': A Conversation with Günter Gaus," in *Essays in Understanding*, 2.
72. Arendt, "Socrates," 27.
73. Arendt, "What Is Authority?" 114–15.
74. Arendt, *Denktagebuch*, 198. In the original *der Mensch*, *der* underlined.
75. For instance Eric Voegelin: "If Plato's evocation of a paradigm of right order is interpreted as a philosopher's opinion about politics, the result will be hopeless nonsense, not worth a word of debate" (Eric Voegelin, *The Collected Works*, v. 16, *Order and History*, v. III [Columbia: University of Missouri Press, 2000], 125).
76. Miguel Abensour, "Against the Sovereignty of Philosophy over Politics: Arendt's Reading of Plato's Cave Allegory," trans. Martin Breaugh, *Social Research*, 4, no. 74 (2007): 975.
77. "The German word *Bildung* clearly indicates the essence of education in the Greek, the Platonic sense," Jaeger, *Paideia*, v. 1, p. xiii.
78. HGA 34, 114G; 83E.
79. HGA 34, 115G; 83E.
80. HGA 34, 116G; 84E.

Chapter 2

The German Idea of *Bildung*

The idea of *Bildung* consists of a whole complex of themes that can be analyzed from many different angles. It is a complicated historical, social, cultural, and literary phenomenon. It is also an idea connected with a specific time and place that has no exact counterpart in other cultural circles.[1] This is also the reason why translations, like "formation," "education," or "development," never fully reflect its meaning and their multitude tends to obscure their reference to the specific German cultural phenomenon. Therefore, I will abstain from translation and maintain the original German term. The idea of *Bildung* came to life in the last three decades of the eighteenth century and was systematically developed until the establishment of the University of Berlin in 1809. Its reactivation at the beginning of the twentieth century is owed to the great study of Eduard Spranger[2] and to the publication of some previously unknown writings of Wilhelm von Humboldt.[3]

In the perspective of this book and the place *Bildung* takes in its structure, two problems seem to be the most interesting. First, to what extent the German idea of *Bildung* is a philosophical idea: how it is entangled in the dilemmas of the philosophy of the time and, to what extent it legitimizes philosophy by bestowing on her a special role in the structure and idea of a modern university. Second, how the philosophical idea of *Bildung* can be inscribed in Hannah Arendt's political concepts, particularly in the problem of Jewish assimilation in German culture.

Although *Bildung* is rightly associated foremostly with Wilhelm von Humboldt (and in its literary dimension with Johann Wolfgang Goethe), when presenting its genesis I cannot entirely omit Johann Gottfried Herder. His work will return in one of the later chapters, since his thought and particularly his vision of history is a relevant reference for Arendt's concept of politics. But since it was Herder who introduced this idea into German culture, I need to acknowledge him in the context of its emergence.

As long as the work of Humboldt testifies to the development of *Bildung* up to its full shape, the prior work of Herder is more an adumbration of this development, a premonition of a new epoch. Herder is in many aspects a thinker on the dividing line between the Enlightenment and Romanticism and his idea of *Bildung* emerges from his protest against the systematic rationalism of the Leibniz-Wolff school, dominant at that time. It turns against the hopes of the Enlightenment of mastering the world and human beings by reason. Here, the two contexts of this protest are relevant: the esthetic and the historical.

In Herder, "image" (*Bild*) as a model (*Vorbild*) for *Bildung* acquires an ethical and pedagogical meaning.[4] For the individual, the meaning of images relies on the power of imagination, that is, the power of displaying the world in one's soul: "Impressions deliver the raw material to the soul: the soul imprints on the material its own image, according to its own nature and previous experience."[5] The idea of autonomy, so important for *Bildung*, also emerges here: The soul, through a sensual image, connects with beauty, with the ideal of beauty, independent from other ideals and norms.[6] Herder mentions the privilege of human being for art and undermines Rousseau's conviction that a human being is only a destroyer of nature: "A certain sort of art is the nature of man."[7] In Herder the formation of man consists not only in the developments of nature, but also in its shaping through the aesthetic ideals of beauty and harmony.

According to Herder, education is not the accelerator of natural development, which would otherwise proceed by itself. Neither is it a process of shaping the individual according to a universal ideal of humanity. It is a never-ending process of becoming this concrete human being; it is not mechanical, but it is an unpredictable outcome of the mutual influence of internal dispositions of the individual and a coil of external circumstances: both natural and cultural, or historical. The theses of Herder are independent from such humanisms that are based on the premise of an ultimate fulfillment of humanity. His works testify to the emergence of a new idea of humanism, later undertaken and developed by Humboldt, which emphasizes humanity not as an established characteristic of man, but as his vulnerability to formation and education.[8]

At the next stage of this analysis we need to undertake the question of the philosophical background of the Humboldtian idea of *Bildung*, specifically his stance toward the role of the state in general education. It is important insofar as the liberal attitude of Humboldt does not stay the same throughout his life. The turning point will be the historical events preceding his appointment to the head of the Department of Confessions and Education in the Prussian

Ministry of Internal Affairs, the battles of Jena and Auerstedt, and the occupation of Prussia by Napoleon's troops. Within this context we can discern two periods in the development of *Bildung* since Herder: on the one hand, the early but already mature work of Humboldt, that is, the last decade of the eighteenth century, which resulted in the neohumanistic *idea* of *Bildung,* and on the other hand, the years immediately preceding and immediately following the reform of public education in Prussia, when the neohumanistic idea of *Bildung* became the social and cultural *ideal.* The exact dates of the second period cannot be defined. But we can assume it is between the battle of Jena (1806) and the Vienna Congress (1815); then the idea of university was not only constituted, but also realized by the foundation of the Friedrich Wilhelm University in Berlin.

HUMBOLDT:
IDEALISM—NEOHUMANISM—LIBERALISM

Out of the many facets of Humboldt's oeuvre, the most relevant to our topic are freedom and individuality. Not only are they central to his conception of *Bildung*, but they are also the source of the power of its pedagogical promise. Therefore, the basic philosophical assumptions of the Humboldtian idea of *Bildung* in the first period of its development will be analyzed from the viewpoint of its most important element, the idea of freedom.

I

The political liberalism of Wilhelm von Humboldt is based on an assumption arising from his theory of *Bildung*: Any positive action of the state exceeding interventions necessary for maintaining the substantial safety of citizens is harmful for the development of human powers. It is because these actions put limitations on freedom and the variety of situations in which humans find themselves, and these are the necessary conditions for their development. From this assumption, combined with the critiques of the absolutist state on the one hand, and the French revolution on the other,[9] emerges the classical liberal program, described in *The Sphere and Duties of Government (The Limits of State Action)* from 1792. In this writing, Humboldt puts serious limitations on the role of the state: "The state is to abstain from all solicitude for the positive welfare of the citizens, and not to proceed a step further than is necessary for their mutual security and protection against foreign enemies; for with no other object should it impose restrictions on freedom."[10] The liberal activity of the state, concerned only with security, is based on an anthropological premise: Safety is the only thing a man cannot attain by himself, individually. And since it is, at the same time, the prerequisite of freedom, it needs to be externally secured for the sake of individual development. The only limitation placed on the freedom of the individual is the freedom of other individuals. Any institutions, whose purpose exceeds substantial security, are harmful. State institutions, as such, weaken the powers of the nation. It is because "State measures always imply more or less positive control; and even where they are not chargeable with actual coercion, they accustom men to look for instruction, guidance, and assistance from without, rather than to rely upon their own expedients."[11]

The counterpart to the individual ideal of *Bildung* is a political ideal, with freedom as its most important prerequisite: "What is to flourish in man, needs to emerge from himself and not to be imposed on him."[12] This kind of freedom is a positive one that always leads to the development of individuality. Freedom is a necessary condition, and if it is not fulfilled, any governmental or educational activity, no matter how beneficial it seems to be, is corruptive: "Whatever man is inclined to, without the free exercise of his own choice, or whatever only implies instruction and guidance, does not enter into his very being, but still remains alien to its true nature, and is, indeed, effected by him, not so much with human agency, as with the mere exactness of mechanical routine."[13]

Humboldt differentiates between education, which he understands as imposing an external goal, from the individual *Bildung*. That is why he is essentially an opponent of public education, which, by its nature, more often serves external state goals than individual formation. One can see the conspicuous influence of Rousseau here: Public education, which is always aimed at raising a citizen, necessarily neglects formation of a human being. Although Humboldt, unlike Rousseau, did not see "citizen" and "human being" to be contradictory terms, he was afraid of colonization of the latter by the first. "The freest development of human nature [*Bildung*], directed as little as possible to the ulterior civil relations, should always be regarded as paramount in importance with respect to the culture of man in society."[14] Public education, since it is haunted by the spirit of government, shapes a human being according to a citizen form and endangers the development of individuality. Therefore, public education, like other spheres, should find itself outside governmental influence.

II

The liberalism of early Humboldt is not purely political thought, for its basis is informed by humanist anthropology and the theory of *Bildung*. As already said, the neohumanist ideal of man is founded on two principles: freedom and individuality. It is these anthropological principles that imply the negative role of the state, described above. This is why, in the *Limits of the State*, where Humboldt analyzes the limits of state influence on its citizens, we also find a concise and meaningful conceptualization of this ideal:

> The true end of Man, or that which is prescribed by the eternal and immutable dictates of reason, and not suggested by vague and transient desires, is the highest and most harmonious development [*Bildung*] of his powers to a complete and consistent whole. Freedom is the grand and indispensable condition which the possibility of such a development presupposes; but there is besides another essential—intimately connected with freedom, it is true—a variety of situations.[15]

The first imperative of *Bildung* is the development of powers toward a whole. This is a leitmotif in all Humboldt's writings on education. In subsequent works he acknowledges the different conditions of this development and also its anthropological premises.

Whereas in *The Limits* Humboldt analyzes *Bildung* from the perspective of freedom, one year later, in *Theorie der Bildung des Menschen* ("Theory of the Bildung of Man," 1793), he emphasizes mostly the multiversity of situations: *Bildung*, although its higher principle is individualism, and maybe because of it, needs relationships with the external world. Human powers need an object resistant to them, through which they could shape themselves. Pure thought is a form needing material, and humanity requires struggles with the external world.[16] Although Humboldt uses the classical scheme of form and matter, his premises are of Kantian origins. The conditions of the possibility of experiencing the world are in the subject: "The very nature of man compels him to transcend himself towards objects. It is very important that in this alienation he does not lose himself [. . .]. He must approach this plurality of objects and press the form of his spirit onto this material, so that they become more alike."[17] Like in Kant, in Humboldt it is the subject that is a condition of the possibility of the object and beyond this relation we can only speak of things themselves that escape any attempts at description. Nevertheless, Humboldt exceeds Kant insofar as he does not limit himself to the description of the transcendental conditions of the possibility of a relationship between subject and object. For him this relationship is also a tangible and mutual influence of man and the world, whose sense lies in the strengthening of spiritual powers: "The ultimate task of our existence: to confer as much content as possible to the idea of humanity in our person [. . .]; this task can be fulfilled only by interconnecting our self with the world and by making of this interconnection the most general, lively and free mutual impact."[18]

In *Über den Geist der Menschheit* ("On Human Spirit," 1797), Humboldt is looking for the absolute measure, an ideal of humanity. But this ideal cannot be defined, it remains "something unknown." Its description, even if it is done with philosophical methods, remains individual, since neither the freedom nor self-assertion of man can be hindered. Without this elusive measure man could not acquire his surroundings or influence it in any way, he would be unable to "translate the world into his individuality and leave an imprint of his individuality on the world."[19] This measure is not a general and common idea, rather, an ideal, created individually: "It is impossible to assess man other than asking: what content did he confer to the form of humanity? Provided that he is the only example of humanity, what idea of humankind would one get after meeting him?"[20] Human spirit is a kind of mediator between man and the world; spirit also makes the difference between sheer acquisition of knowledge and *Bildung*, because: "Cognition educates us truly only when, having acquired the form of our spirit, it develops an affinity with our nature."[21] In this way we can approach the Humboldtian understanding of human powers: These are not in-born abilities (as they were in Herder), but have a certain abstract potential, which can be identified and concretized only in a relationship with the world.[22] This spiritual potential can never be grasped ultimately, since the process of *Bildung* is unlimited in time and space: "What makes man great does not know any limits of fulfillment. He forms himself towards infinity, there is no point to be his ultimate destination."[23]

III

Although the work of Humboldt cannot be considered without its philosophical sources in speculative thought—Kant (active subject), Fichte (the non-transparency of the self), Leibniz (the idea of power)—equally important was Herder's influence, although slightly neglected by Humboldt himself. "Among the whole of images in history, none turns more of our common and lively attention than an image of people and diversity of their ways of life [. . .]."[24] The theoretical background for the idea of *Bildung* cannot be only pure philosophy, but also history and comparative anthropology.[25] Their task consists in the combination of empirical observations with the generality of philosophical reflection. It is not an easy enterprise, for the acquisition of knowledge about the human being carries double the risk: On the one hand, we have Scylla of overgeneralizations and loss of detail, on the other we have Charybdis of limitations of too particular and individual observation: "In order to know man exactly as he is and at the same time to be able to assess, in what direction he can develop, the practical sense of observation and the philosophical spirit have to cooperate."[26] Comparative anthropology is thought of as a synthesis of philosophy and empirical anthropology. In this way it reflects the dual nature of man being a sensual and super-sensual creature at the same time. Thus, the aim of anthropology is also double: It recognizes the multifariousness of human characters on the one hand, while on the other it can assess them, outline the paths of their future development and their mutual influence in the whole.[27]

The diversity of Humboldt's thought, the tensions arising from the combination of two different perspectives, the purely philosophical and anthropological-historical, bring about the aspect that the theory of Humboldt cannot be considered as a fully harmonious relationship between man and the world. The *Bildung* of man consists in the dialectic of alienation and the return from alienation.[28] Humboldt's freedom is surely not the freedom of an idealist subject. Anthropology, history, language, supported by the power of imagination are the necessary conditions of mediation between the self and the world.

Next, I will analyze the idea of *Bildung* in its political application, in its encounter with the historical circumstances in which Prussia found itself at the beginning of the nineteenth century.

HUMBOLDT: THE IDEA OF UNIVERSITY

It is impossible to analyze the meaning of the Prussian reform of education without taking into account the situation of higher education before Humboldt's time. Up to the eighteenth century, universities were institutions reigned over mostly by scholasticism. Their task was to develop the doctrine and preserve the scientific status quo rather than support the avant-garde methods of emerging new sciences. Their aim was not research (this function was fulfilled by royal academies), but training the future doctors, lawyers, and clergy.

Under the influence of the Enlightenment, the position of scholasticism as the only doctrine spread at the universities was significantly weakened. University education in the Enlightenment functioned mostly according to the rules of utilitarianism and specialization: "In the early modern states universities made up a part of the administrative apparatus; their purpose lay not in the cultivation of arts and sciences, but in the education of state officials and—after the schism in the Church—spreading the denomination of particular rulers."[29] There were certain significant exceptions to this pattern in Germany, to which belonged Göttingen, Jena, and Halle, but more and more often they were endangered by liquidation and replacement by practical and specialized schools, the state institution preparing diligent and conscientious candidates for the public service. Their criteria of quality were to be exclusively effectiveness and profitability.[30]

I

The reform of education was the last of the series of constitutional, administrative, social, and economic Prussian reforms (known as the Stein-Hardenberg Reforms). These reforms had been planned in 1807 after the battles of

Jena and Auerstedt and the Treatises of Tilsit, by virtue of which Prussia lost half of its territory. Wilhelm von Humboldt belonged to the group of reformers, who took responsibility for raising Prussia from the debasement resulting from its defeat by Napoleon and the ensuing occupation of the country. Humboldt's task consisted in laying the foundations for a new educational system. Although Humboldt held the head position in the Department of Confessions and Education for only sixteen months, "his actions gave a fresh impetus to educational policy whose effects have been felt right down to the present day."[31] The structure of public education was based on the prerequisites of humanistic *Bildung*. Since neohumanism rejected the utilitarian pedagogy of the Enlightenment, the first premise of Humboldt's reform was the absolute priority of general education over specialist and vocational training, on every level of schooling. Humboldt's activity in the ministry meant a temporary victory over pragmatism, continuing specializations, and vocationalization of education as well as subjugating education to the interests of the churches.

The general framework of the reform of universities, embodied by the foundation of the University of Berlin in 1809, were enclosed in the writing "On the Internal and External Organization of the Institutions of Higher Education in Berlin" (1810). The University of Berlin was a model institution of modern higher education, followed by other German and European universities. Humboldt was inspired by the idealist, Fichtean idea of pure science, which, combined with the principles of freedom and individualism of neohumanistic education, enabled formulation of the ideal of solitude and freedom in scientific research. But he supplemented the idealist concept of science with a new streak, which, put in the context of freedom, constituted the power and originality of the reform. It is the ideal of science as an open problem, always incomplete, always *in statu nascendi*, and which has not been completely discovered and developed, and never will be.[32]

The ideal of open (incomplete) science supported the second famous principle for higher university education, that is, the principle of education by research. It released science both from the limitations of the scholastic doctrine and the encyclopedic tradition of the Enlightenment. When Humboldt was trying to define the tasks of the university anew, he consciously undermined the traditional division of functions between teaching universities and research academies. The necessity of research at universities was also derived from the principle of free development of spiritual powers, based on interaction with the external world. The university has to function in a different way than schools: While the task of the school is to teach established knowledge, the task of the university is different—the professor's role is not to transfer the ready outcomes of research, but to actually research together with his students and to add to the development of knowledge or even to the concept of science itself. It was something completely new: the definition of science as a never-ending process of research, discerning university didactics from school didactics and combining university teaching with research itself, forming the principle of unity of teaching and research, and subsequently shaping the specifics of German universities.[33]

II

As we can see, the idea of the German university is strongly based on the fundamental assumptions of *Bildung*: Its main postulate is freedom and the highest possible development of the spiritual powers of man. The main principle of this university is the academic freedom of "living in ideas," which needed protection from political influences. Humboldt basically maintained his early liberal idea of the limits of state action. The state has to be faithful to the idea of the university. The autonomy of the university consists in separating the university from state actions. The state has no right to intervene in university affairs. The state is only the external form of society and has to be aware of its harmful influence on public and private matters.[34] Nevertheless, we can see here a very subtle and at the same time significant shift from the classical liberal program I have described above. While *The Limits* expresses Humboldt's purely anti-state standpoint, in the first years of the nineteenth century, undoubtedly under the influence of historical events, we can see a gradual development of political and state responsibility in Humboldt. It is not only that Humboldt, as a man of public duty in the Department of Education, cannot simply reject public education. There is more to it than that: The deep crisis of German sovereignty modified and mollified his radical liberal ideas.

Moreover, we have to keep in mind that what we today call the "Humboldtian university" is not exclusively the work of one man. The rights to the authorship of the idea of the German university go also to, among others, Friedrich Schleiermacher, Johann Gottlieb Fichte, and Friedrich Wilhelm Schelling. Each of them in the founding period of Berlin University took part in the public discussion of the idea and organization of universities. Although they have much in common, the differences between them are significant. Humboldt as a writer could have ignored them, but as a public officer he had to take them into account and attempt reconciliation.

It was difficult, particularly in the case of Fichte who was outright suspicious of the abundance of academic freedom. He imagined the university not as an institution of free *Bildung*, but, rather, as an organization whose task is the education (upbringing) of the nation.[35] His image of the university depicts an institution of strict discipline, a sort of scientific monastery. Neither he nor Schelling shared the liberal attitude of Humboldt and his careful description of the relations between the state and the university. For Schelling in turn, the state is an objectification of the world of ideas. The state is an external form of the unified system of knowledge. In this way he closely bonds university and state. They have not only a common goal, but also an analogous structure.[36] Fichte went even further here: He projected in detail the future constitution of Berlin University as reflecting the constitution of the ideal state under the rule of law.[37] He replaced the congruence of goals and the structural analogy with a state-like organization of the university, comprising the detailed regulations of academic life. The closest to Humboldt's liberalism seems to be Schleiermacher, who, contrary to the other two, does not refer to a concept of an ideal state, but analyzes the historical circumstances and emphasizes the limited interest of state mechanisms in supporting science.[38] He is aware of the tension between science and politics and of the dangers for scholars involved in politics. It is also Schleiermacher who emphasizes the role of academic freedom.

Humboldt was entirely in accordance with Schleiermacher's idea of freedom of studies, unrestricted student life, and the freedom of teaching and research. At the same time, Schleiermacher's idea that the spiritual life of the nation has its highest point in the institutions of higher education also became Humboldt's conviction and led to a reconciliation between university and state. Although Humboldt remains much more liberal and much more careful than Fichte and Schelling were, as far as the relations between state and university are concerned, in him also, the goal of the university eventually becomes congruent with the higher goal of the state.

It is a significant shift: The former unavoidable tension between the freedom of the individual and state power fades or even disappears. The former negative concept of the state is modified; now the state has a positive goal exceeding security. The development of individuals is now a counterpart to the development of societies. Science is a chance for individuals to flourish, which on the societal level brings freedom. Good scientific institutions are in accordance with the spiritual life of man. The autonomy of science has to be organized by government, whose role is to keep an eye on universities so that they do not transform into secondary schools or specialized institutions. Nevertheless, the state still has no right to demand that the university fulfills the state's goals.

III

The traditional idea of university, on the one hand understood as *universitas magistrorum et scholarum*, the community of teachers and learners, and on the other as *universitas litterarum*, the unity of sciences, was saved in Humboldt, but filled with new content. The community of professors and students now meant being together in research and in philosophical thinking. Humboldt also reformulated the traditional idea of the unity of sciences based on philosophy. He drew back from Kant's idea from *The Conflict of the Faculties*, according to which the faculty of philosophy, in contrast with theology, law, and medicine, is entirely free in its search for truth, for it is the only discipline not bound by an external authority. Philosophy, unlike in the traditional university structure, should have a primary role and rule over other sciences. It is because philosophy is not one of the sciences but a sphere of free reason and therefore a critical instance that controls them. This postulate was saved by the reformers, although the justification varied. As we will see, mostly it was not the philosophical critique in the Kantian meaning anymore, but the unity of sciences guaranteed by philosophy.

As we have seen, the authors of the idea of university are not completely in accordance and sometimes the differences in their approaches are conspicuous. Nevertheless, the three disputants of Humboldt seem to agree on one matter: All of them believe in the "organic" unity of science: "Education in one concrete discipline has to be preceded with cognition of the organic unity of sciences"[39]—with this statement of Schelling, Fichte and Schleiermacher would also concur. All of them consider philosophy to be a science of special status within the structure and organization of the university. One needs to remember that the faculty of philosophy was understood to be much wider than nowadays and usually comprised everything not covered by law, medicine, and theology. But there was also the so-called pure philosophy (metaphysics) and a paramount role was assigned to it. The faculty of philosophy was to reflect the natural organization of the sciences.

Humboldt himself, careful about the relationship between the state and the university, was also careful about the primary role of the philosophy faculty. He was not a philosopher per se and did not consider philosophy as a queen of sciences or the only possible means of communication between the sciences. But the position of philosophy was not inferior either. As long as philosophy facilitates the fulfillment of *Bildung*, it should reign in any spiritual activity and diffuse all disciplines. Indeed, if we remember the basic premises of the idea of *Bildung*—freedom, individuality, the ideal of open science, and the role of research in education—we understand that "research" here has nothing to do with the empirical methods of the natural sciences; it is, rather, the free inspiration of the teacher, thinking, the search for sources, and individual study, all that Humboldt called "living in ideas." We can see that the basis is also philosophical here and that apart from all the differences between the father founders of the modern university, it was founded on a common philosophical basis. Philosophy is a central element of all studies.

IV

To sum this up, first, the Humboldtian university was bound with, a more or less carefully formulated, reconciliation of the idea of the university with the idea of the state. Since the idea of the university is based on the neohumanistic idea of *Bildung*, this ceased to be the purely liberal idea, insofar as the former contradiction between *Bildung* and state power disappeared. Second, the idea of the Humboldtian university was founded on the distinguished role of philosophy in the structure of the sciences, and, what follows, on the distinguished role of philosophy in the organization of the university. So far, I have considered these two matters separately. Now they will have to be connected and the possible consequences of this connection need examination.

In the context of the German idea of *Bildung,* the classic Platonic conflict between philosophy and politics shifts into the sphere of the relation between the state and the university. The solution of this conflict was provided by the idealist philosophy of reconciliation, which, as we could see, also unified the goal of the state and the goal of the university. The connection between the idea of the university and the idea of the state does not give rise to any objections and does not endanger academic freedom as long as the state is liberal (in a political, not economic sense, of course), respects the autonomy of the university, and does not attempt to directly influence academic affairs. But this connection bears potential dangers and they will have to be acknowledged in both historical and philosophical dimensions.

Historically, the state of harmony postulated by Humboldt, where politics has only an ancillary role to play, turned out to be very fragile. In Germany, only after liberalism yielded to the conservative reaction that came to the fore after the Vienna Congress, the influence of the state on universities and schools turned out to be contradictory to the postulates of the creators of Friedrich-Wilhelm University in Berlin. The state whose only goal was to support the culture of the nation turned out to be a fiction. The great merit of Humboldt was reinstating the universal role of the university. But this also meant that universities as places with which the nation identified itself, and which were to reflect its highest power, became too important to function beyond political influence. Jürgen Habermas stresses that the Humboldtian university had to pay the price of independence for the state organization of its freedom. From the very beginning it was not clear how to unify the role of the university as a crowning of national culture with its political independence.[40]

The Humboldtian model of the university facilitated the overcoming of the inferiority of Prussia against Napoleon through the education of a modern state administration. Up to the revolution of 1848, German universities were centers of liberal and democratic thought, seen as a danger by the Holy Alliance. In 1848 the resistance of university circles was ultimately broken and many professors expelled. From then the elementary university virtue became political neutrality.[41] After the unification of Germany by Bismarck, universities became conservative and nationalist, although still presenting very high academic standards.[42]

When we combine the historical observation about the influence of the state on universities with the factual superiority of philosophical faculties, we can see a new dimension of political influence, putting both the university and philosophy in jeopardy. If the state wants to intervene in academic matters, it will try to influence directly the essence of the university, which in this case is philosophy. One of the possible ways of such influence, unintentionally, Humboldt himself guaranteed when he postulated that the state should fill the vacant university lecterns.[43] When we connect this with a state examination system and state funding, the areas for political influence become quite spacious. Apart from this we can also think of methods of less official pressure. All that amounts to the danger that in unfavorable political circumstances, philosophy becomes a tool of state control and the philosopher a device in governmental hands.

Here, one cannot avoid the association with the infamous Rector Speech of Heidegger. While reading "The Self-Assertion of the German University," we can see that Heidegger's conception of the university, although he referred constantly to the Greek spiritual legacy, was modern to the core. The speech of 1933 is like a prism focusing and magnifying the potential dangers mentioned above. In Heidegger, like in Fichte, yet in incomparably more extreme political circumstances, the principle of the university is "a Volk that knows itself in its state."[44,45] When speaking of science as one of the duties of the university for the nation, Heidegger refers to the Greek concept of science, which is identical to philosophy: "All science is philosophy, whether it knows it or wills it or not."[46] By doing so, although he refers to Aeschylus and uses a different language from that of the authors of the idea of the university, he stays faithful to the tradition of the Humboldtian university and its premise of the unity of science under the guidance of philosophy. Faculties have to fit into the idea of the philosophical or scientific spiritual unity of the nation. But when Heidegger touches on the problem of academic freedom, we cannot speak of the continuity of the Humboldtian tradition anymore. However, it is not a Greek tradition either, but a very modern one—a radicalized Fichtean fear of academic freedom: "The much praised 'academic freedom' is being banished from the German university."[47] University based on national duty is an institution of strong leadership, spirited by discipline and obedience. Obviously it does not mean that any of the authors cited above could be made responsible for Heidegger's statement. But his speech is a good example of how a political helplessness is inscribed into the structure of the German university, not diminishing its intellectual excellence (or more precisely, only in extreme circumstances).

It is not an accident that German universities after 1848, apart from their high academic standards, very rarely became centers of political resistance and so easily gave in to political powers. The case of Heidegger's rectorship is dramatic, because it is a case of fusion, in one person, one of the greatest German minds of the time with a complete lack of political judgment. As a rector of Nazi conferral, Heidegger is a representative of neither Greek *paideia* nor German *Bildung*. But the possibility of such a conferral was potentially present in premises that arose after the political defeat of Prussia over a century earlier.

ARENDT: *BILDUNG* AND ASSIMILATION

The demise of the Holy Roman Empire of the German Nation in the year 1806 was also a turning point in the process of assimilation of Jews, which had started only a few decades before. As we will see, it was also bound with the reshaping of the German idea of *Bildung*, mostly with the increase of its social impact, which came along with the crisis of German statehood and Humboldt's reform of schooling.

I

The period of the emergence of the idea of *Bildung*, the last three decades of the eighteenth century, the time of Herder, Goethe, Lessing, and young Humboldt, was the first period in German history when the chance to integrate the Jews into the German nation arose. It is true, the Prussia of Frederic the Great, where the majority of German Jews lived, was by no means politically very friendly to them and they were subjugated to numerous limitations and prohibitions. But it is also true that at this time the idea of religious tolerance, equality before the law, and universal humanity, unheard of since the Christianization of Europe, appeared in the heads of writers and philosophers and was introduced to the wider public.

In 1743 to Berlin came a young Moses Mendelssohn. After years he became a distinguished German philosopher, respected by Kant, in friendship with Lessing and other great representatives of the Enlightenment. "He was the first of a long line of assimilated German Jews who worshipped German culture and civilization, and whose enterprise, two centuries later, would come to such a horrendous and abrupt end."[48] In 1781 the king's counselor Christian Wilhelm Dohm published a plea for equal rights for Jews ("On the civic advancement of Jews"). To be sure, it was ignored by Frederic the Great and did not bring any practical and political changes, but it contributed to a change in the intellectual climate. In the year 1783 there was the premiere of *Nathan the Wise* by Lessing. The play is an explicit praise of religious tolerance, and refers to the ideal of universal humanity, which is more important than differences between people.[49] At the same time Herder foresaw the influence of Jews on the democratization of Prussia and advocated for the full integration of the Jewish people with Germans, not based on religious tolerance, but on political emancipation.[50]

Apart from any possible differences between Herder, Lessing, and Humboldt, all of them are in unison in one thing: Common humanity finds its voice in the ideal of *Bildung*. This ideal also became a fundamental assimilation medium of that period: a great promise, a passport to the spiritual community of the German people. Mendelssohn's generation wanted to integrate fully into German culture and preserve the Jewish faith. The time of the development of *Bildung* is also the time of the flourishing of salons led by Berlin Jewesses. The life of the salons focused on culture, literature, and self-education. One of the first was League of Virtue (*Tugendbund*), founded by Henriette Herz. Its members were prominent representatives of the Enlightenment, among others the Humboldt brothers. Another such place was the famous Berlin attic of Rahel Levin at Jägerstrasse, with its focus on the Goethe cult. The important feature of these places was their social neutrality: They were open for both Jews and Germans, males and females, people of different social strata, actors, and nobility. Hannah Arendt stressed that what connected the members was not social bonds, but self-education.[51] The salons and the living idea of *Bildung* they embodied released Jews from the need to seek social advancement at all costs. Now, the basis for their acceptance was common culture and striving for its development.[52] *Bildung* was for Jews even more important than for Germans, who won their place in the nation and culture more naturally, simply by being born.

At that time it was believed that the path of Mendelssohn was basically open to any Jew. "Their true home, we know now, was not 'Germany,' but German culture and language. Their true religion was the bourgeois, Goethean ideal of *Bildung*."[53] Since Jews had to find their place in the nation, those who could not count on privileges reserved for the wealthy or on court privileges, embraced education as a visa to Germany. The salons and *Bildung* that inspired them enabled an access to the public world of philosophy, literature, music: the world of culture. However, as it was not a political change, it turned out to be extremely fragile. If "assimilation always meant assimilation to *the Enlightenment*,"[54] along with the downturn of the Enlightenment, the assimilation, almost automatically, was doomed.

II

Neither the ideal of the Enlightenment, the Berlin salons, nor the purely humanistic ideal of *Bildung* stood the test of time. At the beginning of this chapter I analyzed *Bildung* on a theoretical level as an idea of human formation in the Enlightenment and early Romanticism. But, in order to understand the meaning of *Bildung* in the context of the so called "Jewish question," we also need to look at the process in which *Bildung* gained a social meaning.

Apart from being developed as an individual and ethical idea, *Bildung* gradually became an instrument of social stratification. New social-political phenomena appeared at that time, and the most significant was the emergence of society, crucial for Arendt's analyses of modernity. "In the 18th century a new power entered the European scene, which later became extremely important for the character and influence of 'spirit' and its representatives: the social 'sphere' and its spiritual impact."[55] The "social sphere" was of exclusive character and defined itself by a negation of "alien spirit." This means, it defined itself in opposition to the ideals of the former nobility, who in *Bildung* saw a danger for the old order, as well as in opposition to lower classes (peasants, petit bourgeois). Foremostly in the social sphere appeared the wealthy bourgeois, who could follow the ideal of *Bildung,* and that part of nobility, who were ready to forfeit the traditional privileges for the sake of a new aristocracy of spirit. Thus, *Bildung* slowly became an ideal of the new middle class. As such, it was also a mechanism of distancing oneself from the old order: "The 'educated' as a group considered themselves released from the socio-political hierarchy, founded on power-relations, and to be included into a different, social-spiritual hierarchy, competing with the political one. On the top of it stand the educated as an elite."[56] One strived for *Bildung*, because it meant belonging to the elite of the "educated."

The transformation of *Bildung* into a social ideal was coeval with Humboldt's reform of education, which, against the intentions of reformers, supported this process. The reform of schooling in Prussia (especially on the elementary level) was planned according to the ideas of Swiss pedagogue Johann Heinrich Pestalozzi, fully accepted by Humboldt. His mission was to make general education and comprehensive development of personality accessible to all social classes. And yet, after the reform, the full implementation of the new program of education was limited to the higher classes, who could afford the free time for attending high school and university. "In this way, in the epoch of advancement of the bourgeoisie, a new social opposition came into being, which during the nineteenth century, supported by the state system of credentials, resulted in a sort of educational class society (*Bildungsklassengesellschaft*)."[57]

After the ultimate victory over Napoleon, when the external pressure on the Stein-Hardenberg reforms faded and after the Vienna Congress, when conservative powers returned to the political scene, it became clear that the beneficiaries of the reforms were not peasants, craftsmen, or petit bourgeoisie, but the nobility and the wealthy bourgeoisie.[58] The new academic secondary school (*Gymnasium*) allowed for lessening the former distance between the nobility and the bourgeoisie, but it also caused a split in the bourgeoisie, between the wealthy and the poor. The economic differences did not manifest themselves immediately, but they became a source of a distinction between "educated" and "not educated." The new academic secondary schools flourished also as a result of not accepting children from the lower classes. And since they were a necessary condition for university studies, both an actual and formal one, they became a barrier restraining certain groups from overly high educational ambitions: "Humanistic secondary schools and universities developed as institutions of *Bildung* founded on social exclusion."[59]

The early educational careers of Hannah Arendt and Martin Heidegger make a lively example of this dichotomy. Both were exceptional talents. Arendt, a daughter of an assimilated Jewish family, for whom the ideals of *Bildung* were natural, graduates from secondary school on an extramural basis after having attended university lectures in Berlin for a year. Further studies in a freely chosen academic center in Germany and in freely chosen subjects, according to intellectual passions, are a matter of course. Heidegger, a child of a simple family from a little Catholic town, Meßkirch, attends a *Bürgerschule* (non-academic secondary school), because there is no *Gymansium* (academic secondary school) in Meßkirch and his parents cannot afford to send him to another town. After all, his education is enabled not by the liberal humanism of *Bildung*, but by the Catholic Church, which wants to take advantage of the distinguished talents of the teenager for confessional duty. Only owing to a series of church stipends and for the price of intellectual obedience up to habilitation, there opens a possibility, which for a bourgeoisie child like Arendt was taken for granted. Thus, first he attends a *Gymnasium* in Constance, then university—but only within the limits of doctrine and for the price of monastery life.[60]

Thus, along with the inscription of *Bildung* in the political structures, the "free development of powers" turned out to be strictly regulated: "It is a paradox that humanistic thought which referred to what is common to humans above what is bourgeois, specialized, vocational, was used to create a new privileged group in Prussia."[61]

As a response to social and historical changes, a philosophical critique of *Bildung* developed as a critique of society and culture. The first author who dared to severely criticize *Bildung* at the apex of its flourishing was Nietzsche. In 1872[62] he undermined the social economy connected with *Bildung*, foremostly harnessing it to state duty. Although Nietzsche's standpoint is that of an aristocracy of spirit and he is the last to deplore the limitations in the social range of *Bildung*, his observations coincide in sociological analyses on one important point: *Bildung* is being misused by the social economy and the ideal of *Bildung* becomes a coin in social circulation. The true *Bildung* is distorted and, separated from the self, it ceases to mean a personal transformation and becomes only an external form, a social shell that does not concern the human subject any more.

Eventually *Bildung* was by no means only a universal and ahistorical philosophical concept. But its historical range testifies that it was neither a purely ideological component, fixing the *status quo*. *Bildung* carried a potential for social change, less spectacular but analogous to that of the French revolution. In Germany this transformation proceeded differently: through education and through making education an object of desire. As we saw, on the one hand *Bildung* was an emancipation promise for the bourgeoisie, enabling them to have a say in power relations. And it was also a weapon against feudalism, "a breakthrough of a 'bourgeois' subversive thinking, disguised as universal human norms of life and education."[63] On the other hand, within the development of civic society it had the opposite, adaptive function: "In the historical sense, *Bildung* served not only as a weapon against the feudal nobility, but also as an instrument of social distinguishing from the lower classes."[64] This distinguishing function will also be very important in the perspective of the Enlightenment promise of assimilation.

III

The year 1806 and the following years after the defeat of Prussia were also an important caesura in the process of assimilation of Jews into German culture. Along with the crisis of German statehood, the support for assimilation, which had been increasing since the appeal of Christian Dohm, diminished radically. It was a complete change of mood: Enlightened humanism retreated and made space for nationalism and the cult of reason, and human community made room for "the sacred union of church, people and the state."[65] Nationalism, triggered by political events, was strengthened by underscoring the uniqueness of nation or even race, characteristic of Romanticism. "The appropriation by Jews of *Kultur* and the cult of *Bildung* [. . .] threatened the very survival of German nationhood and culture."[66] The old fear of the strangeness of Jewish orthodoxy was replaced by antipathy toward assimilated Jews, whose striving at *Bildung* and German culture was now seen as a danger for the nation.

The Berlin salons also did not survive the French-Prussian war. They fell apart together with the universal ideal of *Bildung*. The old circles, centered on a common cultural enterprise, were now replaced by patriotic associations. Unlike in the salons, the gateway to them was, once again, social position and name. And the important measure was participation in the civil service and the manorial aristocracy. New salons were programmatically political, and the national affairs were supported by the singing of patriotic songs. Arendt comments with characteristic irony: "This was the origin of that odd mixture—found only in Germany—of patriotism and men's glee clubs."[67] Among the most prominent organization of this sort was The Singing Circle, later The Christian-German Table Society. The change in mood was accompanied by the change of criteria upon which one could be accepted as a member: The Table Society excluded all groups that were associated with the Enlightenment: Jews, Philistines, the French, and women.[68] The synonym of philistinism became everything that disagreed with their national ideology.[69] The difference between the old and the new salons Arendt describes again with due ironic distance: "Altogether characteristic of the style of the meetings is that they were held at the noon meal, in contrast to the salons that came together at tea time or in the evening. It is a crucial difference whether one drinks beer or tea."[70] The situation changed not only in terms of old conservatives and nationalists raising their voices. The main problem was that the former representatives of the Enlightenment now moved to new societies: So was the case with Humboldt, Schleiermacher, and Heinrich von Kleist. Humboldt remained, for sure, a liberal and democrat, an advocate of equal political rights, and later paid the price of his political career for this. But people of less stable views inclined toward nationalism or even anti-Semitism. The new wave was not a natural turn in history, it was much more dangerous.

When we associate this history of assimilation, which so soon turned out to be illusory with the transformation of the idea of *Bildung*, we gain a wider context for this history. The paradigm of these changes from the Jewish perspective is the biography of Rahel Varnhagen. The demise of Prussia and the ultimate end of the Enlightenment confirms the intuition of Jews that, in Arendt's words, "the past clung to them as a collective group; that they could only shake it off as individuals."[71]

> The Jews as a whole could no longer assimilate. Mendelssohn was still always able to speak in the name of "the" Jews, whom he wanted to enlighten and to free. He believed—like Dohm—that it was the Jews *as a whole* he would emancipate. The baptismal movement in the next generation shows that the Jewish question had become by then a problem for the *individual* Jew, had become the problem of somehow coming to terms with the world.[72]

The biography of Rahel Varnhagen shows the painful ambivalence intrinsic in the Jewish identity in the Diaspora, additionally intensified by the events in Germany. When the image of the community of *Bildung* occurred to be an illusion, Rahel, as many others, faced a choice: to preserve their national identity at the price of social exclusion, or to strive for social acceptance by becoming an "exceptional Jew"—a person so attractive, apart from her origins, who could still count on respect in society. Nobody believed in the possibility of Mendelssohn's biography anymore: to become a German and a great German and at the same time to remain a Jew. Since the disappearance of the salon, Rahel was subject to an inner war between being a social outsider, who identifies with her Jewishness at the cost of social exclusion, and being an "exceptional Jew" at any cost to find a place in the goy's society, even if the price is to reject one's own Jewishness. Rahel—if we use Arendt's typical terms—was a pariah who tried to become a parvenu.

Along with the transformation of the humanistic idea of *Bildung* into the social ideal of bourgeoisie, education changed its role in assimilation. Like in non-Jewish society, it ceased to be a promise (never fulfilled, in fact) for anybody who had talent and endurance to become an "image of humanity" and was reshaped into a mechanism of separation from lower classes; so for the Jews it ceased to be a universal promise of assimilation and became a way to enter the society at the price of separation from non-educated Jewry. A good illustration here is the history of anti-Jewish riots in 1819, where mobs demolished Jewish houses and shops, first in Würzburg, and then in many other German cities. The reaction of educated Jews was rather inhibited: "The detachedness and the lack of personal identification with the victims on the part of the Jewish upper middle class is an indication that the rich and the largely converted intellectual Jewish elite were turning their backs on the poor and the petit bourgeoisie."[73]

The wave of anti-Semitism (a term coined only later) that flooded Germany, less officially after the battles of Jena and Auerstedt, and more officially after the Vienna Congress, and which intensified on the occasion of any new political or economic crises up to the demise of the Weimar Republic, separated individuals from the Jewish people. One could observe two opposite, though not contradictory, tendencies. On the one hand, the bourgeoisie constituted through *Bildung*, displaced Jews from society: "The Jewish element was expelled from society as soon as the first signs of cultivated middle class society began to dawn,"[74] while on the other hand, Jews tried to preserve their status by becoming transparent as Jews: "Just as every anti-Semite knew his personal exceptional Jews in Berlin, so every Berlin Jew knew at last two eastern Jews in comparison with whom he felt himself to be an exception."[75]

On the margins of the historical development of the German idea of *Bildung* emerges a serious dilemma of integration. The member of a minority people, living somewhat on the outskirts of the society, always faces a difficult choice: to preserve his/her national identity at the price of social exclusion, or to strive for social acceptance as an exception at any cost. In *The Origins of Totalitarianism*, whose first part is a generalization and development of themes undertaken in Rahel's biography, Arendt describes the second attitude as "the parvenu's bad conscience at having betrayed his people and exchanged equal rights for personal privileges."[76] This situation is a painful paradox not only because, like in Rahel's case, it brings about an inner split, but also because it translates into political relations: Whatever improvement of the situation of the oppressed people as a whole endangers the status of its exceptional, socially accepted representatives. The essential difference between them and the rest disappears, they cease to be exceptions, and become members of the oppressed group, eliciting mercy, hatred, or contempt. Thus, they need to distinguish themselves even more, to sacrifice even more for their social acceptance.

The tension between the attitude of the pariah and that of the parvenu discloses the fundamental problem of assimilation and the reason for which it had to turn out to be an illusion. The assimilation of Jews in the German nation was never a political assimilation, understood as an equality of rights: "Such discussions of the Jewish question always remained on a theoretical level and were about the rights of man, not about achieving equal rights for a fellow citizen of a faith different from that of the Christian state and world around him."[77] *Bildung* was a kind of substitute for political assimilation and it came forward to be a social one: founded on differences and reserved for those who could prove to be exceptional. According to Arendt, the self-knowledge of parvenus excluded real political awareness, which compels one to fight for political rights on the margins of society. Meanwhile, the social assimilation proceeded somewhat independently from political assimilation. First, as we know, it was based on the philosophical and literary premises of early *Bildung*, and it referred to universal humanity. But in the real world, the universal humanity, not supported by any political solutions, always turned out to be a too fragile premise, too abstract and too "otherworldly": "One can resist only in terms of the identity under attack. Those who reject such identifications on the part of a hostile world may feel wonderfully superior to the world, but their superiority is truly no longer of this world."[78]

Therefore, in the second stage of its development, *Bildung* made for Jews a different promise than for Mendelssohn's generation: Similarly, as for the bourgeoisie, it became a promise of separation from the lower classes, but for Jews it meant a promise of separation from the Jewish masses. This means, however, that emancipation was firstly of a humanistic, then of a social, but never a truly political character: "Pedagogical reform was the surrogate for political participation: education alone was supposed to ennoble, and thus to conceal, the lack of political hegemony."[79] The Jews were never integrated into the German nation as the Jewish people: "The peculiar fact that in Germany the Jewish question was held to be a question of education was closely connected with this early start and had its consequence in the educational philistinism of both Jewish and non-Jewish middle classes, and also in the crowding of Jews into the liberal professions."[80]

The *Bildung* of the nineteenth century was a false promise for Jews not only because it assumed a separation from political measures for the sake of individual social acceptance, but also because there were other more down-to-earth reasons: The university, the crowning of formal education in the nineteenth century, was at the same time a place where Jews, from its very beginnings up to the victory of Nazism, had limited access. Although the history of Jews at German universities exceeds the scope of this chapter, one thing must be underscored. *Bildung*, at least the aspect connected with the state structures, became a feeble promise for Jews only ten years after the foundation of the University of Berlin. A hundred years later, Max Weber put it succinctly, which would be as true in 1819 as it was in 1919: If the student is a Jew, "of course one says *lasciate ogni speranza*."[81]

CONCLUDING REMARKS

This chapter was an attempt to show in what sense the philosophical idea of *Bildung* carried an unfulfilled promise. Of course, we need to discern between *Bildung* as a buoyant and endurable philosophical and pedagogical idea, still alive in the tradition, from its historical concretizations. The historical and social circumstances that cannot be grasped in purely philosophical analysis, turn out to be relevant for the reason that *Bildung*, to a much higher extent than Plato's *paideia*, made a factual basis for state education. Plato was a great philosopher who bestowed a great promise on pedagogy. In the tradition, it was treated very seriously and had tremendous philosophical and pedagogical impact. But Plato was never an author of historical reform of education, as was the case with German philosophers. It is the reason why *Bildung* had to be analyzed not only from a philosophical point of view, but also from historical and sociological ones. Only such analyses, because of the fact that they take different aspects into consideration, could disclose the ambiguity of the idea that came to the fore when it was faced with historical circumstances.

The theme of this chapter comprised two important things: First, that the idea of *Bildung*, applied in the reform of education, puts philosophy at the top of the paramount institution of *Bildung*, that is, the university. Combined with the state organization of the university, it puts philosophy in a difficult situation: Elevating it in the hierarchy of the sciences, it makes it the most important element of the state organization of the university, and, what follows, a vulnerable object for external ideological pressures. Here the idea of *Bildung* becomes an unsatisfied promise of freedom, expressed in the autonomy of the university. Second, along with the application of *Bildung* into school reform, it became a social value, which served the bourgeoisie for separation from the masses. The power of differentiation, present in the social ideal of *Bildung*, also disclosed the unfulfilled promise of assimilation of Jews into the German nation, present in the neohumanistic idea. It is not an accident that those tensions appeared or came forward in the concrete historical moment of the humiliation of Prussia during the Napoleonic wars. Neither is it an accident that both the unfulfilled promise of assimilation and the project of harmonious relations between universities and the state suffered a complete failure during another crisis of German statehood, and led the Weimar Republic to the catastrophe of the year 1933.

Next, I will analyze a great pedagogical promise of philosophy carried by the early thought of Martin Heidegger, mostly in *Being and Time*.

NOTES

1. See Hans Weil, *Die Entstehung des deutschen Bildungsprinzips* (Bonn: H. Bouvier u. C. Verlag, 1967), 2.
2. Eduard Spranger, *Wilhelm von Humboldt und die Humanitätsidee* (Berlin: Reuther & Reichard, 1909).
3. Foremost is his programmatic writing on university. "On the Internal and External Organization of the Institutions of Higher Education in Berlin," see note 32.
4. Weil, *Die Entstehung*, 68.
5. Johann Gottfried Herder, "Uebers Erkennen und Empfinden in der menschlichen Seele," in *Herders sämmtliche Werke* (Suphan), Band 8 (Berlin: Weidmannsche Buchhandlung, 1883), 252.
6. Weil, *Die Entstehung*, 41.
7. Johann Gottfried Herder, "Ein Gemälde des werdenden Tages der Schöpfung," in *Herders sämmtliche Werke* (Suphan), Band 6 (Berlin: Weidmannsche Buchhandlung, 1883), 152.
8. Weil, *Die Entstehung*, 77.
9. Wilhelm von Humboldt, "Ideen über Staatsverfassung, durch die neue französische Constitution veranlasst," in Humboldt, *Werke in 5 Bänden*, Band I, *Schriften zur Anthropologie und Geschichte* (Darmstadt: Wissenschaftliche Buchgesellschaft, 1960).
10. Wilhelm von Humboldt, *The Sphere and Duties of Government (The Limits of State Action)*, trans. by Joseph Coulthard (A Project of Liberty Fund) http://oll.libertyfund.org/title/589, 30.
11. Humboldt, *The Limits of State Action*, 19.
12. Humboldt, "Staatsverfassung," 36.
13. Humboldt, *The Limits of State Action*, 22.
14. Humboldt, *The Limits of State Action*, 41.
15. Humboldt, *The Limits of State Action*, 13.
16. Wilhelm von Humboldt, "Theorie der Bildung des Menschen." Bruchstück, in *Werke in 5 Bänden*, Band I, *Schriften zur Anthropologie und Geschichte*, 235.
17. Humboldt, "Theorie der Bildung," 237.
18. Humboldt, "Theorie der Bildung," 235–36.

19. Wilhelm von Humboldt, "Über den Geist der Menschheit," in *Werke in 5 Bänden*, Band I, *Schriften zur Anthropologie und Geschichte*, 512.
20. Humboldt, "Geist der Menschheit," 515.
21. Wilhelm von Humboldt, "Das achtzehnte Jahrhundert," in *Werke in 5 Bänden*, Band I, *Schriften zur Anthropologie und Geschichte*, 410.
22. Alfred Schäfer, *Das Bildungsproblem nach der humanistischen Illusion* (Weinheim: Deutscher Studien Verlag, 1996), 40.
23. Humboldt, "Geist der Menschheit," 512.
24. Wilhelm von Humboldt, "Über die Gesetze der Entwicklung der Menschlichen Kräfte." Bruchstück, in *Werke in 5 Bänden*, Band I: *Schriften zur Anthropologie und Geschichte*, 43.
25. See also Hans-Josef Wagner, *Die Aktualität der strukturalen Bildungstheorie Humboldts* (Weinheim: Deutscher Studien Verlag, 1995), 17.
26. Wilhelm von Humboldt, "Plan einer vergleichender Anthropologie," in *Werke in 5 Bänden*, Band I, *Schriften zur Anthropologie und Geschichte*, 338.
27. Humboldt, "Plan einer vergleichender Anthropologie," 344.
28. Schäfer, *Das Bildungsproblem*, 36.
29. Reiner Künzel, "Politische Kontrolle und Finanzierung—die Zukunft staatlicher Steuerung," in *Mythos Humboldt—Vergangenheit und Zukunft der deutschen Universitäten*, ed. Mitchell Ash (Wien: Böhlau, 1999), 181.
30. Eduard Spranger, *Wilhelm von Humboldt und die Reform des Bildungswesens* (Tübingen: Max Niemeyer Verlag, 1965), 13; Joachim Knoll and Horst Siebert, *Wilhelm von Humboldt. Politik und Bildung* (Heidelberg: Quelle & Meyer, 1969), 30.
31. Gerd Hohendorf, *Wilhelm von Humboldt (1767–1835)*, "Prospects: The Quarterly Review of Comparative Education" (Paris, Unesco: International Bureau of Education), 23, nos. 3–4 (1993): 613.
32. Wilhelm von Humboldt, "Ueber die innere und äussere Organisation der höheren wissenschaftlichen Anstalten in Berlin," in *Werke in 5 Bänden*, Band IV, *Schriften zur Politik und Bildungswesen* (Darmstadt: Wissenschaftliche Buchgesellschaft, 1964), 257.
33. See also Peter Lundgreen, "Mythos Humboldt in der Gegenwart: Lehre—Forschung—Selbstverwaltung," in *Mythos Humboldt*, 147.
34. Humboldt, "Ueber die innere," 257.
35. Johann Gottlieb Fichte, "Deduzierter Plan einer zu Berlin zu errichtenden höheren Lehranstalt, die in der gehöriger Verbindung mit einer Akademie der Wissenschaften stehe," in *Die Idee der deutschen Universität. Die fünf Grundschriften aus der Zeit ihrer Neubegründung durch klassischen Idealismus und romantischen Realismus*, ed. Ernst Anrich (Darmstadt: Wissenschaftliche Buchgesellschaft, 1956), 145, 217.
36. Friedrich Wilhelm Joseph Schelling, "Vorlesungen über die Methode des akademischen Studiums," in *Die Idee der deutschen Universität. Die fünf Grundschriften*, 61.
37. Fichte, "Deduzierter Plan," 216.
38. Friedrich Schleiermacher, "Gelegentliche Gedanken über Universitäten in deutschem Sinn," in *Die Idee der deutschen Universität. Die fünf Grundschriften*, 226–27.

39. Schelling, "Vorlesungen," 4.

40. Jürgen Habermas, "Die Idee der Universität—Lernprozesse," in *Die Idee der Universität. Versuch einer Standortbestimmung* (Berlin-Heidelberg: Springer Verlag, 1988), 150.

41. Knoll and Siebert, *Wilhelm von Humboldt*, 48.

42. Hans-Joachim Meyer-Abich, "Die Universitäten und die deutsche politische Kultur der Gegenwart," in *Mythos Humboldt*, 235.

43. Humboldt, "Ueber innere," 265.

44. Martin Heidegger, "The Self-Assertion of the German University," trans. William S. Lewis, in *The Heidegger Controversy: A Critical Reader*, ed. Richard Wolin (Cambridge, MA: The MIT Press, 1998), 30.

45. See Fichte, "Deduzierter Plan," 139.

46. Heidegger, "The Self-Assertion," 31.

47. Heidegger, "The Self-Assertion," 34. Thus, any analogies that can be made between a Heideggerian reading of Plato's allegory of the cave and his political engagement, which are also present in this book, need to take into account the distance of modern philosophy between Plato's and Heidegger's thought. Although Heidegger consciously rejected the modern legacy, he remained dependent on its mediation to some extent.

48. Amos Elon, *The Pity of It All: A Portrait of the German-Jewish Epoch, 1743–1933* (New York: Picador, 2002), 11 (Scribd).

49. "Is Jew or Christian rather Jew or Christian/than man? May I have found in you another/Who is content to be esteemed a man?" Gotthold Ephraim Lessing, *Nathan the Wise*, Act II, scene V, trans. Ellen Frothingham (New York: Leypold & Hold, 1871), 79.

50. Johann Gottlieb Herder, "Adrastea," Band IV, *Unternehmungen des vergangenen Jahrhunderts zu Beförderung eines geistigen Reiches*, chap. 5. *Bekehrung der Juden*, in *Herders sämmtliche Werke* (Suphan), Band 24 (Berlin: Weidmannsche Buchhandlung, 1886), 63.

51. Hannah Arendt, "Berlin Salon," in *Essays in Understanding*, 59–60.

52. Hannah Arendt, *Rahel Varnhagen: The Life of a Jewish Woman* (New York: A Harvest/HBJ, 1974), 27.

53. Elon, *The Pity*, 9.

54. Hannah Arendt, "Original Assimilation: An Epilogue to the One Hundredth Anniversary of Rahel Varnhagen's Death," in Hannah Arendt, *The Jewish Writings*, eds. Jerome Kohn and Ron H. Feldman (New York: Schocken, 2007), 22.

55. Weil, *Die Entstehung*, 193.

56. Weil, *Die Entstehung*, 9.

57. Wilhelm Richter, *Der Wandel des Bildungsgedankes. Die Bruder Humboldt, das Zeitalter der Bildung und die Gegenwart* (Berlin: Colloquium Verlag, 1971), 66.

58. Dietrich Benner, *Wilhelm von Humboldts Bildungstheorie. Eine problemgeschichtliche Studie zum Begründungszusammenhang neuzeitlicher Bildungsreform* (Weinheim und München: Juventa Verlag, 1990), 175.

59. Knoll and Siebert, *Wilhelm von Humboldt*, 38.

60. The social-economic relations in the context of Heidegger's biography are brilliantly described in Rüdiger Safranski, *Ein Meister aus Deutschland. Heidegger und*

seine Zeit (Frankfurt am Main: Fischer Verlag, 2006). English: *Martin Heidegger: Between Good and Evil*, trans. Ewald Osers (Cambridge, MA: Harvard University Press, 1998).

61. Richter, *Der Wandel*, 66.

62. Friedrich Nietzsche, *On the Future of Our Educational Institutions*, trans. John McFarland, Archive.org.

63. Weil, *Die Entstehung*, 222.

64. Hans-Christoph Koller, *Bildung und Widerstreit. Zur Struktur biographischer Bildungsprozesse in der Postmoderne* (München: Wilhelm Fink Verlag, 1999), 105.

65. Elon, *The Pity*, 136.

66. Elon, *The Pity*, 137.

67. Arendt, "Berlin Salon," 62–63.

68. Arendt, "Berlin Salon," 63, *Rahel Varnhagen*, 123, Elon, *The Pity*, 138.

69. The intellectual representative of which became Fichte. In the *Addresses to the German Nation*, delivered in the years 1807–1808, he defines "humanism" and "liberalism" as "alien words, which in German is more truly called slackness and unworthy conduct" (8). Fichte regards Germans as a synonym of nation, whose purity requires protection from "admixture of, or corruption by, any alien element" (135–36). Johann Gottlieb Fichte, *Addresses to the German Nation*, trans. R. F. Jones and G. H. Turnbull (Chicago: The Open Court Publishing, 1922), Archive.org.

70. Arendt, "Berlin Salon," 64.

71. Arendt, *Rahel Varnhagen*, 30.

72. Arendt, "Original Assimilation," 23.

73. Elon, *The Pity*, 147.

74. Arendt, *Rahel Varnhagen*, 58.

75. Arendt, *Rahel Varnhagen*, 85.

76. Hannah Arendt, *The Origins of Totalitarianism* (New York: A Harvest Book, Harcourt, 1985), 67.

77. Hannah Arendt, "Antisemitism" in *The Jewish Writings*, 62.

78. Hannah Arendt, "On Humanity in Dark Times, Thoughts about Lessing," in Hannah Arendt, *Men in Dark Times* (New York: A Harvest Book, Harcourt Brace, 1995), 18.

79. Jacob Taubes, "The Intellectuals and the University," trans. Charlotte Elisheva Fornobert et al., in Jacob Taubes, *From Cult to Culture: Fragments toward a Critique of Historical Reason* (Palo Alto, CA: Stanford University Press, 2009), 291.

80. Arendt, *The Origins*, 60.

81. Max Weber, "Science as a Vocation," in Max Weber, *Essays in Sociology*, trans. H. H. Gert and C. Wright Mills (New York: Oxford University Press, 1946), 134. The quote is from Dante, *The Divine Comedy: Lasciate ogni speranza, voi ch'entrate*: "Abandon all hope you who enter here."

Chapter 3

Authenticity
The Pedagogical Promise of Heidegger

In this chapter I will analyze the early period in Heidegger's philosophy, especially *Being and Time*, his *opus magnum* of 1927. It is a work in which a new, and at the same time familiar, educational promise is hidden. But while concepts such as *paideia* and *Bildung* make a connection between philosophy and education in an obvious way, the analysis of Heidegger's philosophy in the part titled *Philosophical Tradition and Education* requires some justification. Before we move to an analysis of *Being and Time* as a new answer to Plato's problem, we need also to refer to a possibility of an interpretation of early Heidegger in the context of the idea of *Bildung*. Irrespective of all the critical remarks of Heidegger against *Bildung* (chapter 1), his pedagogical agenda can be interpreted as an answer to the critical situation of the Weimar Republic, which, in the view of his contemporaries, was also a crisis of education.

CONTEXTS

The beginnings of Heidegger's academic career were marked by the tensions of the historical context of the catastrophe of the First World War. These tensions are present at the heart of Heidegger's thought. They also make his view on the university more complicated than interpretations that want to see in them a linear movement toward his infamous rectorate.

Just as in the situation after the defeat by Napoleon, after WWI, Germany again fell into a deep crisis. And, just as after 1806, also after 1918, the revival of the sciences and the reform of the university were regarded as ways toward the spiritual renewal of the nation. But there was no public agreement as to how this renewal was to be initiated. Schematically speaking, the spiritual climate of postwar Germany was split into two opposite, even contradictory stances.[1] One is expressed in Oswald Spengler's *The Decline of the West*.[2] The representative of the second is Max Weber: His lecture *Science as a Vocation* was an answer to an atmosphere of which Spengler's book was, at the same time, a trigger and a symptom.

The Decline of the West (already outlined before the war) is framed by sharp dichotomies. The fundamental one is a dichotomy between culture, understood as a living being with a soul, and civilization, understood as the dead remnants of culture, in which all the spirit has been replaced by mechanical forms of survival. Civilization, according to Spengler, is in an agonal state of a declining culture. From this basic opposition further dichotomies emerge: the juxtaposition of spirituality and intellect, wisdom and calculative intelligence, people bound with the earth, and the amorphous city crowd. The final agony of the modern culture of the West came in the nineteenth century: "A century of purely extensive effectiveness, excluding big artistic and metaphysical production—let us say frankly an irreligious time which coincides exactly with the idea of the world-city,"[3] which was also a time of demise. Western culture petrifies and dies and the triumph of press, parliamentary democracy, and economy belong to its convulsive, agonal movements. This process can endure for centuries but is irreversible: "We cannot help it if we are born as men of the early winter of full civilization."[4]

The task of this, surely simplified, presentation of Spengler's views is less to stay true to its full content and more to show how it functioned in the public consciousness. It was one of the rare situations when a philosophical book, not easy to read, but reduced to slogans, perfectly fit in its own time. After the war Spengler's fatalism was fertile soil for heroic appeals for spiritual responses to the crisis, reverberating also from university lecterns.[5]

By contrast, Weber's lecture *Science as a Vocation* (1919) was delivered as a voice of protest against the pretentions of academic prophets (not only the followers of Spengler, but also representatives of the mystic George-Kreis), who desired to take over the role of spiritual leaders of the youth. Weber criticizes the tendency of replacing meticulous academic work, which is always a precondition of valuable ideas with new idols for youth: "personality" and "personal experience." "In the field of science only he who is devoted *solely* to the work at hand has 'personality.'"[6] He appeals for intellectual honesty, for bracketing the political and religious views in research, the lack of which bears not only the danger of indoctrination of students but also badly influences a multispectral view of reality and facilitates the manipulation of facts for the sake of worldview and belief. Karl Löwith, who was present at the lecture, recalls: "After the innumerable speeches of literary activists, Weber's words were like a salvation."[7]

What can be astonishing for those who are inclined to interpret Heidegger's thought as a linear development from his early contributions to the infamous rector's speech (e.g., Victor Farias and Richard Wolin) is that Heidegger did not support Spengler's position, which would be only logical in the light of such a linear interpretation of his intellectual biography. Moreover, his writings and lectures preceding *Being and Time* refer outright to the Weberian spirit. In the first post-war Freiburg semester (winter 1919) Heidegger appeals for the renewal of the university as an awakening of a truly scientific consciousness and combats the prevailing tendencies to identify philosophy and worldview: "The personal stance of the philosopher must be—as in every science—excluded."[8] Heidegger also emphasized a total freedom in research, with truth, the only limitation: "The theoretical sphere is a sphere of absolute *freedom*, and I am obligated only to the idea of scientificity."[9]

Already in 1911, while still being under the influence of Catholicism, even if only institutionally, in the periodical "Akademiker" Heidegger published an appeal for philosophy, which is not a game of subjective opinions and moods, not a "personal experience."[10] Over the following years this appeal gains more and more content and acquires more and more conceptual sharpness. In 1925 (Arendt was already present), Heidegger refers directly to Weber and scolds his critics: "Taking Weber's standpoint to be that of despair and helplessness, one wanted to restore meaning to science and scientific work and sought to do so by cultivating a world view of science and constructing from it a mythical conception of the sciences."[11] The critique of understanding philosophy as a discipline in which conceptual rigorousness is unnecessary and of identifying philosophy with a worldview appears in subsequent lectures up to 1930.[12]

Heidegger also desires a spiritual renewal of the nation. But the program of this renewal is still clear-headed in the Weberian way: instead of ecstasies of the soul and clinging to a worldview (let alone an ideology), a return to the things themselves—analysis of the structures of being, which are conditions of the possibility of worldviews, science, and philosophy. The longing for sense, so pertinent to this epoch, was also Heidegger's longing. But he strived at it not as a provincial "conservative antimodernist,"[13] but foremostly as a professor of the German university, observing the rules of scientific honesty and conceptual rigor, while at the same time creating a program of a complete renewal of academic philosophy. This does not mean that Heidegger was working on "value-free philosophy." His phenomenological "ontology of crisis" will combine a precise philosophical analysis with existential appeal. But it has to be remembered that *Being and Time*, for Arendt always the most important text of Heidegger, was emerging in the atmosphere of conceptual and logical discipline, analytical decency, and meticulous critical reading of the texts of philosophical tradition.

In the works Arendt wrote with the intention of publication, we will not find many direct references to Heidegger. The open discussion with Heidegger appears only toward the end of the lives of both in the *Life of the Mind*.[14] However, if we chart such documents as *Denktagebuch* or her correspondence with Heidegger (and with Jaspers), it turns out that Arendt was not only continuously reading Heidegger (after the twelve-year break of the Thousand-Year Reich, as she ironically put it), but was also grappling with it all the time. After the reconciliation of 1950, her records referring to Heidegger obviously comprised primarily new texts that Heidegger kept sending Arendt, and which she always read, and which already belong to his post-war, after-the-turn writings. But it would be misleading to think that the philosophy of the 1920s was overshadowed by them in Arendt's reception. Elisabeth Young-Bruehl is right when she states that Arendt "had reservations, always, about Heidegger's thought, and she always felt that *Being and Time*, not the later work, was his greatest contribution."[15] In the letter of May 8, 1954, Arendt is trying to describe the outline of *The Human Condition* and comments: "I would not be able to do this, if indeed I can, without what I learned from you in my youth."[16] Arendt has in mind the first semesters of her studies in Marburg: the lecture of the winter term 1924–1925 on Plato's *Sophist*,[17] the summer term 1925 (*History of the Concept of Time*[18]) and the winter-term 19251926 (*Logic: The Question of Truth*).[19] All these lectures belong to the period of *Being and Time*.

In this chapter I will try to consider *Being and Time* as the third (after Plato's *paideia* and German *Bildung*) promise of philosophy for education, which can still be interpreted within the framework of the positive relationship between the two fields. I will also undertake a reconstruction of Hannah Arendt's almost unspoken criticism of Heidegger's *opus magnum*.

Heidegger makes a complicated problem for both philosophy and education for many reasons. On the one hand, he is rightly regarded as a philosopher who challenged the philosophical tradition and during the 1920s discovered the past anew with the methods of phenomenological ontology, which was also a deconstruction of Western metaphysics. Rüdiger Safranski describes the first lectures of Heidegger not only as a manifest against the predominant post-war philosophy of life and worldview philosophy, but also as a provocation against the pathos of Man, Value, Beauty, and Good: "a dadaist episode in philosophy."[20] For instance, when talking about experience, he "took his students' breath away, although accustomed to far more strident experiences in the war."[21] As we will see, Arendt shared the conviction of the novelty of Heidegger's interpretations of Western thought.

On the other hand, however, from Arendt's viewpoint, Heidegger's encounter with the Western philosophical tradition where he undermines this tradition from within, still operating with its categories, was not and could not have been radical enough. For Heidegger, while radicalizing the tradition, fell for certain traditional opinions. The aim of this and following chapters is not squeezing Heidegger back into the framework of tradition or denying him originality. It is, rather, showing the demarcation line, presenting Heidegger as an ambivalent figure, situated both within and outside the tradition. If we look at *Being and Time* from this perspective, it will emerge that Heidegger's ingenious description of everydayness discloses his affinity with Plato's allegory of the cave.[22] This also legitimizes my reading of *Being and Time* as a continuation of the traditional relationship between the philosophical tradition and education.

Since Arendt basically identified the philosophical tradition with the tradition of political thought, the pedagogical promise of Heidegger's early philosophy will have to be considered also with respect to its possible political implications. The leitmotif of both aspects will be two excerpts of Paul York in his letters to Dilthey. The context suggests Heidegger's identification with them.

THE PEDAGOGICAL DIMENSION OF *BEING AND TIME*

Toward the end of *Being and Time* a quotation appears that sheds light on the general intention of the work: "The practical aim of our standpoint is the pedagogical one in the broadest and deepest sense of the word. It is the soul of true philosophy and the truth of Plato and Aristotle."[23] Although it is a quotation from a correspondence between Paul York and Wilhelm Dilthey, it can certainly be assumed that Heidegger uses it on his own behalf. In order to understand the power of this claim, we need to remember the fundamental idea of *Being and Time*.

Being and Time is an attempt to lay the foundations for a completely new ontology, but at the same time drawing back on the greatest struggles in the field of the question of being within Western culture. This ontology is based on a deconstruction of the traditional convictions of what it means to *be*.

A clear indication of the direction of this deconstruction we find in a much later text from 1961:

> If we recall once again the history of Occidental-European thought, then we see that the question about being, taken as a question about the being of beings, is double in form. It asks on the one hand: What are beings, in general, as beings? Considerations with the province of this question come, in the course of the history of philosophy, under the heading of ontology. The question "What are beings?" includes also the question, "Which being is the highest and in what way is it?" The province of this question is called theology. The duality

of the question about the being of beings can be brought together in the title "onto-theo-logy."[24]

In *Being and Time,* the interpretation of Western metaphysics as ontotheology was not yet clearly expressed. But the whole endeavor proceeds toward exposing the sense of the Western questioning of being. This question is not simply one of many philosophical problems. Our understanding of being has always constituted the relation of man toward beings and himself. The task of the Heideggerian deconstruction is to reach deeper than metaphysics: The metaphysical *statements* of philosophy are here interesting as *answers* to the hidden question of being behind these statements. Deconstruction is a way to expose the question itself.

In Heidegger's view, Western metaphysics, since Plato, understood being on the basis of the highest being. It was the highest being that defined the sense of the being of man and the world. Since the highest being (Plato's idea, a personified God and philosophers' gods of all sorts, like the Absolute of German idealism, for instance) has been always characterized by time categories as a perennial entity, as an "eternal now," something beyond time, a present that never passes, our understanding of being became a derivative of this timelessness. Thus, we have had a metaphysical tendency to understand our own being and being of the world as versions of the present time, or as Heidegger would say, the presence-at-hand. The metaphysics of the West is a metaphysics of presence where being lost its primary bond with time. The loss of time-horizons resulted in a situation where the problem of being slipped out of human understanding, and—as an outcome of our metaphysical helplessness—transformed into an empty logical term. That is why in logic and philosophy a dogma reigns, supported by the authority of Kant and Hegel, that *being* is a most universal, indefinable and self-evident concept, the pondering of which is a waste of a philosopher's time.

The fundamental agenda of Heidegger is very simple: to show that *being*, counter to traditional beliefs, *means* something and, moreover, that abandoning this concept as not demanding philosophical care is a mistake and not only a theoretical one. Heidegger wants to revive the long forgotten "Battle of Giants concerning Being." Now we better understand the quotation from York and the way in which Heidegger identifies with its message: The revival of the question of being transgresses theoretical and academic borders. Its aim is pedagogical: The deconstruction of the Western ontology is to change our understanding of ourselves. The correlation of being and time in the title has the purpose of (although in a constant struggle with the giants of Western thought) reversing our thinking and founding a new understanding of being, within the perspective of finite time. This means that our interpretation of being cannot derive its understanding from the highest being or the whole of beings (it cannot be another version of onto-theo-logy), but it has to begin with what is closest and at the same time accessible only with difficulty. That is, ontology has to begin with a single being that combines two features: It is accessible in experience and somehow understands being. These two conditions fulfills only one being: man. But our traditional understanding of the human being as, for example, the combination of body and soul or transcendental subject has to be bracketed here. The human being in Heidegger is being-there, encountered here and now in concrete circumstances: *Da-sein*. To put it in other words, man, because he or she constantly refers to being, is the only timely being in the primary sense of the word. There is no other way of learning something about being as such than through a description of human *Dasein* and its ways of being. They are always modes of understanding of being as such.

Thus, we need to start from the basic, pre-philosophical ways of being of a human being, that is, from a description of everydayness. But it would be misleading to think that the description of everydayness is a simple and everyday affair. Although we have to describe what in the *ontic* sense is closest to us, that is, ourselves, it does not mean that from the *ontological* viewpoint of being we have a direct access to ourselves. More often than not, we do not understand ourselves as beings who relate to our own existence, but we derive an understanding of ourselves from the being of other entities. "No arbitrary idea of being and reality, no matter how 'self-evident' it is, may be brought to bear on this being in a dogmatically constructed way,"[25] says Heidegger, having in mind both traditional philosophical or scientific conceptions and common anthropological beliefs.

Here the Heideggerian method becomes clearer: On the one hand, it is a deconstruction of the history of ontology, that is, "a loosening of the sclerotic tradition" and a "demonstration of the provenance of the fundamental ontological concepts, as the investigation that displays their 'birth certificate.'"[26] On the other hand, since *Dasein*'s access to the understanding of being is not self-evident, a phenomenology will be needed. Heidegger takes over Husserl's motto "to the things themselves!" But he understands it differently: not as a description of the content of consciousness, which bracketed the knowledge of existence of itself and the world, but just the opposite: as a description of being of what shows itself. But since usually we encounter entities without questioning their ways of being, the being of entities is hidden and it does not appear to us. That is also why Heidegger's understanding of a phenomenon is not the same as its simple appearance. A phenomenon is, rather, "something that does not show itself initially and for the most part, something that is *concealed*. [. . .] But at the same time it is something that essentially belongs to what initially and for the most part shows itself, indeed in such a way that it constitutes its meaning and ground."[27] Therefore, it is "not this or that being but rather [. . .] the *being* of beings."[28] An analysis of the structure of existence requires not only conceptual consistency, but also a new language, "not only words, [. . .] but also the 'grammar.'"[29] This new language has to be phenomenological and deconstructive at the same time.

Thus, *Being and Time* is nothing more than an anti-traditional phenomenological description of the structures of *Dasein* with respect to its fundamental time-structure.

I

Since Heidegger was trying to grasp the basic ways of being of man, it is understandable that he started with the elementary dimension of human existence, that is, being-in-the-world. In his view, the being of the world, "wordliness," can be adequately described only as a correlate of a being, who as the only being is truly "in-the-world," that is, *Dasein*. The world grasped in such a mode does not appear as an object or a totality of entities, but as a meaningful whole, a structure, whose meaning is related to the human ways of being. The phenomenological description of everydayness, which is prior to philosophical or scientific accounts, reveals the world primarily appearing as a home full of useful things, tools, where everything has its pre-given place. The world as a correlate of *Dasein* is a structure of tool-like, significant relations. In such a world there are no objects, but ready-to-hand (handy) things: They always relate to other things and, ultimately, to the goal of all relations, which is always *Dasein*. A tool is not an object, it is always hidden behind its usefulness and reference. The basic way of being in the world is using tools, or "*association in* the world *with* innerwordly beings (*Umgang*)."[30] This way of being has its particular way of seeing, which Heidegger calls *circumspection* (*Umsicht*). In this place it has to be noted that Heidegger understands "tool," "useful thing," and "handiness" very comprehensively: anything that relates to something else in the way of what-for is a tool (so a tool is not only a hammer, but also a street, the stars, etc.). A sign is also a tool, which refers to something external to itself (e.g., traffic sign). And it is the structure of a sign that reveals the ontological character of the world clearly. A sign can refer to something only because we come across it within a certain pre-given total relevance (*Bewandtnisganzheit*). The simplest arrow contains a complicated contexture, without which it would be nothing, that is, it would mean nothing. The whole system of involvement relates ultimately to *Dasein*, is for-the-sake of it, and forms a background in which particular things can reveal their meanings. Thus, *Dasein* is in such a way that the world is always already a priori open as a certain total relevance. The world as a structure of relevance is always a significant structure, a structure of *significance* (*Bedeutsamkeit*).

That is why in the lectures directly predating *Being and Time,* Heidegger can say: "The character of the being of the entity which we call world, [. . .] shall be terminologically conceived as a worldhood, [. . .] understood not as a character of the being of the entity but rather as a *character of being of Dasein,* and only through it and along with it that of the entity!"[31]

In his search for a more original way of encountering the world than that described by modern philosophy, Heidegger is trying to overcome the, predominant since Descartes, helplessness of philosophy in an adequate grasping of the existence of other human beings. Initially it appears that his ontological concept of the world as a total significant relevance remedies this helplessness. In this structure others are already inscribed: They are encountered together with the world as coexisting *Daseins.* Just like a tool-like structure of references, the existence of other people comes prior to a subject-object relation. A reference to another human being or beings is a structural element of the handiness of the world; they are also here-and-there, tools and signs also refer to them: "On the basis of this *like-with* being-in-the-world, the world is always already the one that I share with the others. The world of Da-sein is a *with-world.* Being-in is being-with others."[32] Being-with is an existential category just as the world is. *Dasein* exists in such a way that others are a priori already there. "As being-with, Da-sein 'is' essentially for the sake of others."[33]

II

For Arendt, the inscription of others into the ontological structure of the world must have sounded like a promise. In the first draft of her essay *Concern with Politics in Recent European Philosophical Thought* from 1954, she writes: "It is almost impossible to render a clear account of Heidegger's thoughts that may be of political relevance without an elaborate report on his concept and analysis of 'world.'"[34] Heidegger took an important step to overcome the modern philosophy of subjectivity: The attempt of the ontological description of the common world situated this description within "elementary human experiences within this realm itself, and implicitly discards traditional concepts and judgments, which have their roots in altogether different kinds of experience."[35] This promise, however, remained unfulfilled; already in the next step of his analysis (§ 27), this description is informed by another perspective, the dichotomy of authenticity and inauthenticity. The last sentence of the analysis of being-with-others reveals: "In being absorbed in the world of taking care of things, that is, at the same time in being-with towards others, Da-sein is not itself."[36] It is followed by the famous ominous description of an impersonal subject of everydayness: *das Man, The one, The they,* public opinion that swallows up our identity, levels it down, and makes everyone exchangeable.

In this moment we deal with a turn in the structure of *Being and Time*. The description of the basic mode of being of man as being-in-the-world turns out to be a description of a form of existence, which is universal and at the same time burdened with a fundamental existential shortcoming. "Idle talk," "curiosity," and "ambiguity"—the three public forms of being-in-the-world—mean a distortion of this being by the distortions of speech, sight, and understanding of the sense of being. Thus, we can almost feel Arendt's disappointment when we read: "We find the old hostility of the philosopher toward the *polis* in Heidegger's analyses of average everyday life in terms of *das Man* (the 'they' or the rule of public opinion, as opposed to the 'self') in which the public realm has the function of hiding reality and preventing the appearance of truth."[37] This does not mean that Arendt did not appreciate this description of the anonymous subject. On the contrary, she writes that "these phenomenological descriptions offer most penetrating insights into one of the basic aspects of society and, moreover, insists that these structures of human life are inherent in the human condition as such, from which there is no escape into an 'authenticity' which would be the philosopher's prerogative."[38] What Arendt rejects, is not pointing out of the structure of *das Man* from the public sphere and even less the suggestive and to-the-point account of this structure (corresponding as it does with her own description of the conformist "noble society"); it is the reduction of the whole public sphere to inauthenticity.

Moreover, although Heidegger put "world" at the center of *Being and Time*, his description of the public world turns out to be an account of fabrication and completely neglects action. The "world" of *Being and Time* has been reduced to a workshop-like and instrumental dimension. And it is only in this dimension that Heidegger inscribed other people—they are always co-creators and co-users. This is the reason why Heidegger, despite having worked out certain categories that could have served a political philosophy, stands by his instrumental (mis)understanding of human action. And this understanding reduces his analysis of being-with merely to a dimension of total relevance. Since in the workshop-world there are no irreplaceable people, being-in-the-world, understood as using handy things (remembering the wide concept of a handy thing in Heidegger), loses its identity:

> As everyday being-with-one-another, Da-sein stands in *subservience* to the others. It itself *is* not; the others have taken its being away from it. The everyday possibilities of being of Da-sein are at the disposal of the whims of the others. These others are not *definite* others. On the contrary, any other can represent them.[39]

Thus, the description of the world limited to instrumental categories results in the description of interhuman relations only in instrumental categories. With the use of other words, Heidegger repeats the sin of many preceding philosophers, who, once having defined *vita activa* from the viewpoint of *vita contemplativa*, interpreted *vita activa* in a monolithic way, blurring the fundamental distinctions within the active life.[40]

Heidegger tried to convince us that his account is entirely value-free: "Our interpretation has a purely ontological intention and is far removed from any moralizing critique of everyday Da-sein."[41] Indeed, the account of the world as a structure of total relevance is a neutral account. But the atmosphere of this account changes at one point so that one can no longer believe in Heidegger's neutrality. The moment of this change is not accidental. The account of the existential structure loses its ontological neutrality exactly when Heidegger is trying to grasp human plurality. Now the reader has the impression of him looking for another language and it sounds more familiar than the neutral code of phenomenology, since it resembles the language of Plato's allegory of the cave. "Publicness [public opinion] obscures everything,"[42] says Heidegger. Along with the description, the feeling of dimness intensifies. The public sphere is a sphere of illusions. *Uneigentlichkeit*—in English, "inauthenticity"—also means "unreality." In the public sphere man is not himself and things are only shadows: "Everything looks as if it were genuinely understood, grasped, and spoken whereas basically it is not."[43] The modes of speech and listening in the public sphere, the idle talk, brings it about that "one understands not so much the beings talked about, but one does listen to what is spoken about as such."[44] The word alienates itself from the thing and becomes only its echo, weaker and weaker through "*gossiping and passing the word along*"[45] (in his Marburg lectures Heidegger simply identifies idle talk with sophistry).[46] Things look similar with sight: Under the influence of others, the everyday mode of seeing, the circumspection (*Umsicht*), characteristic for taking care of the world, alienates itself from the mode of understanding, characteristic for being concerned and becomes a sheer curiosity, the urge to see without understanding what one sees, the criterion being novelty and distraction. In the mode of curiosity we encounter only appearances, "shadows" of things. We are again like the prisoners in the cave, whose only contact with reality is shadows and echo, but who are unable to recognize their situation and the shadowy nature of their perceptions. "Dasein entangles itself,"[47] says Heidegger.

Plato's cave was a metaphor and a thought experiment. That is why the setting-free happened in a way of deus ex machina. Heidegger's account is a description of factual structures of existence. Therefore the possibility of setting-free has to be in these structures themselves. Heidegger finds this possibility in *angst*, which differs from casual fear (*Furcht*). First, angst is a primordial phenomenon that is a condition of the possibility of popular fears. Second, whereas fear always concerns a concrete entity in the world, angst is an attunement that cuts off our connection with concrete entities and discloses the world and ourselves in the mode of pure existence, that we *are* at all. Thus, angst discloses the irrelevance of our connections to the world, and even more, the public interpretation of our being. Angst is also a great chance for *Dasein*: having alienated it from familiar structures of everyday being and forcing it to confront itself. Only such a confrontation opens up the possibilities of authenticity and inauthenticity. Dasein becomes free toward its ownmost being. But the prize of this freedom is a complete solitude: "*Angst* individualizes and thus discloses Da-sein as '*solus ipse*.'"[48]

The Heideggerian version of the "exit from the cave" has to have a different sense from that in Plato. His world is stripped of the positive possibility of transcendence. In this framework we find no idea, no *telos*, which constituted the promise of ancient and Christian philosophies. *Angst*—the predominant state of mind in *Being and Time*—is lacking the mode of being of Greek philosophers, *thaumadzein*, the awe and admiration for being, which provokes questions about the whole. *Angst* is liberated from common opinions, idle talk, curiosity. But it is not a liberation toward a true Being as metaphysical power, but non-being, "nothingness," which now becomes overwhelming. It is only owing to this facing of nothingness that we become free and become self. The final circle of understanding available to *Dasein* is its ownmost possibility of existence: death. The possibility of non-being is the only possibility that cannot be overtaken by others, the only one where we are irreplaceable. In the face of "its ownmost nonrelational potentiality-of-being"[49] any being-with-others becomes meaningless. But, apart from this immanent relation to one's own being, the attitude of "resolute" *Dasein* is reminiscent of the attitude of the philosopher who ascended from the cave: "In being-toward-death this possibility must not be weakened, it must be understood as *possibility*, cultivated as *possibility*, and *endured as possibility*."[50] Plato says: "The entire soul must be turned away from this changing world, until its eye can *bear* to contemplate reality" (518c). It is right to note that what can be lost in the double translation is entirely clear: In both Schleiermacher's translation of Plato, which was relevant for Heidegger, and in *Sein und Zeit* we have the same verb: *aushalten* (to endure, to bear).

The phenomena of angst and death are indispensable for ontological reasons, and are necessary to understand being in the temporal horizon. Since the only entity that reveals the being of beings is *Dasein*, the understanding of being in the temporal horizon requires grasping all the dimensions of the temporality of *Dasein*. Since *Dasein* usually interprets itself on the basis of the public mode of understanding and this mode is inclined to understand everything as present, thus, in order to disclose the temporal structure of being in only one time-dimension, one needs to refer to the borderline phenomena: *Angst* reveals our "having-been" as being thrown into this world, and being-toward-death reveals *our* "coming toward" as a projection toward the final possibility of our existence. Both phenomena, referring us to nothingness, at the same time disclose the circular and finite structure of being human.[51]

The turn in the purely ontological description reveals the ambiguity of the Heideggerian analyses. Even behind the most value-laden conceptual choices we can find some ontological reasons. The ominous account of the public sphere also had some phenomenal basis, although one could not be mistaken about the evaluations preceding this account. Another turn happens in the moment where Heidegger, having outlined the basic structures of authentic and inauthentic existence, looks for the confirmation of the ontology of authenticity in the factual attitude of *Dasein*. He finds it in the phenomena of resoluteness, conscience, and guilt. Resoluteness is the opposite pole to falling-prey and consists in conscious being-toward-death, not masked by the They. It is a response to the challenge of angst.

In Heidegger's conceptual framework, conscience means an appeal of *Dasein* to *Dasein* itself, to free itself from inauthentic identity and become itself. The uncanniness we experience in angst brings about distance to our public existence and enables us to turn to ourselves. The call of conscience is not a voice of a transcendent entity, but silence—an authentic version of speech liberated from the public sphere and confronted with nothingness. The phenomenon of "guilt" shows even more connections to nothingness and negativity; it has nothing to do with the concerned being-with-others, but "we define the formal existential idea of 'guilty' as being-the-ground for a being which is determined by a not—that is, *being-the-ground of a nullity*."[52] The call of conscience is an appeal for recognition of the "nullity" of everyday existence. The possibility of negation of existence, of its confrontation with nonexistence, is a condition of freedom. Resoluteness is an attitude emerging from our being confronted with non-being and consists in the affirmation of this confrontation, "*reticent projecting oneself upon one's ownmost being-guilty which is ready for* Angst-*resoluteness.*"[53]

As with any phenomenological description, *Being and Time* has to start with experience. Thus, Heidegger begins with the everyday understanding of being. But exactly here a difficulty appears: If he wants to disclose a sense of this experience, he cannot rely completely on its pure description, he has to reach deeper. But, on the other hand, if he wants to remain faithful to his own agenda, that is, the project of the deconstruction of metaphysics, he has to make his analysis independent from traditional metaphysical and theological structures. Hence, he also refers to such experiences that exceed everydayness and reveal nothingness, and negation as belonging to being. Although the choice of these negative experiences is certainly not arbitrary, it is definitely not purely ontological but relies on a historical (ontic) basis. On that account, the Heideggerian analyses can hardly be considered as neutral phenomenological descriptions.

Heidegger is aware of this difficulty: "But does not a definite ontic interpretation of authentic existence, a factical ideal of Da-sein, underlie our ontological interpretation of the existence of Da-sein? Indeed."[54] Heidegger would never repeat the foundationalist mistake of modern metaphysics, which kept seeking the zero point of consciousness: "Philosophy will never seek to deny its 'presuppositions,' but neither may it merely admit them. It conceives them and develops with more and more penetration both the presuppositions themselves and that for which they are presuppositions."[55] Heidegger's hermeneutics strived at grasping the whole of *Dasein*. For that reason the existential analysis had to understand it as a temporal and finite being, living within the borders of *Angst* and resoluteness: so, exactly where being meets non-being.

Regardless of Heidegger's methodological consciousness when writing *Being and Time*, one cannot ignore the ethical project of the work. This project becomes unavoidable in the very moment when it turns out that an understanding of being has to start with human being. It is also the moment of the neutral description being fractured for the first time. The understanding of being has to become an "anthropology" and at the same time it also becomes an "ethics." But there is more to it: If at the basis of *Being and Time* we have a factual ideal of *Dasein*, the work becomes pedagogical in the more direct sense than that present in the ontological analysis. It becomes a positive call for life in the resoluteness and openness to the voice of conscience. This call is bound with a promise of freedom. Although authentic existence does not have much in common with the philosophical ideal of contemplation, its negative condition is similar: setting-free from the limitations of human plurality, escaping from the sphere of opinions and complete solitude.

III

To sum this up, on the one hand, Heidegger dismantles traditional metaphysical structures, but on the other, his attempt to give an account of human plurality remains within the circle of Western philosophy. In Arendt's view, his phenomenology takes over the limitations of that philosophy: the impossibility of an adequate description of the intrahuman world. Heidegger, like Plato and his followers, subdues the public sphere to the needs of a philosophizing individual. "The plurality [of people] bothers man from Plato (to Heidegger)," notes Arendt in her *Denktagebuch*.[56] Now, we need to follow Arendt in considering the reasons of these limitations in Heidegger's thought.

When Heidegger wrote that public opinion obscured everything, he had in mind the covering of a true, resolute, and finite existence with the opinion of others. Arendt was so impressed by this statement that she made it the leitmotif of her book *Men in Dark Times*.[57] But unlike Heidegger, for Arendt this obscurity is by no means an ontological dimension of human existence. Heidegger's claims of the public sphere are in fact remarks on the German society of the Weimar Republic: "What was happening then in the public sphere actually obscured everything that by essence belongs to that sphere."[58] Heidegger lived in dark times as much as other figures in Arendt's book (e.g., Gotthold E. Lessing, Walter Benjamin, Rosa Luxemburg). But Heidegger, unlike them, reacted in a typically philosophical way: He assumed that there was no other escape from the triviality of everyday existence but "withdrawal from it into that solitude which philosophers since Parmenides and Plato have opposed to the political realm."[59] He was not protected from the grave fallacy of other philosophers: He treated the historical and contingent dangers of the common world as essential to, and inscribed in, any public sphere, and designed his philosophy as an escape from that sphere (and later as its "renovation" according to the rules of philosophy). And because of certain prejudgments on the public sphere, taken from tradition, he identified the oppressive and unifying society with the political. He did not understand that "the 'they' is not political but a social phenomenon."[60]

The account of society as something fundamentally different from the public sphere of politics, and at the same time dangerous to the latter, is one of the leading themes of *The Human Condition*. The rescue from the pressures of "the they" is not a withdrawal into privacy, but individual identity, possible only in the public world of human differences. Heidegger never abandoned his philosophical views on action: "The experiences of the philosopher—insofar as he is a philosopher—are with solitude, while for man—insofar as he is political—solitude is an essential but nevertheless marginal experience."[61] In Arendt's view, Heidegger's transgression of the tradition was not radical enough. For this, Heidegger was too much of a philosopher and as almost any other philosopher, too hostile against the *polis*. It can be said, without much exaggeration, that Arendt's thought can be read as an attempt to correct the Heideggerian version of philosophical blindness toward politics.

But there is one more thing to it: Heidegger's philosophy is not only a repetition of the question of being. It is also a repetition of the ancient pedagogical promise of philosophy: This time it is the promise of freedom, which is to be fulfilled not as authentic knowledge, like in Plato, but as an authentic existence.

BEING AND TIME AS POLITICAL PHILOSOPHY?

At the beginning of this chapter I tried to demonstrate the equivocal way in which the early thought of Martin Heidegger fits in the classic dichotomies of its epoch. We have seen that Heidegger's views of that time cannot be simply situated within Spengler's gloomy accounts of Western culture. Heidegger does not downplay their salience, since they are an actual voice of the time, but approaches them critically. At the same time he shows sympathy for and shares intellectual affinities with the sober scientific agenda of Weber. *Being and Time*, if one can say so, is a work oscillating above the Spengler-Weber dichotomy. The phenomenological description of ontological structures (the Weberian spirit) reshapes itself into an existential call (the Spenglerian spirit) only to again become a description.

The pedagogical message of *Being and Time* requires positing the question of the political message of the text. The question would be the extent to which Heidegger's pedagogical agenda implies a political philosophy. I believe the following quote of Paul York also sheds some light on the political aspect of *Being and Time*: "To dissolve elemental public opinion and, if possible, to make possible the shaping of individuality in seeing and regarding, would be a pedagogical task of the state. Then instead of so-called public conscience—instead of this radical externalization—individual conscience, i.e., conscience, would again become powerful."[62]

As we have seen, from Arendt's point of view, *Being and Time* is a political philosophy in a completely *negative* sense. Nevertheless, due to the context of Heidegger's biography, there were many attempts at retrospective interpretations of *Being and Time* as a *positive* political philosophy. In order to understand the possibility of such interpretations, we need to look at the fundamental ontology from the perspective of the final chapters of Heidegger's *opus*. In chapter 5 of the second division, Heidegger sets up an ontological analysis of history. The problem of history emerges as a consequence of the earlier analyses in the following sense: It is all about disclosure of the sense of being as such; but access to being we have only as beings that understand being. An adequate understanding has to take in the whole of *Dasein*, that is, as authentic temporality. And as any other phenomena, history also derives its double sense from the two basic modes of *Dasein*, authenticity and inauthenticity. *Dasein* is essentially historical, but not all interpretations of history are adequate; only those that are based on an authentic understanding of temporality are, that is, as authentic being-toward-death. We remember that being-toward-death turns us to possibilities emerging from our "being thrown" into the world. But here this thrownness has a richer meaning than in the preceding pages of *Being and Time*; it refers to the possibilities residing in heritage. Only authentic being-toward-death ensures that these possibilities are not accidental (drawn from everydayness). The authentic possibilities of *Dasein*'s heritage Heidegger calls fate (*Schicksal*). The critical moment for the political interpretation of these considerations is when individual fate becomes common destiny (*Geschick*). Fate is individual, but it opens up a horizon of destiny emerging from heritage. It turns out that the individualistic anthropology of *Being and Time* is somehow transposed on the existence of the people (*Volk*), being something more than a sum of individual fates: "In communication and in battle the power of destiny first becomes free. The fateful destiny of Da-sein in and with its 'generation' constitutes the complete, authentic occurrence of Da-sein."[63]

The later role of Heidegger in the Nazi power apparatus shed new light back on the content of the 74th paragraph of *Being and Time*. It was read not only as a political philosophy,[64] but also as an outright fascist theory. One of the earliest such interpretations is Karl Löwith's essay of 1939 (a first draft of *Mein Leben* of 1946).[65] According to him, the national-socialist content is present in the nihilism of *Being and Time*. Human existence, whose sense emerges from the ultimate possibility of death, is based on nothingness. Nothingness as a fundamental problem of Heidegger's thought is responsible for "resoluteness" being stripped of traditional theological context and becoming a decision for the actual possibility of the destruction of the old order. Many years after Löwith, Richard Wolin repeated his critique in a wider historical context and at the same time radicalized it. He also saw in resoluteness "the gateway to Heideggerianism as a political philosophy."[66] But he took a huge step when he interpreted the existential modes of authenticity and inauthenticity: "The political philosophy that corresponds to that ontological dualism suggests that human beings are divided by nature into leaders and followers."[67] With this step he drifts away from Löwith and gets dangerously close to the persecutory work of Victor Farias,[68] from whom he wanted to distance himself.

The final chapters of *Being and Time* were often connected with the texts of the late 1920s and early 1930s, mostly with *The Introduction to Metaphysics* and the rector's speech. A continuity of work as well as a correspondence between Heidegger's philosophy and his practical life were sought. But it must be remembered that the possibility of community in *Being and Time* emerges entirely from the individualistic authentic temporality. Common destiny is founded on individual fate (based on individualization of death), not the other way round.[69] If there is a quasi-political experience underlying this description to be found, it is, rather, the generational experience of the trenches of WWI than anything else: the feeling of momentary brotherhood (in the sense of *Augenblick*) implied in the total equality of imminent death, which is solitary anyway. It is the solitude of being-toward-death, suddenly actualized, and not the rhythmical march that is a foundation of this community. Even less is it a mass-movement based on very modern propaganda, public opinion expressed in acts of acclamation and mass-media, as Hitlerism was.

Whereas Heidegger's commitment to National Socialism is a historical fact, it can hardly be derived from the ontology of authenticity. The authentic being-toward-death is always ultimately individualizing and situating a man not only outside society, but also outside any community that swallows up the individuality and complete solitude of a human being. Even the remarks of the generational destiny, which elicited so much criticism, should be considered in a wider context. They are followed by no positive political appeal (certainly not for being a leader, as Farias claims). They can be understood as an attempt at an ontological founding of the philosophy of history in a dialogue with Dilthey and York (and Hegel). Heidegger quotes extensively from their correspondence, which is noteworthy if we notice that he almost never quoted anything. Let us in this context once again read the second part of the above-cited York's words of the role of the state: If the role of the state is to form individualism, "then instead of so-called public conscience—instead of this radical externalization—individual conscience, i.e., conscience, would again become powerful." It is, indeed, difficult to read it as a prefiguration of a mass-movement.

Within the whole range of attempts at intellectually coming to terms with the juxtaposition of historical facts and the philosophical complexity of *Being and Time*, the stance of Rüdiger Safranski must be highlighted. Very far from exonerating Heidegger, he at the same time avoids a one-sided reading of Heidegger's work:

> Heidegger's authenticity rejects any conformism. [. . .] a community of dense homogeneity is bound to seem to him rather suspect. However, Heidegger will draw other political conclusions from his ethics of authenticity. He will see the National Socialist revolution as a collective breakout from inauthenticity and therefore join it. But these conclusions do not inevitably follow from the worldview of *Being and Time*. Others have drawn different conclusions from it.[70]

These others are Hannah Arendt, Hans-Georg Gadamer, Hans Jonas, Jean-Paul Sartre, Leo Strauss, and Herbert Marcuse, to name just the most prominent ones. Within *Being and Time,* the *ontological* possibility for a collective authenticity is either nonexistent or very scarce. But this would mean that in Heidegger's life and thought, or even in the thought itself, there is a fracture.

Arendt, and her opinion is most relevant here, basically reads Heidegger's philosophy independently from his political commitment. Even the most critical text (*What Is Existential Philosophy?*[71]), where Arendt undertakes postwar reckonings with Heidegger's thought, is free from drawing political conclusions from this thought. The reason for this is much deeper than the emotional relations between them. Arendt's own political thought is built on the feud with Heidegger, but this feud is pervaded with a conditional affirmation. It is not only that Arendt reversed the Heideggerian categories; it is also the case, and Seyla Benhabib was right in her evaluation of *The Human Condition*, that "Being-unto-death is displaced by natality; the isolated Dasein is replaced by a condition of plurality; and instead of instrumental action, a new category of human activity, action, understood as speech and doing, emerges."[72] But there is more to it: From the point of view of Arendt's thought, the most important achievement of Heidegger was the dismantling of the teleological structures of existence, which Arendt transforms into a dismantling of the teleological models of action. It will be done at the same time in accordance with Heidegger and against him. In the following chapters we will see different disclosures of this struggle. Now the most important thing is that Arendt's thought is a tangible demonstration of Safranski's thesis: From *Being and Time*, different conclusions can be drawn from those Heidegger drew himself.

To put it differently, with a reference to the analogies between Plato and Heidegger, in the period of *Being and Time* Heidegger almost fulfills all the conditions of the philosopher who escaped the cave. All but one. The deconstructive, anti-teleological ontology, although it founds something faintly resembling Platonic contemplation, is stripped of a very important aspect leading the philosopher back down into the cave: the idea of Good as a measure of human affairs. In Heidegger's philosophy this measure is absent, if we do not count the elusive moment of resolution. But this, as I tried to show above, is unsuitable for such a measure. Arendt's opinion was that the concept of finite historicity meant that "the philosopher has left behind him the claim to being 'wise' and knowing eternal standards for the perishable affairs of the City men, for such 'wisdom' could be justified only from a position outside the realm of human affairs and be thought legitimate only by virtue of the philosopher's proximity to the Absolute."[73]

Now we can see the complexity of Heidegger's relation to tradition. He was a thinker who broke with metaphysical premises of the philosophical tradition and his philosophy is rightly regarded to be novel. This break opened "the way to a re-examination of the whole realm of politics."[74] But, to be able to fulfill this promise, Heidegger's thought turned out to be too much of a continuation of traditional convictions concerning the nature of the public sphere. The line between traditionalism and innovation in Heidegger is a line between political thought and philosophy. The premises for a new concept of politics, which Arendt saw in *Being and Time*, remain undeveloped, and his philosophy of politics is purely *negative*.

This presentation of the educational potential of *Being and Time* closes the part on the traditional and "natural" connections between philosophy and education. If we seriously approach Arendt's thesis of the "broken thread of tradition," we will have to question these connections. Of this, the "anti-philosophical" and "pedagogical" effort of Arendt's thought will emerge: putting the question of action anew. But before it can be unfolded, we need to follow the further paths of Heidegger's philosophy as a result of this breach in tradition.

NOTES

1. The cultural antinomies of the Weimar Republic in the context of the intellectual development of Heidegger are comprehensively outlined in Safranski's biography (Safranski, *Martin Heidegger*, 89–93) to which my analysis in indebted.
2. Oswald Spengler, *The Decline of the West: Form and Actuality*, trans. Charles Francis Atkinson (New York: Alfred A. Knopf, 1926), Archive.org.
3. Spengler, *The Decline*, 44.
4. Spengler, *The Decline*, 44.
5. A good example is pedagogue Ernst Krieck, who in 1931 lost his position for Nazi agitation at the university. In a few years he was reinstated.
6. Weber, "Science as a Vocation," 137.
7. Karl Löwith, *My Life in Germany Before and After 1933: A Report*, trans. Elisabeth King (Champaign: University of Illinois Press, 1994), 17.
8. Martin Heidegger, *Zur Bestimmung der Philosophie*, Gesamtausgabe II Abt., Band 56/57 (Frankfurt am Main: Vittorio Klostermann, 1999), 10; English: Martin Heidegger, *Towards the Definition of Philosophy*, trans. Ted Sadler (New York: Continuum, 2008), 8. Further quoted as HGA 56/57 with reference to both the original (G) and the translation (E).
9. HGA 56/57, 213G; 159E. With reference to philosophy, Heidegger uses the German term *Wissenschaft*. It is a neutral and wide concept of science, which is not limited to natural sciences or empirical methods. This can be surprising for the readers of Heidegger's later philosophy, accustomed to expressions like "science does not think" or "science technology" with a reference to positive natural science. Young Heidegger, while obviously not being a positivist, treats the sciences very seriously as concretizations of philosophy.
10. Martin Heidegger, "Zur philosophischen Orientierung für Akademiker," in Martin Heidegger, *Reden und andere Zeugnisse eines Lebensweges 1910–1976*, Gesamtausgabe I Abt., Band 16 (Frankfurt am Main: Vittorio Klostermann, 2000). 11 (GA 16). Further quoted as HGA 16.
11. Martin Heidegger, *Prolegomena zur Geschichte des Zeitbegriffs*, Gesamtausgabe II Abt., Band 20 (Frankfurt am Main: Vittorio Klostermann, 1994), 3; English: Martin Heidegger, *History of the Concept of Time*, trans. Theodore Kisiel (Bloomington: Indiana University Press, 1985), 2. Further quoted as HGA 20 with reference to both the original (G) and the translation (E).
12. See for instance HGA 24, 5–14G; 5–9E. Toward the end of the 1920s, Heidegger ceases to juxtapose philosophy and science with worldview and shows the connection between the two phenomena. See the winter term 1928/29: Martin Heidegger, *Einleitung in die Philosophie*, Gesamtausgabe Abt. II, Band 27 (Frankfurt am Main: Vittorio Klostermann, 1996), further quoted as HGA 27. But still in the next semester (Spring 1929) appears the positive reference to Weber and the critique of anti-intellectualism. Martin Heidegger, *Der deutsche Idealismus (Fichte, Schelling, Hegel) und die philosophische Problemlage der Gegenwart*, Gesamtausgabe II Abt., Band 28 (Frankfurt am Main: Vittorio Klostermann, 1997), 349; further quoted as HGA 28. Nevertheless, in this lecture new tones start to come forward: the reform

of science through the inner metamorphosis of *Dasein*. In the following semester Heidegger juxtaposes philosophy with both science and worldview. See Martin Heidegger, *Die Grundbegriffe der Metaphysik. Welt-Endlichkeit-Einsamkeit*, Gesamtausgabe II Abt., Band 29/30 (Frankfurt am Main: Vittorio Klostermann, 1983), 1–5; English: Martin Heidegger, *The Fundamental Concepts of Metaphysics. World, Finitude, Solitude*, trans. William McNeill and Nicholas Walker (Bloomington: Indiana University Press, 1995), 1–3. Further quoted as HGA 29/30 with reference to both the original (G) and the translation (E). The concept of "scientific philosophy" will gradually disappear from his lectures. With passing time Heidegger shifted accents toward existential engagement (see the next chapter). But the demand of conceptual precision would never be abandoned in the lectures.

13. See for instance Richard Wolin, *The Politics of Being: The Political Thought of Martin Heidegger* (New York: Columbia University Press, 1990), 22–23.

14. With the one exception of *What Is Existential Philosophy*, see Preface.

15. Elisabeth Young-Bruehl, *Hannah Arendt. For Love of the World* (New Haven, CT: Yale University Press, 2004), 304.

16. Hannah Arendt to Martin Heidegger, May 8, 1954, *Letters*, 120.

17. See chapter 5.

18. HGA 20.

19. Martin Heidegger, *Logik. Die Frage nach der Wahrheit*, Gesamtausgabe II Abt., Band 21 (Frankfurt am Main: Vittorio Klostermann, 1976); English: Martin Heidegger, *Logic. The Question of Truth*, trans. Thomas Sheehan (Bloomington: Indiana University Press, 2010). Further quoted as HGA 21 with reference to both the original (G) and the translation (E).

20. Safranski, *Martin Heidegger*, 99. On the basis of this example we can see how difficult it is to inscribe Heidegger into the standard oppositions, for instance as a conservative. If he was a "conservative anti-modernist," he was so in his own distinguished way, escaping the classical dichotomies of the epoch. More about the language of Heidegger and the background of the Weimar Republic the reader finds in George Steiner, "Heidegger, Again," *Salmagundi*, 82/83 (1989): 31–55.

21. Safranski, *Martin Heidegger*, 100.

22. See also Jacques Taminiaux, *The Thracian Maid and the Professional Thinker. Arendt and Heidegger*, trans. Michael Gendre (Albany: State University of New York Press, 1997), 45.

23. Martin Heidegger, *Sein und Zeit* (Tübingen: Max Niemeyer Verlag, 2001), 402. Martin Heidegger, *Being and Time: A Translation of Sein und Zeit*, trans. Joan Stambaugh (Albany: State University of New York Press, 1996), 367; further quoted with a double reference as BT and SZ.

24. Martin Heidegger, "Kant's Thesis about Being," trans. Ted E. Klein Jr. and William E. Pohl, in *Pathmarks*, 340.

25. SZ, 16; BT, 14–15.

26. SZ, 22; BT, 20.

27. SZ, 35; BT, 31.

28. SZ, 35; BT, 31.

29. SZ, 39; BT, 31.

30. SZ, 67; BT, 62.
31. HGA 20, 228G; 169E.
32. SZ, 118; BT, 111–12.
33. SZ, 123; BT, 116.
34. Hannah Arendt, "Concern with Politics in Recent European Philosophical Thought," in *Essays in Understanding*, 446 (endnote).
35. Arendt, "Concern with Politics," 432.
36. SZ, 125; BT, 118.
37. Arendt, "Concern with Politics," 432–33.
38. Arendt, "Concern with Politics," 433.
39. SZ, 126; BT, 118.
40. See also Taminiaux, *The Thracian Maid*, 199.
41. SZ, 167; BT, 156.
42. SZ, 127; BT, 119.
43. SZ, 173; BT, 162.
44. SZ, 168; BT, 157.
45. SZ, 168; BT, 158.
46. HGA 20, 377G; 273E.
47. SZ, 348; BT, 319.
48. SZ, 188; BT, 176.
49. SZ, 255; BT, 235.
50. SZ, 261; BT, 241.
51. Arendt wrote her doctoral dissertation under Jaspers' supervision. But her main inspiration remained the analysis of the temporality of *Being and Time* (Hannah Arendt, *Love and Saint Augustine*, trans. Joanna V. Scott and Judith Ch. Stark [Chicago: The University of Chicago Press, 1996]).
52. SZ, 283; BT, 261.
53. SZ, 296–97; BT, 273.
54. SZ, 310; BT, 286.
55. SZ, 310; BT, 286–87.
56. Arendt, *Denktagebuch*, 79–80.
57. Hannah Arendt, *Men in Dark Times* (New York: A Harvest Book, 1995), ix.
58. Arendt, *Denktagebuch*, 664. See also Seyla Benhabib, *The Reluctant Modernism of Hannah Arendt* (Lanham, MD: Rowman & Littlefield, 2003), 56.
59. Arendt, *Men in Dark Times*, ix.
60. Arendt, *Denktagebuch*, 664.
61. Arendt, "Concern with Politics," 443.
62. SZ, 403; BT, 368.
63. SZ, 384–85; BT, 352.
64. See W. R. Newell, "Heidegger on Freedom and Community: Some Political Implications of His Early Thought," *The American Political Science Review*, 78, no. 3 (1984): 775–84.
65. Karl Löwith, "The Political Implications of Heidegger's Existentialism," trans. Richard Wolin and Melissa J. Cox, *New German Critique* 45 (1988): 117–34. Löwith finds a counterpart of the Heideggerian resoluteness in the decisionism of

Carl Schmitt. But it must be noted that two years later Löwith himself warned of hasty identifications of existential philosophy with nihilism and Nazism. Karl Löwith, "Heidegger: Problem and Background of Existentialism," *Social Research* 15, no. 3 (1948).

66. Wolin, *The Politics of Being*, 35.
67. Wolin, *The Politics of Being*, 56.
68. Farias is a representative of the extreme stance in the so-called Heidegger controversy. His book is devoted to justification of the thesis that Nazi strains had been present in Heidegger since adolescence. He goes so far as an attempt at comparing certain passages from *Being and Time* with Hitler's *Mein Kampf*. Victor Farias, *Heidegger and Nazism*, eds. Joseph Margolis and Tom Rockmore (Philadelphia: Temple University Press, 1989). This direction of reading Heidegger initiated by Farias also inspired his translator: Tom Rockmore, "Heidegger after Farias," *History of Philosophy Quarterly* 8, no. 1 (1991): 81–102.
69. SZ, 386; BT, 353.
70. Safranski, *Martin Heidegger*, 168.
71. See Preface.
72. Benhabib, *The Reluctant Modernism*, 107.
73. Arendt, "Concern with Politics," 432.
74. Arendt, "Concern with Politics," 432.

Part II

PHILOSOPHY AND EDUCATION AT A CROSSROADS

Antonia Grunenberg, in her "history of a love," commented in a radical way on Arendt's attitude toward the fact that some intellectuals and philosophers supported the regime with their own authority: "In Arendt's view, with the arrival of totalitarianism the educational mission of philosophy was discredited."[1] In the following chapters, I will undertake an attempt to challenge this radical diagnosis. The meaning of Grunenberg's quote will have to be "unpacked." Thus far, I have interpreted the relationship between education and philosophy as a relationship of mostly unquestioned positive interdependence: Philosophy offered education and pedagogy a promise, expressed in terms like "freedom," "individuality," and "authenticity." Nevertheless, if we are to understand Grunenberg's statement, we need to consider a question concerning the end of this relationship, resulting from the end of Western tradition. We will also have to question the role of Heidegger in this end (chapter 4). But the subsequent question to this about the end will be that of the beginning: the beginning of a new thinking about politics, a new pluralistic ontology, a new world. In order to answer this question I will confront the early inspiration that Arendt found in Heidegger's lectures with her own reading of the Greek tradition. The leitmotif will be the Marburg lecture on Plato's *Sophist* from the winter term of 1924–1925, the first one Arendt attended as a student (chapter 5). In what follows, I will analyze the most important concept in Arendt's philosophy: the concept of the world (chapter 6). The last part of the book will be an exploration of the positive consequences of the end, that is, to reposition the question of the relationship between philosophy (thinking) and education.

NOTE

1. Grunenberg, *Hannah Arendt and Martin Heidegger*, 262.

Chapter 4

The Broken Thread of Tradition and Heidegger's Breaks

"The break in our tradition is now an accomplished fact. It is neither the result of anyone's deliberate choice nor subject to further decision,"[1] says Arendt. The only thing we can do is to describe this fact in order to understand it, and to understand its consequences: for politics, for philosophy, for education. To be able to untangle the complicated knot of meanings hidden under Arendt's expression of the "broken thread of tradition," we need to make a few distinctions. This is necessary, for the categories Arendt used are not always unequivocal and are often dependent on what she was actually interested in.

Firstly, Arendt explicitly distinguished tradition from both the past and from history: "The end of our tradition is obviously the end neither of history nor of the past, generally speaking."[2] Arendt learned the difference between the past and tradition from Heidegger as early as her first semester of studies. Heidegger taught: "Philosophical questioning [. . .] is not concerned with freeing us from the past but, on the contrary, with making the past free for us, free to liberate us from the tradition."[3] Only then can we approach things themselves, hidden in the past. For Arendt, as it was for Heidegger, the break in the tradition is not the same as a loss of the past. The end of tradition means that the thread connecting us with the past is broken. Tradition no longer delineates our attitude toward the past, which, of course, makes this attitude problematic. But the break of the thread of tradition—Arendt was never less conservative than in this moment—means also that we freed ourselves from "the chain fettering each successive generation to a predetermined aspect of the past. It could be that only now will the past open up to us with unexpected freshness and tell us things no one has yet had ears to hear."[4]

Secondly, when we are talking about the broken thread of tradition in Arendt's thought, we need to examine tradition in a wide context, that is, the tradition of the West, bearing in mind the whole gamut of cultural and historical phenomena that constitute the continuity of our civilization. In Arendt, such tradition is basically of Roman origin and builds a unity with authority and religion: "The famous 'decline of the West' consists primarily in the decline of the Roman trinity of religion, tradition, and authority."[5] Arendt belonged to this generation of German Jews, for whom the year 1933 was the end of the world: the final failure of the ideals of the Enlightenment and assimilation, accompanied by unprecedented barbarism. Tradition in this basic, general meaning ended with the rise of twentieth-century totalitarianism. Arendt did not share the convictions of thinkers such as Adorno or Voegelin, who traced totalitarianism back to some modern or even premodern phenomena: the Enlightenment, or "gnosis." Arendt has in mind exactly this general meaning of tradition when she tries to grasp the cause of the break in history: "This sprang from a chaos of mass-perplexities on the political scene and of mass-opinions in the spiritual sphere which the totalitarian movements, through terror and ideology, crystallized into a new form of government and domination."[6] The most representative account of how Arendt understood the decline of the West is presented in *The Origins of Totalitarianism*.

Thirdly, when Arendt writes on tradition, one has to keep in mind that sometimes she understands the term not in the totality as described above, but as different intellectual traditions: "the tradition of political thought," or "the Western philosophical tradition." The creators of these specific traditions, in plural, were Plato and Aristotle, not the Romans.

Obviously, these different ways of understanding the concept of tradition are not to be considered in isolation. Tradition per se comprises different intellectual and philosophical traditions. But it is not an accident that the end of European tradition approximately coincided with the end of traditional philosophy and of traditional political thought. The announcement, not the cause, but a harbinger, of the end of tradition comes at the highest and at the same time declining moments of political (Marx), religious (Kiekegaard), and philosophical thought (Nietzsche). These were the last modern thinkers, "standing at the end of the tradition, just before the break came."[7] These otherwise different philosophers have one thing in common: They experienced something new and could not describe it without the old categories of thought. Even though they rejected the authority of tradition, they did not undermine its conceptual framework. They questioned the basic assumptions of traditional religion, politics, and metaphysics and consciously turned upside down the traditional hierarchy of concepts. But these turns of the thinkers of the declining tradition are not simply turnings of traditional oppositions. Their writings are the accounts of great minds struggling with new phenomena, for descriptions of which they did not have adequate terms yet. These terms will be worked out only in the spiritual formation of the twentieth century.

In this chapter I will be interested mostly in the break in tradition in the context of the ideological entanglement of Heidegger. Hannah Arendt, although at first very critical of Heidegger, after their reunion in 1950 tended to diminish the relationship between Heidegger's thought and his membership of the National Socialism. If we accepted that Heidegger's political involvement had no relation to his philosophy and remained an error of judgment, it would not be worthwhile to give too much attention to this. But, if there is a relationship between Heidegger's thought and his *quasi*-political action, we need to question the pedagogical role of philosophy in this context. Of course, the break in the tradition is a much wider phenomenon than the so-called Heidegger controversy. But the consideration of this break in this particular context allows for a depiction of his history as a symptom of something more general. The break in the tradition also means the end of the traditional promise of philosophy for education and pedagogy. Hitherto, we have approached three revelations of this promise: Plato's *paideia* (chapter 1), the German idea of *Bildung* (chapter 2), and the promise of fundamental ontology (chapter 3). As we will see, Heidegger in the 1930s breaks with all these promises: First, he distances himself from his own philosophy of the 1920s and from the pedagogical promise of individual authenticity that it implied; second, he turns away from the promise of *paideia*, present in Plato's philosophy; and third, he rejects the promise of the idea of university: the idea of independent science and free education.

The reading of the political involvement of Heidegger as a split from the philosophy of *Being and Time* is counter both to his self-understanding (Heidegger treated his own thought too seriously to accept having committed a philosophical mistake and his life too seriously to disconnect it with his thought to acknowledge a political mistake) and to many interpretations seeking the origins of the political commitment in Heidegger's early thought (see chapter 3). Moreover, the presented interpretation of the rectorate as a break with the Platonic moments of his own thought counters both Heidegger's self-understanding (it is obviously not accidental that Heidegger in the early 1930s delivered a lecture on the allegory of the cave) and the way some contemporaries, Arendt included, favored Heidegger with a comparison to the traditional mistake of the philosopher who wanted to teach a tyrant. Arendt depicted Heidegger's political involvement on the occasion of his 80th birthday.[8] But since we have reasons to treat this text with caution as a testimony of Arendt's interpretation of Heidegger,[9] we need to take a risk to "understand the author better than he understood himself" and show the reasons why Heidegger of the years 1933–1934 was not Plato. I will look for these reasons both in the documents of the time (mostly in Heidegger's lectures, the greater part published only after both thinkers had died, therefore unknown to Arendt) and in Arendt's political categories.

Chapter 4

HEIDEGGER ESTRANGED FROM HIS OWN THOUGHT

Hannah Arendt accepted without reservations, and repeated, Heidegger's diagnosis concerning the moment Western philosophy was overcome. The only philosopher who could compete with Heidegger's innovative way of thinking was Nietzsche. Heidegger, after several years of fascination with Nietzsche, also the years of his support for Nazism, toward the end of the 1930s made a radical shift in his interpretation. Now Heidegger's Nietzsche is the last metaphysician, who turned Platonism upside down[10] and drew the final conclusions from this turn, which were the idea of eternal recurrence and will to power.[11] Heidegger's after-the-turn philosophy is an attempt to ultimately overcome metaphysics. The leitmotifs of this are, on the one hand, the terms of thinking about the essence of metaphysics (the critique of technology as "enframing"), and on the other, the postulate of the human relinquishment of being the master of being (man as a shepherd of being and *Gelassenheit*).

In her *Denktagebuch*, Arendt derived her understanding of Nietzsche wholly from Heidegger's lectures.[12] In her published texts Heidegger's name does not appear in this context, but Arendt maintains that Nietzsche was unable to liberate himself from the traditional conceptual dichotomy between the ideal and sensual worlds. His rebellion against the transformation of ideas into values (so conspicuous in the early writings, for example, the critique of the "value of *Bildung*," with which we are already familiar) was reshaped into a philosophy as "trans-valuation of values." In this way Nietzsche, proclaiming new, higher values, "was the first to fall prey to delusions which he himself had helped to destroy, accepting the old traditional notion of measuring with transcendent units in its newest and most hideous form."[13]

Thus, the break of the thread of the tradition of Western philosophy was accomplished, according to Arendt, not by Nietzsche, but by Heidegger. While he can be inscribed into the tradition as far as the approach to politics is concerned, if we take into consideration the experience of thinking and the critique of Western metaphysics (Nietzsche inclusive), it was Heidegger who removed the ruins of traditional thinking and dared to think beyond philosophical schools and the traditional division of philosophy into subdisciplines. It was the origin of the great project of *Being and Time*.

I

Heidegger not only broke with the metaphysical tradition, inaugurated by Plato and crowned by Nietzsche. In the 1930s he also broke with the premises of his early philosophy, while maintaining its rhetoric. The aura of Heidegger's philosophy, which surrounded the genesis of *Being and Time*, began to change at the end of the 1920s. The second part of *Being and Time* was never published.[14] Never published was also the third division of the first part, titled *Time and Being*. Heidegger undertakes the theme of this division in the summer term of 1927 (*The Basic Problems of Phenomenology*), in which he, for the first time, explicitly develops the problem of ontological difference. Nevertheless, the path leading to the question of being as such would come out as an illusion. "Anyway, I was then [January 1927, P. S.] convinced to be able to, within a year, express everything clearer. It was an illusion," Heidegger would say in 1941.[15] The accomplished deconstruction of the tradition seems to be insufficient. The analytic of *Dasein* turns out to be a *cul-de-sac*, still dependent on the philosophy of the subject and transcendentalism. Heidegger, once having situated the question of being on the horizon of *Dasein*, cannot find and exit toward fundamental ontology, toward the question of being as such. Meanwhile, *Being and Time* is being read as everything it was not meant to be: as philosophical anthropology and existentialism. The first part of the masterpiece does not end—according to Heidegger's initial plans—with "the explication of time as the transcendental horizon of the question of being,"[16] in which "everything is reversed,"[17] but with an analysis of *human* historicity, which turned out to be politically controversial (see chapter 3).

Before, in the mid-1930s, in Heidegger's philosophy a turn begins to emerge (not *Dasein*, but being alone as the primordial phenomenon), he had been in a philosophical void for a few years already. The individualistic premises of *Being and Time* were not to be maintained, while the terms (or better: "forest paths") of the later philosophy were still to be worked out (for they were a later reaction to his personal political failure). The most important terminological difference within the early texts and lectures consists in that Heidegger supplements the analytic of being with thinking of nothingness, already suggested in *Being and Time*, but not developed. Now he writes to Elisabeth Blochmann: "Prevailing is this element of *negativity*: to put *nothing* on the path towards the depth of *Dasein*."[18] Heidegger develops the problem of nothingness and its affinity with being in lectures and writings at the turn of decades, foremostly in his inauguration lecture of 1929, titled *What Is Metaphysics?* Nevertheless, Heidegger was still in a void, and it was not a void emerging from nihilistic philosophy, but a creative slump (such as often follows a great success, in the case of Heidegger crowned with his victorious debate with Cassirer in Davos), accompanied by the great ambition of creating a philosophy "for the time." In 1930, Heidegger rejects the first calling to Berlin, this time not yet as a result of a desire to stay in the provinces (such a justification first appears after the second nomination in 1933), but out of the genuine feeling of having to start everything anew and not being able to take over such a responsibility yet. "I do not feel now, having just approached a beginning of a sure (*sicher*) work, ready to fulfill the Berlin professorship in a way I would have to demand of myself and anybody else. The truly resistant philosophy can only be a philosophy for its time, e.g., is able to reign this time," are Heidegger's words of justification of his refusal to the minister Adolf Grimme.[19] Toward the end of 1931, Heidegger confesses to Jaspers to be scared of the "dubious" success of *Being and Time*: "I have dared to go far beyond my own existential power and without clearly seeing the confines of what is materially in question for me."[20] In what follows, Heidegger describes his role as an overseer in a gallery, whose task is fulfilled by making sure that the great works of tradition are rightly illuminated: "I only read and work on the history of philosophy."[21] At the beginning of 1932, he will write in his private notes (the infamous *Black Notebooks*): "Today (March 1932) I am in all clarity in a place from which my entire previous literary output (*Being and Time*, 'What Is Metaphysics?' Kantbook, and 'On the Essence of Ground' I and II) has become alien to me."[22]

Simultaneously, toward the end of the 1920s the ambivalent balance, present in *Being and Time*, is being breached: It was a balance between crisp, argumentative analysis and an existential call, between transhistoric fundamental ontology and concrete historicity. This ambivalence made the early *opus* of Heidegger so difficult to read unequivocally as existential philosophy; it made it also dubious to straightforwardly interpret it politically and according to the predominant tendencies of the time (which we saw on the basis of the Weber-Spengler opposition). However, toward the end of the decade this ambivalent balance begins to wobble and starts to move toward pedagogical leadership and, a little later, political engagement.

First of all, Heidegger departs from the agenda of phenomenology, even from his own understanding of phenomenology, worked out in a critical dialogue with Husserl. At the same time he breaks with "scientific philosophy" (in the wide sense of the German *Wissenschaft*) and the Weberian ideal of neutrality. Concurrently, he starts to modify his so far negative attitude toward worldview. In the summer term of 1927, Heidegger sees the necessity of a philosophical analysis of worldviews, but still rejects the possibility of a "world-view-philosophy." Worldview, he stresses, is based not on theoretical knowledge, but on a belief that more or less immediately defines action. Worldview means a stance toward entities, and has—unlike a philosophical questioning of the being of entities—not an ontological, but *ontic* character. The difference between philosophy and worldview is based on ontological difference, and therefore a radical difference, which puts expressions like "world-view philosophy" on the same status as "wooden iron"—that is, absurd.[23] What follows is that the aim of philosophy is not an attitude toward entities or guidelines for action. In the last Marburg lecture (the summer term of 1928) Heidegger still criticizes anti-intellectualism as "the revolt [of slaves] against rationality."[24] At the same time, in this lecture he ceases to see "world-view philosophy" as a contradictory concept: "There is in fact, a philosophical world-view."[25] But he works out such an understanding of worldview that has not much in common with current approaches: worldview as a result of philosophy, practical guidelines for life; to philosophize means to remain "untouched by all the idle talk of the day."[26]

II

The important caesura, when it comes to the problem of the relationship of philosophy to science and worldview, is Heidegger's transfer to Freiburg and the assumption of Husserl's lectern. In the first lecture of the winter term of 1928–1929 (*Introduction into Philosophy*), the bond between philosophy and science becomes loose: Philosophy is a source of science and itself cannot be science. Along with the fracture between philosophy and science (*Wissenschaft*), the problem of the relationship between philosophy and worldview appears in a new light.[27] Heidegger derives from the ontological structures of *Dasein* two basic forms of worldview: being-thrown is now interpreted as being immersed in beings that have power over man. It is accompanied by the possibility of a worldview that guarantees safety and familiarity with entities (*Geborgenheit*).[28] The concrete forms of this type of worldview are, for instance, mythical forms of cults. This type of worldview does not yet open the possibilities of questioning entities, and it does not potentially entwine into philosophy or science. For this, another type of worldview is necessary, which Heidegger calls "world-view as an attitude (*Haltung*)." The possibility of this type is rooted in the human ability to exceed entities and to project itself on being (now Heidegger uses the word "transcendence"). Exceeding beings, "challenging them" is the opposite direction to the attempts to safely situate oneself within entities. While in the first type of worldview, entities were primary, in the second type primary is the existing *Dasein,* which asks entities questions about their way of being. And depending on the kinds of these questions, philosophy or science comes into being.

In this way Heidegger manages to unify philosophy and worldview: Philosophy is a way of practising worldview as a conscious questioning of the fundamental way of being of entities. Philosophy is grounded in the possibility of worldview as an attitude, it is an actualization of the ontological difference, present in all explicit questioning of being. Nevertheless, this bond between philosophy and worldview does not mean that philosophy should create worldviews. Philosophy *is* a worldview in a basic, existential meaning.

Concerning the role of university lectures Heidegger draws further conclusions. Since philosophy is a possibility of the very existence of *Dasein*, the introduction of students into philosophy is not introducing them into a new field of "knowledge about philosophy," but an awakening of the dormant possibility of existence: "Philosophizing should become an event of our own *Dasein*,"[29] adding "our *Dasein* here and now, in this very moment (*Augenblick*)."[30] We can see now, how existential accents begin to dominate over crisp ontological-existential analysis. Indubitably, Heidegger as a teacher feels now, more than earlier, obligated to invoke in his students the philosophy hidden in them: "I liberated myself from the school constraint, the contorted science-orientation and all these things."[31] Along with this, the exalted tones of philosophical vocation and leadership appear; now, philosophy becomes an "obligation to take over the leadership in the whole of historical being-with."[32] This leadership should be inconspicuous and in this way "to have a more powerful impact within the whole of human community, defining the moment (*Augenblick*) of our present *Dasein*."[33] Toward the end of the lecture Heidegger connects this kind of leadership with worldview: "Two powers define our *Dasein* at the university: science and leadership, or world-view."[34] At the same time, this desire of philosophical leadership is still accompanied by a creative block: A year later Heidegger still underscores the ambiguity of philosophy, its uncertainty and fragility. "Philosophy is opposite to comfort and assurance. It is turbulent (*Wirbel*)";[35] "No knower necessarily stands so close to the verge of error at every moment as the one who philosophizes,"[36] says Heidegger, giving an account of his own existential situation.

In the fall of 1929, Heidegger continues with the direction taken after his arrival in Freiburg: He stresses weaker and weaker the necessity of conceptual analysis and distanced phenomenological research, which pervaded his earlier lectures. Now, the awakening of students to philosophy consists in creating the right attunement (in the ontological meaning, of course) and being *gripped* (*ergriffen*) by philosophy.[37] Heidegger begins to sway between conceptual analysis and pathos. He asks his listeners: "Why are we here? Do we know what we are letting ourselves in for?"[38] The fundamental task of the lecture, Heidegger says openly, is "awakening a fundamental attunement in our philosophizing,"[39] even though, not so long earlier, he insisted that "it is surely no criterion for the genuineness and intrinsic legitimacy of a science or philosophical discipline that it does or does not appeal to students."[40]

In the first part of the lecture of 1929 Heidegger delivers a master analysis of attunement, referring to the analysis of moods from *Being and Time*. But this time the distinguished mood is not, as it was then, *angst*, whose role consisted in individualizing *Dasein* in the face of being-toward-death. This time Heidegger analyses the phenomenon of *boredom*. Starting with everyday phenomena, he gradually descends deeply into *Dasein*'s structures in order to extract what he calls a "profound boredom." The existential structure of this boredom resembles the structure of angst: It leads us beyond being concerned (bored) with entities and makes *Dasein* face entities as a whole, disclosing the finitude of human temporality. Entities in this profound boredom appear less fearsome, but they become elusive, they "decline cooperation," become indifferent and unresponsive, they become a void. The profound existential boredom is not "my boredom": It is not that I am bored, "*it is boring for one (es ist einem langweilig).*"[41]

Despite the structural proximity with the analyses of *Being and Time*, we can see in this lecture an important shift in accents: In *Being and Time* (and the lectures of this time), Heidegger seeks to describe angst as a distinguished mood, in this way to reveal something or even to appeal for something. But he does not *evoke* in listeners the described mood. This would be the domain of public opinion, of *das Man*.[42] Apart from this, angst emerges from the core of *Dasein* but, unlike other moods, cannot be evoked, it comes by itself. Now, Heidegger not only strives at the description of the phenomenon of boredom, he also strives at putting the listeners into this state of mind (which is, of course, not to be misunderstood as simply being bored with the lecture), which is the fundamental attunement for philosophy (since it makes *Dasein* face the entirety of entities). Philosophy is not "a matter of method, but one of engagement (*Einsatz*) and of the *possibility of engagement pertaining to a philosophizing existence*,"[43] says Heidegger, who in *Being and Time* wrote: "The expression 'phenomenology' signifies primarily a *concept of method.*"[44]

We can see now how Heidegger, gradually withdrawing from "scientific philosophy," shifts the individualistic categories of his early philosophy toward the level of history and community. The analysis of angst from *Being and Time* was of both an ontological and existential character, that is, it referred to concrete, individual *Dasein* and at the same time described one of the universal structures of being-in-the-world; although one could find in this analysis traces of generational experience, it remained independent from this. Now, by the description of boredom, Heidegger foregoes transhistorical fundamental ontology. Boredom is not a structure of *Dasein* in general, but a fundamental mode of attunement that "*today perhaps determines our* Dasein *here and now.*"[45] Contemporary *Dasein* is doomed, melancholic, and voided, apparent in superficial crises and half measures of overcoming them: "*Has man in the end become boring to himself?*"[46] Heidegger does not strive at finding a remedy for the crisis of culture, although in this context Spengler's name crops up. But Spengler follows Nietzsche's opposition between spirit and life, which makes him unable to present human being ontologically: "Such philosophy attains merely the setting-out [*Dar-stellung*] of man, but never his Da-sein."[47] Heidegger wants to go deeper than Spengler, but now he heads toward basically the same direction.

Thus, he strives at leading the *Dasein* of students toward the fundamentals of the predominant mood of the time, to deepen the pervasive boredom to make them face the void of existence, from which one can glance off in the moment of resolution: "We are asking concerning one profound boredom, concerning *one*—i.e., one *in particular*, i.e., one of *our* Dasein, not just about profound boredom in general or universally."[48] This is the opposite direction to that of the analyses of *Being and Time*, where Heidegger always asked about the phenomenon as such, making particular concretizations secondary and explanatory. But there is one more important difference: We know angst to be an individualizing mood that excluded *Dasein* from interhuman relations, especially from the power of the collective subject, *das Man*. Meanwhile, in the analyzed lecture, attunement gains a collective character: "Attunement is not some being that appears [. . .] but the way of our being there with one another."[49] The question of the possibility of individual *Dasein* becomes the question of "our *Dasein*"; now Heidegger asks, not as he used to do earlier, who is *my Dasein*, but "Who, then, are we? What do we mean here in referring to '*us*'?"[50] One of the following questions goes: "*Do things stand ultimately in such a way with us that a profound boredom draws back and forth like a silent fog in abysses of Dasein?*"[51] Now it's *us*, not me.

This analysis of boredom, completed during this lecture, becomes an answer to the needs of *Dasein* in that particular historical situation. Boredom is revealed as a mode of attunement predominant in the time of the demise of the Weimar Republic, tormented with deep crises. In this way Heidegger slowly departs from the ideal of philosophy, which is always "untimely." He criticizes the philosophies of culture for their superficiality and strives at thought that in a more fundamental and philosophically original way would respond to the current situation, which the two above-described lectures are good testimonies of. The new tones, which I have pointed out, are accompanied by the great analyses of tradition in the old style. Heidegger devotes the following semesters to "illuminate" Kant, Aristotle, Hegel, and Plato, and no intellectual effort is spared to his students. But the new tones that emerge at the turn of the 1930s do not disappear.

Obviously, Heidegger never understood reading the philosophical tradition as a history of philosophy in its classic academic version. The works of a philosopher have always had to speak to us today—this is the principle of Heidegger's hermeneutics from the very beginning. They are not a detached past, but are *our* having-been, they are us, we are they. Reading Greeks, medieval authors, or the representatives of German idealism means repeating the same question of being in different languages, which always refers to *Dasein*. But earlier, Heidegger never wanted philosophy to be "timely" or "up-to-date," only meaningful. The contemporary meaning of philosophy consisted in overcoming the old schools (mostly the nineteenth century) of its practice and enlivening the tradition on the way to its deconstruction: It was the origin of *Being and Time*. But in the 1930s, Heidegger wants more: He wants "timely," current philosophy, which would make for a metaphysical unity with history. In the lecture on Plato of the winter term of 1931–1932 (we know it from chapter 1), Heidegger undertakes the theme of the philosopher as a liberator of people chained in the cave: "Being free, being a liberator, is to act together in history with those to whom one belongs in one's nature."[52] He wants to come back to the cave and to answer the concrete problem of the epoch: The present is "something to be *overcome*. Genuine historical return is the decisive beginning of authentic *futurity*."[53]

I have read through Heidegger's lectures of the late 1920s and early 1930s in order to show the tension that accompanied his membership of the NS. Heidegger was in a creative block: In the lectures of the early 1930s, we find no new *philosophy*. This would come only later as a reaction to the political catastrophe. What we find are the old categories of *Being and Time* in a new, *political* disclosure. Heidegger ceases to think distanced from reality and begins to translate the individualistic and at the same time universal terms of *Being and Time* into the rhetoric of German nationalism. *Dasein* is no longer a structure of human being as such and becomes the existence of the German people. *Augenblick* is no longer the individual and incommunicable moment of recognition of one's own being-unto-death and becomes the moment of a national upsurge toward collective authenticity. Similar shifts happen to the concepts of conscience and guilt.

With these translations, Heidegger had to *compromise* the premises of his own philosophy. He used the old categories in a context completely alien to them. But since he referred to the same words, some interpreters drew the conclusion of a continuity between the early philosophy of *Being and Time* and his political commitment (chapter 3). But the problem seems to be more complicated: Toward the end of the 1920s, Heidegger's attitude to philosophy and his role as a lecturer begins to change. The new content that appears now is not newly philosophical, but newly "political." Heidegger fills the old categories with collective national content and distorts their meaning. Where he wants to not only think, but also "act," his own concepts function as "empty shells." Heidegger does not have any "national socialistic philosophy," but as Habermas notices, "The basic concepts (left unchanged) of fundamental ontology were given a new content."[54] Heidegger himself believed to be in accordance with his old philosophy. And this explains how he can in 1936 say to Karl Löwith that the conception of historicity from *Being and Time* is the basis of his political commitment.[55] Interestingly, Heidegger pointed exactly at historicity (which from the perspective of political events constitutes the most controversial element of his *opus magnum*), and did not mention any of the key categories of *Being and Time*, which he later translated into the alien quasi-rhetoric of Nazism. However, I contend, this declaration is by no means a testimony of a real continuity,[56] but a record of the false self-knowledge of the philosopher. Indeed, the educational promise of *Being and Time*—the promise of an individual overcoming of inauthentic collective identity in an act of existential resolution—is a completely different promise from that which Heidegger offers his students in the years preceding the Third Reich and in the first years of its existence: Now it is a promise of becoming a tool in the national revolution and a cell in the collective organism. The shift of existential categories to the level of *Volk* is not a change of measure. Along with this shift we have a reversal of characters: Now the voice of conscience indeed becomes "'*das Man*' at the height of reign."[57]

Heidegger's estrangement from the premises of his own philosophy also has consequences in the field of politics and tradition. Heidegger's early philosophy could be read in Arendt's mode as disinterested in the specifics of the political, or as considering it from the point of view of contemplation, in short, as a political philosophy in a *negative* sense. For this reason, Heidegger's early thought could be interpreted as a continuation of the tradition of political thought initiated by Plato. Now, even if we limit ourselves "only" to the academic texts of the 1930s, Heidegger cannot be read as politically disinterested anymore. The break with the premises of his philosophy will also be a forfeiting of its apolitical character. Despite certain analogies, Heidegger-rector and member of the NSDAP is not a Platonic philosopher who wants to impose philosophical standards on politics. Heidegger, still not understanding the nature of the political, fuses together philosophy and politics, with the result of negating both. In this he is much more radical than Plato.

TRADITION DEFEATED: HEIDEGGER BREAKS WITH PLATO AND THE IDEA OF UNIVERSITY

At first glance, *Being and Time* showed a non-obvious affinity with Plato's cave, but after a closer look it appears inescapable. The direction of Heidegger's analyses led then, so to say, outside the cave of *the they*. However, fundamental ontology did not possess transcendental concepts that would show a philosopher the way back to the cave. Within the horizon of *Being and Time*, the return to the cave of inauthenticity has by no means the features of political leadership, but is a natural movement of falling into the world, the unavoidable moment of every human existence. Apart from this, Heidegger the philosopher had no ambitions exceeding an accurate description of existential structures and making them the path to understanding being as such.

I

At the beginning of the 1930s, the situation seems to be the same and, oddly, at the same time different: Heidegger deconstructed metaphysics and still does not possess the transcendental norms to be applied in politics. Neither does he have an understanding of politics that would make such norms abundant. At the same time, his ambitions are different. He describes Plato's stance and we get the feeling he is writing about the current historical situation:

> The authentic guardians of human association in the unity of the πόλις must be those who philosophize. He does not mean that philosophy professors are to become chancellors of the state, but that philosophers are to become φύλακες, guardians. Control and organization of the state is to be undertaken by philosophers, who set standards and rules in accordance with their widest and deepest freely inquiring knowledge, thus determining the general course which society should follow.[58]

But Heidegger not so much establishes the philosophical measure for politics, like Plato, but, rather, *identifies* philosophy with politics. In Safranski's words: "He intends to be the herald of a historical-political and, simultaneously, philosophical epiphany [. . .]. Now he has to be vigilant, lest he miss the moment (*Augenblick*, P. S.) when politics can and must become philosophical and philosophy political."[59] Slowly, the philosophical leadership at the university, and the awakening of the philosophical spirit of students, become unsatisfactory for him.

The remarks, which in the lecture on Plato in 1931–1932 are ambiguously interwoven into the interpretation of the allegory of the cave, gain immediate power in the semester during which Heidegger is elected to be the rector. In the spring of 1933 he begins the lecture with the words: "The great historical moment (*Augenblick*) the German people go through is known to academic youth."[60] The moment (Heidegger openly refers to National Socialism) is historical, because the people found their leader. "We want to make philosophy real"[61]; "Not to speak about questions but to act questioningly and dare to commit."[62] Instead of "who is *Dasein*?", the fundamental question of philosophy now sounds: "Who is this people in history and what is its destiny in the foundations of its being"?[63]

The idea, that each *Dasein*, grasped individually, is potentially a philosophical being, is an essentially democratic idea. Every man, understanding being, unconsciously discerns being from entities, lives in the ontological difference. The philosopher is the one who makes this distinction consciously, but the distance between him and other men is, rather, quantitative. Nonetheless, the idea of philosophical *Dasein* changes dramatically when *Dasein* is separated from individualism (Heidegger poses a question of what philosophy is not and answers: "it is not a concern with the existence of the individual"[64]) and identified with a concrete historical collective: *Volk* as a "German *Dasein*." Philosophy now refers not to an understanding of being, characteristic to every man, but to history and a national mission, where there is no place for individual questioning of being. A new metaphysics emerges, stripped of questioning subjects. The German *Dasein* becomes an instrument of higher powers, and it is being itself that speaks now: "We are the people who must only *win* its own metaphysics and who *will do it*."[65] A semester later, when repeating the lecture on Plato, Heidegger emphasizes that at stake is not truth in general, but "the truth, the only truth which for our *Dasein* now constitutes law and support."[66] In what follows, Heidegger refers to Heraclitus and we have a disquisition on combat and foes, a disquisition of which Carl Schmitt could have been the author as well. Now, the distinguished mode of attunement is not *angst* (with World War I in the background) or *boredom* (of the failing Weimar Republic), but a "primordial courage."[67]

II

Heidegger in 1945 summed up the time of his rectorship with remarks titled *Facts and Thoughts*.[68] The "facts" that Heidegger referred to are known due to the historical study of Hugo Ott[69] and turned out to be, euphemistically speaking, not entirely congruent with Heidegger's account. We are but now interested in thoughts, particularly one thought: Heidegger's conviction about the continuity and consistency of his philosophical beliefs. Heidegger himself maintained that his acts as the rector were only conclusions from the necessity of the renewal of university, which he had advocated already in 1929. Nevertheless, Heidegger's later belief that philosophy unites with politics in the great metaphysical revolution made him radicalize the postulate of the reform that resulted in an almost physical attack on the tradition of the German university.

Toward the end of the 1920s, Heidegger raised a motif of the crisis of university, not untypically for the time. "Academic studies are questionable today,"[70] says Heidegger to students in 1929. The symptoms of the crisis sound familiar: the specialization, vocationalization, the inability of students to grasp science as a whole. "Do we not miss the essence of everything at the university?"[71] Heidegger asked rhetorically. Similarly, in the inauguration lecture of the same year:

> The scientific fields are quite diverse. The ways they treat their objects of inquiry differ fundamentally. Today only the technical organization of universities and faculties consolidates this multiplicity of dispersed disciplines; the practical establishment of goals by each discipline provides the only meaningful source of unity. Nonetheless, the rootedness of the sciences in their essential ground has atrophied.[72]

In this lecture, Heidegger points to the right ground for the sciences in the question of being and nothingness. Thus, it is an attempt, by way of a new philosophical questioning, of reinstating the organic unity of the sciences founded in philosophy, as postulated already by the creators of the German university of the nineteenth century.

Nonetheless, in the first half of the 1930s Heidegger is not so much convinced about the crisis of the traditional university, but of its complete fall.[73] He no longer attempts to rescue the unity of science or protect the university from harmful external influences, but, surfing on the revolutionary wave, strives at its complete redefinition: "We need a new constitution of the university [. . .]. Not to give what is present at hand a 'build up' and a new gloss but to destroy the university. This 'negativity' however, will be effective only if it finds its task in the education of a new species."[74]

Heidegger's rector speech is a peculiar document. On the one hand, the condition of the possibility of its creation was the structure of the German university, worked out at the beginning of the nineteenth century, and Heidegger still referred to certain premises of Humboldt's reform, like the above-mentioned organic unity of science under philosophical leadership. Even the questioning of academic freedom in the name of nationalism, so radically contradictory to Humboldt's legacy, can be somehow related to Fichte's ideas, or to the factual dependence of the German university on the state. Also, Heidegger's critical attitude toward the idea of *Bildung* can be inscribed into the immanent self-critical logic of the institution. All of this, the conviction of the fundamental crisis included, is not new and is compatible with the general attunements of interwar Germany.

On the other hand, this speech is an actual split with the German cultural tradition in general and German university in particular: coupling labor, military service, and science at the service of the state,[75] he destroys the elementary distance toward political reality that the university held on to even in difficult political moments. He also destroys the fundamental conditions of study, this "living in ideas," which makes him challenge not only Humboldt, but also Fichte, who emphasized that the care of physical existence and work do not fit in academic study.[76] A few months later, Heidegger goes on to speak to his students, and describes this destruction in a succinct way: "Let not propositions and 'ideas' be the rules of your being. The Führer alone *is* the present and future German reality and its law."[77] Of course, the three services of labor, military service, and science are designed by Heidegger to reflect Plato's triad of workers, guardians, and philosophers. But in Plato, who understood the specifics of contemplation, we nowhere find the idea that one person fulfills all these duties simultaneously, switching from one to another.

Heidegger stylizes his speech to sound Platonic, but at the same time he distorts the spirit unrecognizably. By doing so, he departs from another founder of the idea of university: Friedrich Schleiermacher. The speech ends with the quotation from Plato: *ta megala [. . .] panta episphale* (*Republic*, 497d). But Heidegger, who so far willingly referred to the classic translation of Schleiermacher, now translates the fragment awry.[78] Instead of "for all great things are prone to fall, and, as the saying goes, fine things are really hard to achieve,"[79] we have (literally): "All that is great stands in combat," or as the English translations of Heidegger go, "All that is great stands in the storm" (*Alles große steht im Sturm*[80]). Heidegger not only cuts out the middle of the sentence, which makes the words that originally refer to "fine things" in his quotation refer to the greatness, but also distorts the meaning of the Greek word *episphales* (on the verge of falling, dangerous, unsteady) to put it into a military context and incorporate Plato into "the battle community of teachers and students."[81] Thus, what in Plato is an expression of the doubts of the philosopher in the face of overwhelming intellectual enterprise he set for himself and an expression of reservations about his ability to fulfill this task, in Heidegger it transforms into "the glory and greatness of this new beginning."[82] The linguistic level of Heidegger's speech invokes unequivocal associations: "*Sturm*" in Plato's sentence is designed to create an analogy with the *Sturmabteilung* (SA) in the totalitarian state. Karl Löwith describes Heidegger's speech as "a minor stylistic masterpiece": "At the end of the speech, the listener was in doubt as to whether he should start reading the pre-Socratics or to enlist in the SA."[83]

That military exercises and labor service were not only concessions to the state, but that Heidegger in the time of the rectorate really identified them with the essence of study, corroborate numerous occurrences of that time. When we read them, for example, the speech on the occasion of matriculation of 1933–1934, we gain the impression that, for the moment, the search for truth is completely irrelevant, since it revealed itself as *aletheia* along with the political change, and the primary duty of the student is to *make it real* in a physical sense; the old academic values of higher education are dead; now, the "student becomes a worker."[84] This coupling of learning with physical labor is an expression of the desire of *realization* of philosophy in the NS state. Since the political and metaphysical revolutions are one and the same thing, it no longer makes any difference whether one is digging trenches or reading Parmenides: Both activities stand equally at the service of being.

Thus, in Heidegger's attitude to university we also have to do with a split: "It is surprising that Heidegger, who until then had always wished to keep the spirit of true scholarship and philosophy free from any considerations of utility or practical orientation, is now calling for an instrumentalization of scholarship for national goals."[85] Toward the end of the 1920s, Heidegger wanted to overcome the specialization and vocationalization of academic study. In the 1930s, through organizing, as a rector, labor camps for students, he "overcame" the difference between thinking and labor, idea and matter. "A new reality is present in the work camp,"[86] says Heidegger. Indeed, it was a new reality that as yet revealed its power within the Albert-Ludwig-University.

III

This does not mean, however, that the Heideggerian version of "identification" of philosophy and "politics" in the form of a metaphysical revolution was in agreement with factual Nazi ideology. In *Facts and Thoughts,* Heidegger claimed to be criticized by the ministry for avoiding the program of the party and particularly the ideology of race[87] and on this particular point we have no reasons not to believe this testimony, as it is corroborated even by his *Black Notebooks*. The openly anti-Semitic remarks, which appear in them, never have a biological-racist grounding. On the contrary, Heidegger's anti-Semitism is of a "metaphysical" nature: Jews contribute to the forgetfulness of being and the triumph of "calculative thinking." But they are not the only representatives of the fulfilled metaphysics of modernity: They share a place with Bolsheviks, Americans, the English, certified psychologists, and others. "The question of the role of *World-Judaism* is not a racial question, but a metaphysical one."[88]

It seems, rather, that Heidegger had a certain imagined version of Nazi ideology. The Nazis never desired his metaphysical revolution and had no intention of listening to the philosopher-leader. In the spring of 1934 Heidegger planned to deliver a lecture on "Science and State," but in connection to the events preceding his retreat from the rectorate, he changed the title at the last minute and addressed the Party functionaries present in the lecture room with the words: "I teach logic," which, naturally, discouraged them from attending. Heidegger indeed taught logic. Although the rhetoric identifying *Dasein* with *Volk* and that of historical resoluteness still appears,[89] a new motif emerges, the motif of poetry as a primordial language of the people. Poetry will soon become a niche into which Heidegger, disappointed with the revolution, withdraws. For now he says to the people present: "In order to comprehend this, the Germans, who talk so much today about discipline (*Zucht*) must learn what it means to preserve that which they already possess."[90]

From this moment Heidegger begins slowly to withdraw from political engagement. It does not mean that he at once stops believing in the sense of the national socialistic revolution per se.[91] But his understanding of the revolution starts to depart from the course of contemporary events: "His focus shifted until he regarded National Socialism no longer as a breakout from the modern age but as its especially consistent expression. He discovered that National Socialism was itself the problem whose solution he had once thought it was."⁹² The motif of the critique of modernity will be developed in his later philosophy. For now, we can see the first symptoms of the retreat: The historical destiny of the German people is to be fulfilled not immediately, but through the language of poetry. The winter term of 1934–1935 is not devoted to analysis of Hölderlin by chance. The lecture's aim is not to "offer something catchy and current with regard to the demands of time."⁹³ Heidegger begins to work out the new language—a shelter that allows him to hide from commitment. Thinking slowly starts to connect with the "saying" of poetry, which more primordially than academic philosophy becomes "revealing of Being (*Seyn*)."⁹⁴ Heidegger will also slowly come out from his creative block. With the process, the postulate of the unity of philosophy and political reality will be less and less audible and Heidegger starts to articulate a more or less camouflaged critique of the Third Reich and its ideology.⁹⁵ Simultanously, Heidegger abandons his desire for timely philosophy: "Philosophy is essentially untimely because it is one of those few things whose fate remains never to be able to find a direct resonance in their own time, and never to be permitted to find such a resonance."⁹⁶ When philosophy is trying to be current, "either there is no actual philosophy or else philosophy is misinterpreted and [. . .] misused for the needs of the day."⁹⁷ Neither can we demand from philosophy to "provide a foundation to the current and future historical *Dasein*."⁹⁸

In summing up, although Heidegger accepted many Platonic assumptions on the nature of the public sphere, the political role of Heidegger has not much to do with the role of philosophers in the state, as projected by Plato. Heidegger never possessed any transcendental norm, which defined the relationship between philosophy and politics in Plato. The idea of good subordinated politics to philosophy, but did not lead to their amalgamation. As long as Heidegger was uninterested in politics, his attitude toward the public sphere could be interpreted in Plato's categories. But when he decided to return to the cave, with empty hands, the nature of this return had to be non-Platonic.

ARENDT: THINKING THROUGH THE BREAK

Heidegger's break with his own thought, which resulted in the rectorate, can also be accounted for in Arendt's political categories. Although in the laudation for Heidegger's 80th birthday Arendt grasped his political actions with Plato's traditional motif of Syracuse, this account can be challenged by the wider context of Arendt's own political thought. Arendt could not have known the historical documents, which were made public only in the 1980s, owing to the work of Hugo Ott, and accepted Heidegger's version of the alleged persecution he suffered after his retreat from the post.[99]

As if contrary to her Platonic interpretation of Heidegger's case, the importance and freshness of Arendt's postwar work is rooted in the fact that the events of World War II, which started with the caesura of 1933, she recognized as new phenomena, having their origins in the history of Europe, but principally without precedence.

I

According to Arendt, if we want to understand the events of the twentieth century, especially the totalitarian movements, whose emergence sealed the demise of the triad of tradition, authority, and religion, we need to resist the temptation of drawing these events into the old categories of European thought. The experience of totalitarianism is something new in history, and accordingly, requires new vocabulary and new thinking. We can, of course, try to describe these experiences with the old categories, but only at the risk of losing their phenomenal content. The power of *The Origins of Totalitarianism* rests on the fact that Arendt does not attempt to derive totalitarianism from old forms of government or, even less, to identify it with one of those forms, but accepts that there is a new experience underlying totalitarianism, and that this experience needs a new description, free from the old forms. The sense of this description (it can be called a phenomenological one) is not only of scientific, but also of existential relevance. The understanding of what really happened helps to preserve the events from forgetfulness and make experiences out of them, that is, things that shape our past and our knowledge about ourselves.

But since new experiences tend to slip through our fingers because of the lack of adequate language, we try to save them with the language we have inherited. This can lead to the loss of their specifics and harm our understanding of what really happened. That is why Arendt put so much effort into working out new categories for twentieth-century political thought (not less than Heidegger in a new language of ontology). In the context of the Heidegger controversy, the distinction between authoritarianism, tyranny, and totalitarianism seems to be relevant. Arendt attempts to avoid identification of these phenomena through the reconstruction of *images* of the structures of power, corresponding with these three concepts.

The image of authoritarian rule is a pyramid, where the "seat of power is located at the top, from which authority and power is filtered down to the base."[100] From our point of view, the most important thing is that the source of power is transcendent from the top of the pyramid. Arendt applies this model particularly to medieval theocracies and Plato's republic: The structure of power is defined by an external norm (or idea), drawing its authority from a divine order. A different image is assigned to tyranny: It is still a pyramid, but without the intervening layers between top and bottom. The tyrant rules not with authority, but with a physical menace, and exercises his power "over a mass of carefully isolated, disintegrated, and completely equal individuals."[101] Totalitarianism, however, does not have the structure of a pyramid; its image stems from another *imaginarium*: It is an onion. The leader is situated at the very center and acts from within, not from without the concentric structure: "All the extraordinarily manifold parts of the movement [. . .] are related in such a way that each forms the façade in one direction and the center in the other, that is, plays the role of normal outside world for one layer and the role of radical extremism for another."[102]

If we look at the role of Heidegger in the Nazi power apparatus from the perspective of Arendt's distinctions between authoritarianism, tyranny, and totalitarianism, we need to state that this role does not fit into the authoritarian, Platonic system of power. Heidegger could act in the system just because behind his identification of the Reich's politics and the history of being there was no external authority. Nietzsche's saying "God is dead" (Heidegger referred to it in his Rector's speech), combined with his lack of understanding of human affairs and the public sphere in an immediate political application, turned into an explosive mixture. In 1933, Heidegger could not have been aware of the nature of totalitarianism. But his support for the regime could not be the support of authoritarian rule, exactly because there was no transcendent source of authority in his philosophy (not only a question of his departure from Christianity). What occurred to be philosophically enormously fruitful, was politically dangerous, but the fact that Heidegger could take part in politics at all demanded a distortion of his philosophical thought, as we have seen. As a result, Heidegger, instead of being a lost Platonic philosopher, who at the risk of his life tries to teach the tyrant the rules of government according to eternal cosmic laws, turned out to be a philosopher who with all vehemence strived at creating another layer of an onion around the leader. This layer was to be the German university. The case of Heidegger is not the worst illustration of the phenomenon described by Arendt as "the temporary alliance between the mob and the elite."[103] It was temporary because after the seizure of power, the totalitarian movement was reshaped into a regime and got rid of intellectuals sympathizing previously with the movement. Heidegger was no exception (other examples are Ernst Krieck and Carl Schmitt). But Heidegger's admiration for Hitler, which can hardly be accounted for in intellectual categories, and the rhetoric of the march he used (realized in a factual marching of uniformed participants of an infamous "science camp" in October 1933) are the consequences of "patently absurd propositions" that were easier to accept than "the old truths which had become pious banalities."[104]

II

From Arendt's perspective, the end of the tradition of political thought "came with Marx's declaration that philosophy and its truth are located not outside the affairs of men and their common world but precisely in them."[105] Plato initiated the classic attitude of philosophy toward politics: First turning away from politics, then returning through imposing philosophical standards on human affairs. Marx goes in the opposite direction, that is, the philosopher "turns away from philosophy so as to 'realize' it in politics"[106] (here we have a purely formal analogy to Heidegger's "realization" of philosophy in the 1930s). Marx's thought, along with Nietzsche's and Kierkegaard's, is paradoxical: It combines two opposite poles, that is, it contains a discrepancy between "certain trends in the present which could no longer be understood in the framework of the tradition, and the traditional concepts and ideals by which Marx himself understood and integrated them."[107]

For Marx, a new experience, incongruent with tradition, was the Hegelian transformation of metaphysics into a philosophy of history; a philosopher becomes a historian, "to whose backward glance, eventually, at the end of time, the meaning of becoming and motion, not of being and truth, would reveal itself."[108] Marx responded with a leap from philosophy into politics, a leap from theory into action, and, what follows, the reversal of their hierarchy. For Kierkegaard, a new experience was a modern loss of faith, "not only in God but in reason as well, which was inherent in Descartes' *de omnibus dubitandum est*, with its underlying suspicion that things may not be as they appear."[109] The answer to this tendency was a leap from doubt into faith, which, again, brought about a reversal of known categories (at the same time Kierkegaard introduced doubt into religion). For Nietzsche, in turn, a new experience was the fact that in modern society the transcendent status of ideas and norms was abolished and dissolved "into relationships between its members, establishing them as functional 'values.'"[110] Transcendent and unchangeable ideas were replaced by relative and changeable values. Nietzsche responded with a "leap from the nonsensuous transcendent realm of ideas and measurements into the sensuousness of life, his 'inverted Platonism' or 'trans-valuation of values.'"[111] This "trans-valuation" was another attempt to turn away from the tradition, but, according to Arendt, it "succeeded only in turning tradition upside-down."[112]

All this means that Marx, Nietzsche, and Kierkegaard were not symbols of the breaking of the thread of tradition (in both a political and general sense), but rather representatives of a generation of philosophers, who already could see the end of old reality, but were still not able to find the means of expression to overcome this reality; their "seemingly playful, challenging and paradoxical mood conceals the perplexity of having to deal with new phenomena in terms of an old tradition of thought outside of whose conceptual framework no thinking seemed possible at all."[113]

At the same time, Marx, when it comes to the degree of breaking the thread of the tradition of political thought, was more advanced than Heidegger's early philosophy, insofar as Heidegger in *Being and Time* took over the Platonic opposition between philosophy and human affairs, placing authenticity beyond the public sphere. Whereas Marx, in an attempt to abolish philosophy through its realization, questioned the very opposition between *vita activa* and *vita contemplativa* and was the first to bestow politics with philosophical dignity.[114] This makes Marx difficult to be easily read as a representative of tradition.

The certain hesitation Arendt shows in the question of Marx being within, or without, the tradition arises from two things: first, sometimes Arendt has in mind the tradition of political thought (which Marx could have broken), and at another time the tradition of the West in a more general meaning (which could not have been broken by any thinker, and ended up with the rise of totalitarian rule). Second, there is a difference between Nietzsche and Marx here; Nietzsche, unlike Marx, had to be left within tradition so that Heidegger could be the one to dismantle it first (we remember that Arendt accepted Heidegger's account of Nietzsche's philosophy). However, the space after Marx remained empty and Arendt herself did not feel up to filling it. But the truth is that it was Arendt who overcame the tradition of political thought and she did it in the struggle with both Marx and Heidegger. Contrary to Heidegger, she never claimed to be innovative and often emphasized the alliances she found with the old authors. But all her postwar writings are a great attempt to describe the political events beyond the language of tradition. The tradition of political thought was unable to save all important political experiences of the West:

> This insulation shown by our tradition from its beginning against all political experiences that did not fit into its framework [. . .] has remained one of its outstanding features. The mere tendency to exclude everything that was not consistent developed into a great power of exclusion, which kept the tradition intact against all new, contradictory and conflicting experiences.[115]

For Arendt, tradition, no matter if we speak now of the tradition of the West in general, of the philosophical tradition, or of the tradition of political thought, is an ambiguous category: Guaranteeing safety and stability, it is a blueprint, or even an iron cage, that defines memory in advance and decides what will be transferred onward. In the tradition of political thought, dominated by contemplation, this blueprint was made up of instrumental relations and categories drawn from the private sphere, or, from the experience of thinking. This resulted in the inability of this tradition to understand plurality and the specifics of action, from Plato to Heidegger: "Whatever experiences did not fit into these dichotomies, as outlined in Plato's and Aristotle's political philosophies, simply did not enter the field of political theory."[116] That is why these theories were unfit to give an account of new, unprecedented events, like modern revolutions or twentieth-century totalitarianisms.

CONCLUDING REMARKS

This whole story is paradoxical. If we accept that it was Heidegger who ultimately overcame the tradition of Western philosophy, which for him was identical with the history of forgetfulness of being, in order to posit this question anew, it is impossible to overlook that he himself fell into a Platonic trap: at each stage of his intellectual biography—from the earliest Marburg lectures to the late writings—he was unable to think of human plurality other than in Plato's categories, that is, as an augmented singular. First, it was the impersonal *the they*, then the historical *Dasein* of the people, and at last, a poetic community of mortals. In 1933, he attempted to escape this trap with a shortcut: by abolishing the gap between philosophy and political action altogether. But then he did not simply apply traditional Platonic intellectual tools; neither did he thoroughly think through political categories, but immediately translated his nonpolitical categories into action. If we exclude the rectorate period, we could say that Heidegger's political philosophy remains *negative* by its inscription of the traditional relationship between philosophy and politics.

As a negative political philosophy, Heidegger's thought confirms the traditional philosophical promise for education: the promise of individual liberation from the ontological weaknesses of the public sphere (see chapter 3). As an attempt at application of philosophy into politics, which at the same time was a pedagogical enterprise, it is, rather, a negation of this promise. This brings about the necessity of challenging this promise from the perspective contrary to both traditional philosophy and the opposite stance of Heidegger.

Hannah Arendt's attitude toward "the broken thread of tradition," although the moment of this break defines the greatest tragedies of the twentieth century, is not negative and it evokes in her no conservative desire of returning to, or re-establishing the old hierarchies. The liberation from tradition "is the great chance to look upon the past with eyes undistracted by any tradition, with a directness which has disappeared from Occidental reading and hearing ever since Roman civilization submitted to the authority of Greek thought."[117] The Roman triad of authority, religion, and tradition was destroyed, but the past was not. In her *Denktagebuch*, Arendt states that like the end of tradition did not destroy the past, the demise of religion did not invalidate faith in God. But the question is this: What remains after authority? Arendt, only in private notes, it must be remembered, gives an answer: What remains is education "as introducing new people into the common world."[118]

Perhaps the end of tradition, which also makes the classic relation between philosophy and education questionable, is a chance to dig into the ill-disciplined past and on this basis, to think over the traditional promise of philosophy to education. Thinking beyond tradition is not the same as turning upside down known hierarchies. Questioning the relation between philosophy and education is not equal to overturning traditional answers and negating the possibility of this relation. In the third part of this book I will undertake an attempt to think this relation over with Arendt.

But before this, we need to recover from the past certain premises of this relationship, independent of tradition. A new look upon the past will require replacing the reversals, which always remain within conceptual structures of tradition, with a method of phenomenological deconstruction. This method in Heidegger's application we know already from the analysis of *Being and Time*. Its application by Arendt, that is, an attempt to recover action in the struggle both with the tradition of political thought and with Heidegger, will be the theme of the two following chapters. Nevertheless, in order to understand Arendt's position we need to step back to 1924, when Arendt as an eighteen-year-old student for the first time heard Heidegger's lecture.

NOTES

1. Arendt, "Tradition and the Modern Age," 16.
2. Hannah Arendt, "The Tradition of Political Thought," in *Promise of Politics*, 43.
3. Martin Heidegger, *Platon: Sophistes*, Gesamtausgabe, II abt., Band 19 (Frankfurt am Main: Vittorio Klostermann, 1992), 413; English: Martin Heidegger, *Plato's Sophist*, trans. Richard Rojcewicz and André Schuwer (Bloomington: Indiana University Press, 1997), 285. Further quoted as HGA 19 with reference to both the original (G) and the translation (E).
4. Arendt, "What Is Authority?" 94.
5. Arendt, "What Is Authority?" 140.
6. Arendt, "The Tradition of Political Thought," 26.
7. Arendt, "The Tradition of Political Thought," 27.
8. See Arendt, "Martin Heidegger at Eighty," 54.
9. See Preface.
10. See Martin Heidegger, *Nietzsche*, Volume I, *Will to Power as Art*, trans. David F. Krell (San Francisco: HarperCollins, 1991), 200–10.
11. See Martin Heidegger, *Nietzsche*, Volume III, *Will to Power as Knowledge and as Metaphysics*, trans. Joan Stambaugh, David F. Krell, and Frank A. Capuzzi (San Francisco: HarperCollins, 1991), 187–215.

12. See Arendt, *Denktagebuch*, 133.
13. Arendt, "Tradition and the Modern Age," 34.
14. An attempt of the reconstruction of the possible continuation of *Being and Time* and the reasons why it was never published was undertaken by Theodore Kisiel, "The Demise of Being and Time: 1927–1930," trans. Richard Polt, in *Heidegger's Being and Time: Critical Essays*, ed. Richard Polt (Oxford: Rowman & Littlefield Publishers, 2005).
15. Martin Heidegger, *Die Metaphysik des deutschen Idealismus. Zur erneuten Auslegung von Schelling: Philosophische Untersuchungen über das Wesen der menschlichen Freiheit und die damit zusammenhängenden Gegenstände (1809)*, Gesamtausgabe II. Abt., Band 49 (Frankfurt am Main: Vittorio Klostermann, 1991), 40.
16. SZ, 39; BT, 35.
17. Martin Heidegger, "Letter on Humanism," trans. Frank A. Capuzzi, in *Pathmarks*, 249–50.
18. A letter to Elisabeth Blochmann, September 12, 1929, in Martin Heidegger and Elisabeth Blochmann, *Briefwechsel 1918–1969* (Marbach am Neckar: Deutsche Schillergesellschaft, 1990), 32.
19. Martin Heidegger, "Entscheidung gegen Berlin," in HGA 16, 61.
20. Martin Heidegger to Karl Jaspers, December 20, 1931. Martin Heidegger and Karl Jaspers, *The Heidegger-Jaspers Correspondence (1920–1963)*, ed. Walter Biemel and Hans Saner, trans. Gary E. Aylesworth (New York: Humanity Books, 2003), 232.
21. Heidegger to Jaspers, December 20, 1931. *The Heidegger-Jaspers Correspondence*, 233.
22. Martin Heidegger, *Überlegungen II–IV (Schwarze Hefte 1931–1938)*, Gesamtausgabe IV. Abt., Band 94 (Frankfurt am Main: Vittorio Klostermann, 2014), 19; English: Martin Heidegger, *Ponderings II–VI (Black Notebooks 1931–1938)*, trans. Richard Rojcewicz (Bloomington: Indiana University Press, 2016), 15. Further quoted as HGA 94 with reference to both the original (G) and the translation (E).
23. See HGA 24, 15–17G; 12–13E.
24. Martin Heidegger, *Metaphysische Anfangsgründe der Logik im Ausgang von Leibniz*, Gesamtausgabe II Abt., Band 26 (Frankfurt am Main: Vittorio Klostermann, 1978), 5; English: Martin Heidegger, *The Metaphysical Foundations of Logic*, trans. Michael Heim (Bloomington: Indiana University Press, 1992), 5. Further quoted as HGA 26 with reference to both the original (G) and the translation (E).
25. HGA 26, 22G; 18E.
26. HGA 26, 22G; 18E.
27. See HGA 27, 14–18.
28. See HGA 27, 357.
29. HGA 27, 5–6.
30. HGA 27, 6.
31. Heidegger to Blochmann, December 18, 1929. *Briefwechsel*, 34.
32. HGA 27, 7.
33. HGA 27, 8.
34. HGA 27, 401.
35. HGA 29/30, 28G; 19E.

36. HGA 29/30, 29G; 19E.
37. HGA 29/30, 9G; 7E.
38. HGA 29/30, 6G; 5E.
39. HGA 29/30, 89G; 59E.
40. HGA 26, 5G; 5E.
41. HGA 29/30, 202G; 134E.
42. See SZ, 138–39; BT, 130.
43. HGA 29/30, 231G; 154E.
44. SZ, 27; BT, 24.
45. HGA 29/30, 236G; 157E.
46. HGA 29/30, 241G; 161E.
47. HGA 29/30, 113G; 76E.
48. HGA 29/30, 242G; 162E.
49. HGA 29/30, 100G; 66E.
50. HGA 29/30, 103G; 69E.
51. HGA 29/30, 115G; 77E.
52. HGA 34, 85G; 62E.
53. HGA 34, 10G; 7E.
54. Jürgen Habermas, *The Philosophical Discourse of Modernity: Twelve Lectures*, trans. Frederick Lawrence (Oxford: Blackwell Publishers, 1998), 157.
55. Karl Löwith, "My Last Meeting with Heidegger in Rome, 1936," in *The Heidegger Controversy*, 142.
56. As, for example, Richard Wolin maintains, see *The Politics of Being*, 75.
57. Arendt, *Denktagebuch*, 181.
58. HGA 34, 100G; 73E.
59. Safranski, *Martin Heidegger*, 224.
60. Martin Heidegger, *Sein und Wahrheit*, Gesamtausgabe II Abt., Band 36/37 (Frankfurt am Main: Vittorio Klostermann, 1978), 3. Further quoted as HGA 36/37.
61. HGA 36/37, 4.
62. HGA 36/37, 4–5.
63. HGA 36/37, 4.
64. HGA 36/37, 8.
65. HGA 36/37, 80.
66. HGA 36/37, 84.
67. HGA 36/37, 88.
68. Martin Heidegger, "The Rectorate 1933/34: Facts and Thoughts," trans. Karsten Harris, *Review of Metaphysics*, 38, no. 3 (1985).
69. Hugo Ott, *Martin Heidegger: A Political Life*, trans. Allan Blunden (New York: Basic Books, 1993).
70. HGA 28, 347.
71. HGA 28, 348.
72. Martin Heidegger, "What Is Metaphysics?" trans, David F. Krell in Heidegger, in *Pathmarks*, 82–83.
73. Martin Heidegger, *Die deutsche Universität*, in HGA 16, 287, 301.
74. HGA 94, 115G; 85E.
75. Heidegger, "The Self-Assertion of the German University," 35.

76. See Fichte, "Deduzierter Plan, " 139.
77. Martin Heidegger, "Zum Semesterbeginn" (November 3, 1933), in HGA 16, 184; English: "German Students" (November 3, 1933), trans. William S. Lewis, in *The Heidegger Controversy*, 47.
78. In Schleiermacher's translation the excerpt sounds: "Denn alles große ist auch bedenklich, und wie man sagt das Schöne ist in der Tat schwer." For comparisons with the English translations of Plato, see Wolin, *The Politics of Being*, 90–91.
79. Plato, *Republic*, 497d (Grube and Reeve).
80. Heidegger, "Selbstbehauptung der deutschen Universität," in HGA 16, 117.
81. Martin Heidegger, "The Self-Assertion of the German University," trans. Karsten Harris, *Review of Metaphysics* 38, no. 3 (1985): 479. In Lewis' translation Kampf rendered as "struggle," see *The Heidegger Controversy*, 37. "Die Kampfgemeinschaft der Lehrer und Schüler," Heidegger, "Selbstbehauptung der deutschen Universität," 116. If not indicated otherwise, in other places I refer to the Lewis translation.
82. Heidegger, "The Self-Assertion," 38.
83. Löwith, "The Political Implications of Heidegger's Existentialism," 124–25.
84. Martin Heidegger, "Der deutsche Student als Arbeiter," in HGA 16, 204.
85. Safranski, *Martin Heidegger*, 260.
86. Martin Heidegger, "Arbeitsdienst und Universität," in HGA 16, 125; English: "Labor Service and the Univerity" (June 20, 1933), in *The Heidegger Controversy*, 43.
87. Heidegger, "The Rectorate 1933/34," 490.
88. Martin Heidegger, *Überlegungen XII–XV (Schwarze Hefte 1939–1941)*, Gesamtausgabe IV. Abt., Band 96 (Frankfurt am Main: Vittorio Klostermann, 2014), 243; English: Martin Heidegger, *Ponderings XII–XV (Black Notebooks 1939–1941)*, trans. Richard Rojcewicz (Bloomington: Indiana University Press, 2017), 191. Further quoted as HGA 96 with reference to both the original (G) and the translation (E).
89. See Martin Heidegger, *Logik und die Frage nach der Sprache*, Gesamtausgabe II Abt., Band 38 (Frankfurt am Main: Vittorio Klostermann, 1998), 165; English: Martin Heidegger, *Logic and the Question Concerning the Essence of Language*, trans. Wanda T. Gregory and Yvonne Unna (Albany: State University of New York Press, 2009), 129–30. Further quoted as HGA 38 with reference to both the original (G) and the translation (E).
90. HGA 38, 170G; 142E.
91. See for instance the infamous sentence on NS: "the inner truth and greatness of this movement," Martin Heidegger, *Introduction to Metaphysics*, trans. Gregory Fried and Richard Polt (New Haven, CT: Yale University Press, 2000), 213.
92. Safranski, *Martin Heidegger*, 293.
93. Martin Heidegger, *Hölderlins Hymnen "Germanien" und "Der Rhein,"* Gesamtausgabe II Abt., Band 39 (Frankfurt am Main: Vittorio Klostermann, 1999), 4. Further quoted as HGA 39.
94. HGA 39, 6.
95. See for instance Heidegger's remarks on literary science: "now everything is swallowed by *Volk, Blut und Boden*, HGA 39, 254.
96. Heidegger, *Introduction to Metaphysics*, 9.

97. Heidegger, *Introduction to Metaphysics*, 9.
98. Heidegger, *Introduction to Metaphysics*, 11.
99. "He was served somewhat worse than Plato, because the tyrant and his victims were not located beyond the sea, but in his own country." Arendt, *Martin Heidegger at Eighty*, 54.
100. Arendt, "What Is Authority?" 98.
101. Arendt, "What Is Authority?" 99.
102. Arendt, "What Is Authority?" 99.
103. Arendt, *The Origins*, 326–40.
104. Arendt, *The Origins*, 334.
105. Arendt, "Tradition and the Modern Age," 17.
106. Arendt, "Tradition and the Modern Age," 17.
107. Arendt, "Tradition and the Modern Age," 20.
108. Arendt, "Tradition and the Modern Age," 29.
109. Arendt, "Tradition and the Modern Age," 28–29.
110. Arendt, "Tradition and the Modern Age," 32.
111. Arendt, "Tradition and the Modern Age," 29.
112. Arendt, "Tradition and the Modern Age," 29.
113. Arendt, "Tradition and the Modern Age," 24.
114. See Arendt, "The End of Tradition," in *The Promise of Politics*, 91–92.
115. Arendt, "The Tradition of Political Thought," 47.
116. Arendt, "The Tradition of Political Thought," 56.
117. Arendt, "Tradition and the Modern Age," 28.
118. Arendt, *Denktagebuch*, 460.

Chapter 5

Reading Aristotle

In the philosophical context, the result of the diagnosis of the broken thread of tradition is expressed by Arendt succinctly: "The thread of tradition is broken, and we must discover the past for ourselves—that is, read its authors as though nobody had ever read them before."[1] There is no doubt that Arendt learned this way of reading from Heidegger, whom she considered to be the first thinker able to free himself from the conceptuality of petrified tradition and discover the past anew. In her laudation on the occasion of his eightieth birthday, she describes the fresh breeze attracting students, who longed for a new experience of thinking, to Marburg. Among the post–World War I generation Heidegger was widely considered to be able to have access "to the things themselves" and to unleash the "wind of thought." And although Arendt does not refer to her personal experience, it is clear that she has in mind the time when she, as an eighteen-year-old-student, listened to the first lecture during her studies. It was the winter term of 1924–1925: "Plato was not talked *about* and his theory of Ideas expounded; rather for an entire semester a single dialogue was pursued and subjected to question step by step, until the time-honored doctrine had disappeared to make room for a set of problems of immediate and urgent relevance."[2] The lecture was titled: "Interpretation Platonischer Dialog (*Sophistes*)."

This chapter is an attempt to answer the question of what "set of problems" Heidegger drew forth from beneath the ruins of philosophical doctrines and what this "immediate and urgent relevance" was for Arendt's thinking. If this first lecture sowed the seeds that in Arendt's mind sprouted at once, and after years bore the ripe fruit of her concept of action,[3] we need to briefly recall its content.

HEIDEGGER'S ARISTOTLE

For young Heidegger, Aristotle was a crucial author. What is more, he was an immediate inspiration that directed the 18-year-old Heidegger to the phenomenological studies by Husserl and haunted him with a question that he asked again and again throughout his own life. It was Aristotle's famous sentence from *Metaphysics*: *to on legetai pollachos* ("there are several senses in which a thing may be said to 'be'"[4]) that for the young Heidegger was an illumination which determined his questioning for the rest of his long intellectual life: the question of the meaning of being.[5]

This explains why, although the main theme of his 1924–1925 Marburg lecture was Plato's *Sophist*,[6] Heidegger begins with a detailed analysis of the 6th book of *Nicomachean Ethics*. From Heidegger's point of view, the Aristotelian distinctions had nothing arbitrary in them, but were a phenomenological description of the multifariousness of human experience and a mature version of the most ingenious intuitions of earlier philosophy. Especially when it came to Plato's dialogues, Heidegger believed Aristotle to be the hermeneutic key for understanding them. He recalls "an old hermeneutic principle": to begin with what is clear and proceed to understand what is obscure. For Heidegger this principle means that Aristotle understood Plato better than Plato understood himself.

Heidegger wanted to interpret Plato through Aristotle, so he had to, in turn, understand Aristotle better than Aristotle understood himself. In 1953 in Arendt's *Denktagebuch* appears a record on Heidegger's method of interpretation:

> Heidegger not only presumes that every text contains something unsaid, but also that this unsaid thing forms a crux [. . .], and at the same time an empty spot at the very center around which everything revolves [. . .]. In this spot—at the very center, where the author is absent and which is reserved for the readers and the audience—Heidegger situates himself.[7]

Thus, Heidegger read Aristotle through his own discoveries of fundamental ontology and existential analysis, in other words, in the nascent categories of *Being and Time*. But since these categories contain some Platonic assumptions (chapter 3), it comes to a paradox. Heidegger wants to read Plato through Aristotle, but he reads Aristotle through some semi-platonic premises of his own early philosophy, and it occurs that his analysis turns itself upside down: Heidegger not only reads Plato through Aristotle, but also Aristotle through Plato. The later qualification of such a reading made by Arendt will mean underscoring these Aristotelian streams, which cannot be interpreted through Plato. But this qualification will have its limits, since for Arendt

Aristotle also turns out to be a Platonic philosopher. However, he turns out to be Platonic in a completely different way than Heidegger.

I

In order to grasp the direction of Heidegger's reading we need to juxtapose the style and content of *Nicomachean Ethics* with the style and content of Heidegger's interpretation in the above-mentioned lecture.

The 6th book of *Nicomechean Ethics* is a description of intellectual (*dianoethic*) virtues, "dispositions which will best qualify [the soul] to attain the truth."[8] Among them, two groups can be distinguished: intellectual dispositions to cognition (*epistemonistikon*) of what is unchangeable (*episteme, sophia* and *nous*) and the ability of deliberation (*logistikon*) on what can change (*techne* and *phronesis*). The crux of Heidegger's analysis is distinguishing between technical cleverness (*techne*) and practical wisdom (*phronesis*), and conceptualizing their relationship with philosophical wisdom (*sophia*).

Techne is a mode of discovering the truth characteristic for creation or fabrication (*poiesis*). *Phronesis* is a mode of discovering the truth characteristic for action (*praxis*). The basic difference between *techne* and *phronesis* is that the goal of *phronesis* is not beyond the very act of consideration, like it is the case with the goal of *techne*. The principle (*arche*) of *techne* is an image (*eidos*) in the mind of the creator. The goal (*telos*) of creation is external to the act of creation and is identical with the finished work (*ergon*)[9] whereas the act of practical consideration does not concern anything external; here the goal is not outside the act of consideration, but is intertwined with practical action itself. Thus, *phronesis* overcomes a certain ontological weakness of *techne*: in *phronesis* the principle (*arche*) and the goal (*telos*) of action are intertwined. Action embraces both the principle and the goal. The goal of action is action itself—*hou heneka*. Contrarily, in the case of *poiesis*, the activity of a creator leads to a goal, but it is ancillary to the goal and comes to a stop once the goal has been attained.[10] In the case of creation, work is *heneka tinos*—for the sake of something else. The Aristotelian difference between *hou heneka* (for the sake of itself) and *heneka tinos* (for the sake of something else) turns out to be important for understanding Arendt's concept of action.

Thus far, Heidegger's reading is faithful to Aristotle. But already in his interpretation of the difference between *techne* and *phronesis* one can see a specific Heideggerian agenda: a reading of Aristotle toward *Being and Time*. Since *techne* and technical deliberation refer to something external, *techne* has a heterogeneous element. The case is different with *phronesis*: here the goal of action is nothing external to the action itself, but intrinsic to it, the practical activity and its goal are closely bound to the one who reflects on the action. What is the goal of this reflection or consideration? Aristotle says: "the good life in general."[11] Heidegger translates it as "the right mode of being of Dasein as such and as a whole."[12] Although the Heideggerian "right mode of being" is by no means illegitimate as a translation, it is unquestionable that it tends toward authenticity. As said above, *phronesis* overcomes a flaw characteristic for *poiesis*: its principle (*arche*) and its goal (*telos*) are inseparable. For Heidegger it means that they come together in the being of a human being (*Dasein*). Therefore, the deliberation (consideration) of *praxis* never ends: *Dasein* cannot stop questioning the right mode of being.

Now it is clear in what direction tends Heidegger's interpretation of Aristotle. Already in this brief characterization of *techne* and *phronesis* one can feel the spirit of existential analysis with its fundamental dichotomy of right and wrong modes of human being, that is, authenticity and inauthenticity of existence. For instance, Aristotle says, in full accordance with the classic Greek view, that pleasure or pain can pervert beliefs concerning action, since they can blur the goal of action, which is a good life.[13] Heidegger interprets this fragment: A certain disposition (attunement) can "cover up man to himself and make him concerned with things of minor significance."[14] Such a reading is already very close to a reinterpretation of *poiesis* as an inauthentic mode of being of *Dasein*, which, concerned with (and stunned by) handy things that are not *Dasein*, forgets its ownmost way of being and "falls" to the world. That is why *Dasein* needs the "salvation of phronesis": "It is not at all a matter of course that Dasein be disclosed to itself in its proper being," says Heidegger.[15] The truth of being must be dragged out. So, *phronesis*, which is one of the ways of discovering the truth (*aletheuein*) within *praxis*, can make action transparent: "Φρόνεσις [. . .] is involved in a constant struggle against a tendency to cover over residing at the heart of Dasein."[16] Ultimately Heidegger identifies *phronesis* with conscience (which in *Being and Time* will mean an appeal of *Dasein* to itself for choosing the right way of being).

Now, how does *phronesis* relate to such modes of attaining truth where the object is unchangeable, that is, to theoretical thinking? Of the three modes, *sophia*, philosophical wisdom, is the most interesting, since it combines scientific cognition (*episteme*) with intuitive thinking of first principles (*nous*).[17] Aristotle, like all Greek philosophers, valued modes of cognition on the basis of the way of being of the objects to be cognized. Since everything that can change is ontologically inferior to what is unchangeable (mathematical objects, celestial bodies, Platonic forms), cognition of unchangeable objects must be superior to the cognition of changeable (terrestrial) things. Therefore, *phronesis*, the higher mode of deliberation within changeable human affairs, has to yield to theoretical wisdom within the hierarchy. "For it would be strange to think that the art of politics, or practical wisdom, is the best knowledge, since man is not the best thing in the world,"[18] says Aristotle. *Sophia* concerns itself with the good that cannot be changed and which is the same for all beings, whereas *phronesis*, practical wisdom, is always relative. The cognition of what never changes lets the human soul partake in divinity: It is *bios theoretikos*, life devoted to theory, the life of a philosopher, which is the highest mode of human being. Greek philosophical evaluation of different modes of cognition is always derivative of ontological views.

In *Metaphysics*, Aristotle distinguishes philosophical wisdom from other kinds of knowledge by referring to causes and principles of entities. The ascent toward the higher modes of cognition consists in understanding more and more general causes. The cognition of the highest and first principles, because they are unchangeable, is the most difficult task for man and yet, paradoxically, they are more cognizable than the changeable ones. Such knowledge is not sought for any other advantage, it is a goal for its own sake. It is a divine and most noble kind of knowledge: "Hence also the possession of it might be justly regarded as beyond human power."[19] In Aristotle, philosophical wisdom, the cognition of the first principles, allows men to enter a different, divine realm, in which even the wisest can partake only, so to say, as guests. In *Ethics*, Aristotle says: "Such a life as this however will be higher than the human level."[20]

Hence, while *bios theoretikos* is the highest mode of being accessible to humans, it is not *human* life par excellence. Here, human being needs to transcend humanity bound with the changeable circumstances of life. In Aristotle, practical and theoretical wisdom belong to different dimensions. One of the differences between him and Plato is that having accepted the superiority of *sophia* over *phronesis*, Aristotle does not believe that *sophia* can ever replace *phronesis*. Theoretical wisdom, as noble and divine as it is, is rather helpless in the realm of human affairs, such as ethics and politics.

And yet Heidegger, unlike Aristotle (but more like Plato), strives at unifying those two dimensions, in order to be able to demonstrate the unity of human existence. He interprets Aristotle's view on the superiority of *sophia* over *phronesis*, using characteristic terms: "[. . .] σοφία [. . .] has a priority over φρόνεσις, such that this ἀληθεύειν constitutes the proper possibility, and the genuine possibility of Dasein: the βίος θεωρητικός, the existence of scientific man."[21] Heidegger notices a problem in *Metaphysics*: If theoretical wisdom is a cognition of causes, and the final cause is always a certain good, *sophia* approaches good (*agathon*). In this way, according to Heidegger, it comes closer to *praxis*, which also approaches good. But *sophia* is not *praxis*, it is theory. Heidegger approaches the problem by showing that good is primarily understood in an ontological, not ethical way. Good is an ontological characteristic of an entity, its way of being, and so it can be the object of theoretical contemplation.[22] Nevertheless, he further refers to the excerpt of *Metaphysics*, where Aristotle, when describing theoretical wisdom, actually uses the word *phronesis* instead of *sophia*.[23] In fact, it is not the only technical term whose meaning is not stable in Aristotle to the point that hitherto heterogeneous terms become synonyms (another example would be *techne* and *episteme*). I will not go into the possible reasons of this terminological inconsistency in Aristotle. From our point of view, it is more important what it means for Heidegger. For him such a usage of *phronesis* is not accidental, but it indicates a possibility of unification of *sophia* and *phronesis*. *Sophia* is, so to say, a higher version of *phronesis*: they represent the same kind. *Sophia*, as a higher *phronesis*, becomes the highest possibility of a human being and the highest form of *praxis*.

We can see how Heidegger takes advantage of a minor terminological confusion in Aristotle for his own philosophical reasons. First of all, he needs to understand the reasons why these terms in Aristotle are considered separately: *phronesis* and *sophia* cannot be of the same kind, because man is not the highest being and he is not eternal. Although in a cosmic dimension *phronesis* is inferior to *sophia*, from the point of view of what is good to humans, practical wisdom is more important than cognition of abstract principles. The concrete situation requires a decision based on provisional insight into changeable circumstances. For Heidegger, the most important thing is to grasp the temporal difference between the two modes of knowledge. It is closely connected with the meaning of being that defines the Greek understanding of the world and the hierarchy of human modes of being. The ontological assumptions of the Greeks prevent practical wisdom from becoming superior to theoretical wisdom. This is how Heidegger sums up Aristotle's hesitation on the matter:

> One might suppose that, insofar as his own Being, his own existence, is of decisive importance for a man, that truth is the highest which relates to Dasein itself, and therefore φρόνεσις is the highest and most decisive mode of disclosure. Yet Aristotle says that σοφία, pure understanding, is, with regard to its ἀληθεύειν (and insofar as ἀληθεύειν characterizes the Being of man), the highest possible mode of human existence.[24]

The difference between theoretical and practical wisdom is based on the temporal difference between their objects. Concrete action, which always refers to the actual being of *Dasein*, requires a moment of vision (*Augenblick*)— an instant comprehension of the entirety of the existence of human being. *Sophia*, by contrast, is based on contemplation of what is eternal (*Immersein*), "time (the momentary and the eternal) here functions to discriminate between [. . .] φρόνεσις and [. . .] σοφία."[25] And here emerges the question that is crucial from the perspective of nascent fundamental ontology: Is eternity (*Immersein*) viable to define the right mode of being human? For Heidegger, the Greek concept of time is problematic: How can a mortal man attain the highest mode of existence (*eudaimonia*) through pure contemplation of what is eternal? It is the leitmotif of Greek philosophy: The intellectual approach to what is eternally true bestows the soul with a sort of immortality of eternal truths. It means that eternity and imperturbability are the fundamental meanings of being for the Greeks. But this kind of *eudaimonia* (for Heidegger the Greek term for authenticity) binds the authentic mode of being with (timeless) presence (*Anwesenheit*). The metaphysics of presence defines the sense of human existence from the Greeks on:

> Only [. . .] from the wholly determined and clear domination of the meaning of Being as eternal Being, does the priority of σοφία become understandable [. . .]. For the Greeks the consideration of human existence was oriented purely toward the meaning of Being itself, i.e., toward the extent to which it is possible for human Dasein to be everlasting.[26]

Thus, Heidegger distances himself from the Greek understanding of being. In *Being and Time*, he claims that the "Greek interpretation of being comes about without any explicit knowledge of the guideline functioning in it, without taking cognizance of or understanding the fundamental ontological function of time, without the insight into the ground of the possibility of this function."[27] Heidegger's *opus magnum* will thus be an answer to the Greek understanding of being: the description of the structures of human existence with regard to the temporal finitude of *Dasein*. Fundamental ontology and its temporal dimension, the authentic human being as being-toward-death, a finite being, is a project of deconstruction of the Greek understanding of being as presence.

That is why Heidegger strives at combining *sophia* and *phronesis*: With regard to time, the authentic being of *Dasein* has the character of Aristotle's *praxis*, something that can be different from what it actually is, which in Heidegger's language means a being that temporalizes, a thrown project. But Heideggerian authenticity, the resolute being-toward-death, resembles *sophia* insofar as it puts the human being beyond the community and makes him a self-sufficient individual. Thus, Heideggerian authenticity unifies the autarky of solitary theoretical contemplation with temporality, which is accessible only in practical wisdom, *phronesis*. Briefly, he strives toward such an understanding of *praxis* that supports the thesis: "Da-sein is a being which is concerned in its being about that being."[28]

II

In his *Sophist*, Plato, striving to tell the difference between philosopher and sophist, had to commit what he himself called the "patricide" of

Parmenides[29]—he had to challenge the great Eleatic tradition that being exists and non-being exists not. If we want to depict a sophist in his being and still believe that a sophist is someone who tells un-truths, nonexisting things (the word images of things), then, if we do not want to deny sophist existence, we cannot stay in accordance with the tradition saying that what is un-true necessarily has to be nonexistent. If we want to be able to speak of appearances, falsehoods, and opinions, we need to accept that un-truth also exists in a way, and that *non-being also exists* in a way.

Very important here is innovative hermeneutics: Plato gains access to an understanding of being, ontology, starting from a concrete human existence, that of a philosopher. The being of a philosopher (different from that of a sophist) leads Plato to the question of being as such. Owing to the fact that Plato finds the basis for his questioning in a concrete situation, and not in abstract contemplation, he can tell the difference between various modes of being, and he can, for the first time, put the question of the being of nothingness. Aristotle undertook this question and pursued it toward philosophical excellence reflected in the opening sentence of the seventh book of *Metaphysics* ("there are several senses in which a thing may be said to 'be'"), where the difference between being and entities was expressed explicitly. In Heidegger's lecture on Plato's *Sophist*, this early inspiration has already become a mature interpretation: "This idea of 'onto-logy,' of λέγειν, of the addressing of beings with regard to their Being, was exposed for the first time with complete acumen by Aristotle."[30]

This is the reason why Heidegger wanted to read Plato through Aristotle. Like Plato, he started from a concrete human existence (though not of a philosopher's) in order to explain different modes of understanding of being, about which he learned from Aristotle. But at the same time Heidegger interprets Aristotle in the light of Platonic oppositions: The way of being of a philosopher becomes a measure of being as such. Of this emerges a non-true and uprooted way of being in the *polis*, based on the subject-less speech of sophistry. The opposite is the authentic life of philosophers.[31] Thus, Heidegger's assumption that Plato should be read through Aristotle, can be reversed and it can be demonstrated that Heidegger referred to some Platonic oppositions in his interpretation of Aristotle: one of these being the opposition of *aletheia* and *doxa*, truth and opinion. For Heidegger, *doxa* is a covering over of being and an expression of inauthenticity: Ignorance and idle talk prevent *Dasein* from an understanding of its own existence. The philosopher's struggle is not only with discovering the truth, it is also concerned with combating sophistry and rhetoric, which cover up being by words. When Heidegger characterizes different modes of being as different modes of discovering truth, opinions lose their connection with truth, so natural for Aristotle, and become the opposite: a non-being that exists as a semblance.

ARENDT'S ARISTOTLE

The lecture course of the winter term of 1924–1925 was the first semester of Hannah Arendt's studies in Marburg. As we will see, her later thought can be considered a response to this reading of Aristotle. But this also means that Arendt, despite her own original acquisition of Greek thought, worked out in the polemic with the teacher, owes him a truly philosophical inspiration, drawing her attention to the "set of problems of immediate and urgent relevance."

I

In the previous section we could see how Heidegger adjusts Aristotle's concept to the (partly Platonic) premises of his own ontology. The result is a specific interpretation of Aristotle's *praxis* toward authentic existence. But such an understanding of *praxis* requires excluding it from the public world. Therefore, *The Human Condition* will be an attempt at restitution of the public and political strains of *praxis*, against Heidegger's interpretation of Aristotle. The book identifies the authentic human way of being exactly with what Heidegger neglected: public speech and action.

Heidegger turned the attention of the young Arendt to a very important feature in Greek anthropology: For Greeks, *aletheuin*, the drawing out of beings from hiddenness is a basic way of being of man, apparent in the power of speech, the fundamental constitution of *Dasein*: man is *zoon logon echon*, an animal capable of speech.[32] In Heidegger, speech is ontologically connected with truth: It discloses beings in their being. This disclosure is always endangered with closure by an inauthentic mode of speech, idle talk, identified by Heidegger with the realm of *doxa*.

Arendt could not agree with such a reading of Aristotle. In *The Human Condition* she states: "Aristotle's definition of man as *zoon politicon* [. . .] can be fully understood only if one adds his second famous definition of man as *zoon logon echon* (a living being capable of speech)."[33] The capability of speech, as interpreted by Arendt, counter to Heidegger, is a political ability par excellence:

> In his two most famous definitions, Aristotle only formulated the current opinion of the *polis* about man and the political way of life, and according to this opinion, everybody outside the *polis*—slaves and barbarians—was *aneu logou*, deprived, of course, not of the faculty of speech, but of a way of life in which speech and only speech made sense and where the central concern of all citizens was to talk with each other.[34]

Regarded from the public point of view, speech cannot be split into true speech and public idle talk. Moreover, in the original sense *zoon logon* has not much to do with *bios theoretikos*. The realm of speech is a sphere where people have to talk about common matters and where speech is an opposition to *bia*, sheer violence: the realm of the *polis*. Speech, necessary to life in the state, does not claim to concern absolute truths. For in politics it is not truth that is important, but the right opinion. It is neither false nor meaningless idle talk, but an opinion with some reasons behind it. One cannot rigorously demonstrate the rightness of opinion, but one can search for arguments for it. It is here where speech is most needed: It fills in the space between individuals and brings them together. Human plurality and speech are interdependent.

Heidegger, to remain true to his fundamental ontology, had to interpret *phronesis* toward theoretical wisdom and to tie it with the philosophical question of truth. On that account he neglected the fragments of Aristotle that emphasize the public character of practical wisdom and its correspondence with politics and interpersonal relations (debate, legislation, judiciary): "Political wisdom and practical wisdom are the same state of mind";[35] "We think Pericles and men like him have practical wisdom, viz. because they can see what is good for themselves and what is good for men in general."[36] Even if at least one dimension of *phronesis* is political action, it cannot be considered in terms of philosophical truth, but in political categories of righteousness and appropriateness. But these are qualities of opinions. Since *phronesis* is an intellectual virtue concerned with things that can be different to what they actually are, it is identical to the power of producing opinions: "There being two parts of the soul that can follow a course of reasoning, it must be the virtue of one of the two, i.e. of that part which forms opinions."[37] It forms a contrast to Plato's thesis in the *Sophist* spoken by the Visitor: "So the sophist has now appeared as having a kind of belief-knowledge about everything, but not truth."[38]

Aristotle overcame the Platonic opposition, that is, the opposition of truth and opinion, but also the corresponding opposition between real philosophical thinking and sophistic apparent thinking. Having accepted the Platonic distinction, he evaluated it differently. Opinion is not the opposite of truth, but a result of a different rationality than philosophical or scientific truth. Heidegger, by contrast, lists in the same breath Aristotle, Plato, and Socrates as those who struggle against rhetoric and sophistry, which cover truth with idle talk.[39] But whereas it is difficult to ascribe to Aristotle sympathy for sophistry (for this he is too much of Plato's disciple), he explicitly tells it apart from rhetoric. The latter, being the art of evoking opinions, is closely connected with the wisdom of politicians and with practical wisdom. The famous first sentence of *Rhetoric*, "Rhetoric is the counterpart of Dialectic,"[40] is a polemic with Plato's identification of rhetoric and sophistry. "Counterpart" here means an affinity and analogy instead of opposition: "Both alike are concerned with such things as come, more or less, within the general ken of all men [. . .]. Accordingly all men make use, more or less, of both."[41]

The description of man as an animal possessed of the faculty of speech must have been noticed by Arendt when she was listening to Heidegger's lecture, but it gained in meaning later. The faculty of speech would go on to be so important for Arendt that she would even conceive of thinking as an inner dialogue, once again, in rebellion against Heidegger's reading of Aristotle. In his attempts at connecting *phronesis* and *sophia*, Heidegger cross-contaminates them: "Φρόνεσις is, structurally, identical with σοφία; it is an ἀληθεύειν ἄνευ λόγου. [. . .] We have here two possibilities of νοῦς."[42] It is an interpretation of the 11th chapter of the 6th book of *Nicomachean Ethics*, where Aristotle compares practical and philosophical wisdom. Indeed, here Aristotle, contradictory to his earlier distinctions, connects a certain aspect of practical wisdom with intuitive thinking (*nous*): "The intuitive reason [nous] involved in practical reasonings grasps the last and variable fact."[43] However, in an earlier passage we have a typical contradistinction between *phronesis* and *nous*; here *phronesis* is "opposed to intuitive reason; for intuitive reason is of the limiting premises, for which no reason can be given, while practical wisdom is concerned with the ultimate particular."[44] It seems that Aristotle uses here the term *nous* (intuitive reason) with two different meanings (like he did with *techne* and *phronesis*): once in a wider sense, corresponding with a usage of natural language, comprising also an intuition characteristic for *praxis*, another in a narrower sense, congruent with the terminological structure of his philosophy, where *nous* refers to a contemplation of unchangeable entities and is reserved for theoretical cognition. And again, Heidegger takes advantage of this discrepancy in order to legitimize the fundamental philosophical gesture of *Being and Time*, that is, making philosophy the highest form of *praxis*.

In the standard translations of *Nichomachean Ethics* we do not find any suggestion of practical and theoretical wisdom being beyond speech. *Aneu logou*, explicitly "beyond words," means also "beyond demonstration" (*logos* is word as well as reason, proof or argument in Greek) and this is what Aristotle must have had in mind: "that transcend all proof" (Williams), "that cannot be demonstrated" (Peters), or, as quoted above, "for which no reason can be given" (Ross). The impossibility of proving a truth is obviously different from the impossibility of its utterance. Heidegger leaves this expression equivocally in Greek. But it is unlikely to think that he has in mind demonstrations rather than words.[45] It can be assumed that here also he takes advantage of the ambiguity present in Aristotle to drain *phronesis* of any connotations with judgments concerning public affairs and public speech, for they are realms of falling prey to the world and inauthenticity, and to shift its meaning toward wordless contemplation; the Aristotelian practical wisdom becomes here the silent gaze on possibilities of the being of *Dasein* ("authentic speech"), the moment of vision where the whole of finite existence is displayed with one word: It becomes a condition of resoluteness.

II

In order to be able to interpret *Nicomachean Ethics* in the spirit of his own thought, Heidegger had to ignore the aspect of Aristotelian ethics that emerges from his polemics with Plato. Therefore, he had to ignore the fact that in Aristotle ethics is subordinated to politics and not to metaphysics, so it has much to do with public life and public opinion, which for Heidegger were the sources of the they-self and inauthenticity. Thus, good, which is the theme of *Ethics*, is of a different kind from Plato's idea of good. Aristotle introduces clear distinctions, which allow him to address good in many aspects: "The word 'good' is used in as many senses as the word 'is.'"[46] The theme of *Ethics* is not absolute good, this is a theme of metaphysics. This nuancing of philosophical issues allows Aristotle to speak about good and human virtues on many different levels, which also enables him to adjust his method to the aspect of good analyzed. If the theme of *Ethics* is not good in the absolute Platonic meaning, but what is best for men, and it "involves much difference of opinion and uncertainty,"[47] then in ethics, as in politics, we need to be satisfied to achieve "that amount of precision which belongs to its subject matter [. . .]; for it is a mark of an educated man to expect that amount of exactness in each kind which the nature of the particular subject admits. It is equally unreasonable to accept merely probable conclusions from a mathematician and to demand strict demonstration from an orator."[48]

It follows that opinions, *doxai*, cannot be excluded not only from political action and practical wisdom, but also from the philosophical description of these kinds of activities. According to Aristotle, "the right opinion" and a degree of probability that belongs to it, is the highest degree of truth we can count on in these matters. He, insofar as being an ethicist and theoretician of politics, identifies himself rather as an orator than metaphysician.[49]

Therefore, Hannah Arendt has both good reasons and a stable basis for the interpretation of Aristotle in a different direction than that of Heidegger. A good example is the problematic character of the unpredictability of action: fragility, indefiniteness, and elusiveness of human affairs. Heidegger underscores a philosophical solution, that is, he finds in contemplation a remedy for this uncertainty and modifies it in a characteristic way. Firstly, he points out a philosophical remedy for the uncertainty and unpredictability of being-with others: Thus whereas the possibilities of Being with regard to πρᾶξις are dependent on being with others, the pure on-looking upon what always is is free of this bond."[50] Subsequently, he draws a conclusion that by no means can be regarded as congruent with Aristotle: "Therefore they cannot be man's proper [eigentlich] possibilities of Being."[51] As we know, Aristotle shares with other Greek philosophers the opinion of philosophy being the highest form of life. But it is one thing to maintain that contemplation is the distinguished mode of being for pure pleasure and autarky (as Aristotle does) and another to deny the authenticity of other modes of being (as Heidegger does).

That is why Arendt, exactly in this fragility of speech and action, will see specific human activities. Moreover, contrary to Heidegger's interpretation of Aristotle, she will emphasize the alternative, "original" Greek solution to the problem of this fragility: "The original, prephilosophic Greek remedy for this frailty had been the foundation of the *polis*. The *polis* [. . .] grew out of and remained rooted in the Greek pre-*polis* experience and estimate of what makes it worthwhile for men to live together (*syzen*), namely the 'sharing of words and deeds.'"[52] For Arendt, the original Greek solution to the problem of the elusiveness and unpredictability of human affairs consisted neither in their negation in philosophic contemplation nor in an attempt at finding another, "authentic" form of life. The rescue of the fragility of human affairs can be found in them, that is, in a political structure that bestows on them a degree of stability without annihilating them. That is why Arendt emphasizes the political role of poetic and historical narrations, preserving human deeds and words, and protecting them from being forgotten. One of the functions of the *polis* "was to offer a remedy for the futility of action and speech,"[53] for "the organization of the *polis* [. . .] is a kind of organized remembrance."[54]

Thus, in Arendt's conception of action, it is difficult not to encounter any traces of her anti-Heideggerian reading of Aristotle. These traces are conspicuous in *The Human Condition* and form Arendt's understanding of action as a faculty of beginning, not defined by a predictable goal: "It is this insistence on the living deed and the spoken word as the greatest achievements of which human beings are capable that was conceptualized in Aristotle's notion of *energeia* ("actuality"), with which he designated all activities that do not pursue an end (are *ateleis*) and leave no work behind."[55] Action, which for Arendt is pure *energeia*, pure actuality, needs the world, the *polis* with its stories written "in the hope of preserving from decay the remembrance of what men have done and of preventing the great and wonderful actions of the Greeks and the Barbarians from losing their due need of glory."[56]

ARISTOTLE: PLATO'S MOST GENUINE DISCIPLE[57]

From what has been said above about Arendt's reading of Aristotle, some interpreters drew a conclusion that her conception of action is inspired and informed by his views,[58] or even that "Arendt reread Aristotle so as to reveal the ontological features of ethical and political action,"[59] or that she "went on to revive the missing concept of 'praxis.'"[60] The last section of this chapter is devoted to a deconstruction of this myth concerning the Aristotelian residue in Arendt's thought and to the demonstration of the complexity of Arendt's attitude to Aristotle. For sure, Arendt appreciated Aristotle's dispute with Plato and his step toward *praxis* and so she underscored exactly those aspects of *Nicomachean Ethics* that Heidegger neglected. But this is far from justifying a conclusion that Arendt accepted Aristotle's account of *praxis*. This would mean ignoring her explicit statements on the matter, such as this: "Nothing could be more alien to the pre-*polis* experience of human deeds than the Aristotelian definition of *praxis* that became authoritative throughout the tradition."[61] But even if we did not have such testimonies, an understanding of the idea of action in Arendt would lead us to the conclusion of its irreconcilability with Aristotle.

I

It seems that the beginning of *The Human Condition* as well as the essay on Socrates is sufficient proof that for Arendt—let us put it in Dana Richard Villa's words—"the pressing problem is not to *recover* ancient concepts and categories, or to *restore* tradition in some form, but rather to deconstruct and overcome the reifications of dead tradition."[62] Arendt accused the political philosophy of Plato of subordination of action under contemplation and, subsequently, of identification of political action with fabrication. The ideal state, or, the idea of the state, is a model for politics, which belongs to *techne*. Fabrication according to the eternal model was Plato's solution to the fragility of human affairs. Moreover, Plato initiated the tradition of political philosophy with its main feature of the "forgetfulness of *praxis*." Thus, Arendt adapted the Heideggerian strategy of deconstruction she learned from the lectures preceding the publication of *Being and Time*: Her goal was to disclose the phenomenal crux of pre-philosophic Greek political experience by questioning the traditional ontological presuppositions and bracketing the traditional philosophical prejudgments concerning active life: elevating contemplation over action and considering action to be ancillary to contemplation. This leads, according to Arendt, to a blurring of the phenomenal distinctions within active life, especially between *poiesis* and *praxis*, and to the "translation of acting into the idiom of making."[63] Just as the goal of Heidegger was such a thinking of being that would be counter to the petrified interpretative tradition, the goal of Arendt was a description of the phenomenon of action counter to philosophical tradition par excellence, and also counter to the Heideggerian approach.

Aristotle has often been considered, and not untruly so, to be the philosopher who saved or recovered the fundamental distinctions within active life. Nevertheless, as we have already seen, Aristotle, although he cannot be denied intuition in practical matters, shared the conviction of all philosophers of contemplation being superior to active life. This view was so deeply rooted in mature Greek metaphysics that it endured into the Christian era, remained preserved almost intact to our times, only to appear in one of the most recent disciples of Plato: Martin Heidegger. Therefore, Arendt's appreciation of certain aspects of Aristotle's political thought on no account means that she shared the communitarian trust in Aristotle's tradition of political thought and that she wanted to retrieve or enliven it in any form. I will try to support the opposite thesis, for the first time formulated by Dana R. Villa, which was that from Arendt's point of view, Aristotle's conception of action also needs deconstruction. Despite the standard interpretation of Aristotle as a thinker who saved *praxis* from a Platonic identification with *poiesis*, Villa shows that the Aristotelian conception of action is haunted by teleology, while Arendt's autonomy of action excludes any teleological structure. Hence, Arendt's deconstructive strategy was "designed to reveal the instrumentalism at the heart of Aristotle's account"[64]; and "the Aristotelian influence is thus one key to understanding the Arendtian quest for purely political politics. Yet her appropriation of Aristotle is, in an important sense, ironic, since she uses concepts from his political philosophy to deconstruct and overcome his own theory of action."[65]

This thesis seems to be confirmed by numerous excerpts from *The Human Condition* and from *Between Past and Future*,[66] as well as by many records in her *Denktagebuch* (which Villa could not have known when writing his book). In *The Human Condition* Arendt emphasizes Aristotle's naturalistic account of the origin of the *polis*, for instance, "The state comes into existence, originating in bare needs of life, and continuing in existence for the sake of good life."[67] Just this one sentence from *Politics* is sufficient to see the reasons why Arendt had to overcome Aristotle's political thought based on two basic assumptions: firstly, the *polis* being the crowning of the natural order and secondly, that it refers to the goals of a good life, with the virtue and happiness of its citizens being ancillary to these goals. The first assumption can be easily testified: "And therefore, if the earlier forms of society are natural, so is the state, for it is the end of them, and the [completed] nature is the end";[68] "The state is a creation of nature and that man is by nature a political animal."[69] Thus, the state is an entelechy, an actuality of natural human relationships, with its preceding forms having been families and rural colonies. This explains the ontological priority of the *polis* to the smaller communities it stemmed from: "And so what is posterior in the order of becoming is prior in the order of nature."[70]

The second assumption is also unequivocal. Since nature, having a teleological character, "makes nothing in vain"[71] and the goals of the state and individual life are the same, the *polis* is evaluated not according to the sheer possibility of action but according to the conditions of good life, where "the best life, both for individuals and states, is the life of virtue."⁷² And since happiness is an excellence in practicing virtue, the goal of the state is a good life, virtue, and happiness of man, where one is unthinkable without another.

For Arendt this could mean only that despite the promise of the Aristotelian description of *phronesis* and *praxis* as activities whose value lies in themselves and despite discerning them from instrumentality of fabrication, action was ultimately subordinated to heterogeneous structures: the ontological, metaphysical, and ethical ones, its intrinsic value being annihilated. Moreover, the instrumental character of thinking, connected with fabrication, so strong in Plato, is present also in Aristotle. In *Politics* he says: "As the weaver or shipbuilder or any other artisan must have the material proper for his work [. . .], so the statesman or legislator must also have the material suited to him."⁷³ This material is the populace of the city. Further, Aristotle describes political action in a purely instrumental form as looking for the means to a pre-given end. This is how Arendt comments on Aristotle's attitude toward politics: "Work, such as the activity of the legislator in Greek understanding, can become the content of action only on condition that further action is not desirable or possible."⁷⁴

Ultimately, in Aristotle, action becomes a means to an end and the value of politics fulfills the task of making good citizens (as in the 7th book of *Politics*), or in an actualization of the highest good (as in the 1st book of *Ethics*). Good support of the thesis of Arendt's conception of politics and action being not only non-Platonic, but also non-Aristotelian, is the succinct, but telling, record of February 1954 in her *Denktagebuch*: "As Plato sees everything in the perspective of idea, Aristotle sees everything in the perspective of τέλος. But these are only two different ways of interpretation of ποίησις and τέχνη; in πρᾶξις there is neither τέλος nor idea."⁷⁵ For Arendt, philosophical thinking per se, and not only philosophical thinking of a certain kind, is unable to grasp the specifics of action. Philosophy has a predilection for fabrication, for "contemplation and fabrication (*theoria* and *poiesis*) have an inner affinity and do not stand in the same unequivocal opposition to each other as contemplation and action."⁷⁶ It is connected with the concept of idea or model (*eidos*), essential for fabrication, and without which there is no philosophical contemplation.

It is true that Arendt noticed this problem while attending Heidegger's lecture on the *Sophist*. Presenting the natural understanding of being by the Greeks, he pointed out the fundamental relationship between *ousia* and *poiesis* (being and making), or *on* and *pragmata* (the beings and useful things).⁷⁷ Thus, while Plato initiated mature Greek philosophy in the way that he made the idea, taken from the experience of *poiesis*, a criterion of political experience and so identified action with fabrication,[78] Aristotle basically followed this path. In Arendt's view, Aristotle's definition of the goal of *praxis* as *hou heneka* (autonomous action) in opposition to *heneka tinos* (the instrumental reference of action) actually combines the intrinsic sense of an activity (for the sake of . . .) with reference to the external goal (in order to . . .).[79] In other words, when speaking of *praxis*, he does not discern those things consistently enough. This brings about a subtle but most significant confusion: The goal of action is identified with its sense. If we wish to grasp the specifics of action in Arendt, this distinction needs to be treated very seriously.

II

Arendt was suspicious not only of the essence of technology, like Heidegger, but also of the Greek understanding of *poiesis*. The indefiniteness of the means-ends structure, that an end becomes a means to another end, confirms the *utility* of instrumental action, but denies its *sensibility* or *meaningfulness*. Fabrication has no intrinsic sense; it always refers to an external *what for*. Intrinsically sensible and meaningful can be only such action that refers to nothing. The meaning of action is something completely different to the instrumental structure. We are approaching here the crux of the concept of action in Arendt in the context of her reading of Aristotle. The sensibility and meaningfulness of action, contrary to its purposefulness, presupposes freedom.

Since the problem of freedom in Arendt is strictly connected with the phenomenon of the world, its more detailed description will have to wait for the next chapter. Now it is important only insofar as it refers to the interpretation of Aristotle. In the essay "What Is Freedom?" Arendt says: "The *raison d'être* of politics is freedom, and its field of experience is action."[80] For Arendt freedom is foremostly not a phenomenon of will, but "the freedom to call something into being which did not exist before."[81] Thus, Arendt emphasizes the faculty of spontaneously initiating something new (*archein*), for new beginnings are the sense of action. The freedom of action excludes a pre-given goal (*telos*) of a good life or virtue. It also excludes the inscription of action into the natural order of things: "Action, to be free, must be free from motive on one side, from its intended goal as a predictable effect on the other."[82] Thus, action is fundamentally independent from natural causes or reasonable ends of the cosmic order and it cannot be put into a hierarchical structure of causes. Action, freed from both motive and goal loosens the connection between ethics and politics, and abolishes the subordination of politics to virtue. All this makes Arendt's conception of action non-Aristotelian.

The paradigm of the Greek, pre-philosophic understanding of action is for Arendt the funeral oration of Pericles, which for Arendt testifies perfectly that "the innermost meaning of the acted deed and the spoken word is independent of victory and defeat and must remain untouched by any eventual outcome, by their consequences for better or worse."[83] That is why Arendt underscored the performative aspect of action, often referring to the metaphors of theater. The freedom of action is situated in the ability of appearance, disclosing one's own uniqueness, and revealing "who" we are.

Thus, the criterion of an assessment of action is neither utilitarian, nor ethical in a traditional way, but mostly esthetic. In her *Denktagebuch*, Arendt provides a telling example: If I have to betray someone to attain a certain goal, then this goal changes its meaning and becomes something else, because I introduced the betrayal into the human world.[84] Thus, it is this uglifying of the world, and not moral evil of the betrayal that makes it unacceptable. On this account, when Arendt sought allies in such understanding of freedom, she found them on the margins of, or even beyond, the philosophical tradition and not always in archaic times. One of these allies was Machiavelli who knew that "goodness, as a consistent way of life, is not only impossible within the confines of the public realm, it is even destructive of it."[85] So the thesis of Seyla Benhabib that Arendt seemingly reread Aristotle to reveal the ontological features of ethical and political action, which would describe the thought of, for instance, Alasdair MacIntyre,[86] misses as an interpretation of Arendt.

As indicated above, the deconstructive strategy of Arendt refers also to Martin Heidegger, to whom it is indebted. Arendt, as we have already seen in chapter 1, wrote at the same time with Heidegger and against him. And such a way requires a special methodology: She could not recover relevant political phenomena according to the same principle as Heidegger recovered different meanings of being from Aristotle. Philosophy is helpless when the account of the plurality of men and action is at stake, and it is because philosophy is concerned with man, not men. This is also the case with so-called political philosophy.[87] With certain exceptions we need to reach for the testimonies of historians and poets who are not misled by the unifying tendencies of philosophical thinking and in whose works human experience is sediment. In the matter of human experience philosophy needs correction.

Thus, Heidegger, not as much as most philosophers of politics, mixed action with fabrication, but identified the public sphere with *poiesis* and therefore with inauthenticity. Heidegger's *praxis* does not cherish instrumentality, but still it is *praxis* drained of any forms of human plurality and being-with-others. This *praxis* fulfills itself in a solitary being-toward-death, resoluteness and *Angst*, in short, in escape from the common world. The concept of the world in Arendt is an immediate, although implicit, answer to such an account and the stake is freedom.

NOTES

1. Hannah Arendt, "The Crisis in Culture: Its Social and Its Political Significance," in *Between Past and Future*, 201.
2. Arendt, "Martin Heidegger at Eighty," 50.
3. See also Taminiaux, *The Thracian Maid*, 3; Benhabib, *The Reluctant Modernism*, 116.
4. Aristotle, *Metaphysics*, trans. W. D. Ross, Z, VII, 1028a, classics.mit.edu. Further quoted as *Met*, according to Bekker's pagination.
5. See Heidegger's autobiographical account: "My Way to Philosophy," trans. Joan Stambaugh, in Martin Heidegger, *Philosophical and Political Writings* (New York: Continuum, 2003), 70.
6. HGA 19.
7. Arendt, *Denktagebuch*, 353–54.
8. Aristotle, *The Nicomachean Ethics*, trans. H. A. Rackham (Cambridge, MA: Harvard University Press, 1956), 1139b. Further quoted as EN with Bekker's pagination and with translator's name in brackets if other than Rackham.
9. EN, 1140a, Met., 1032b.
10. EN, 1139b.
11. EN, 1139b.
12. HGA 19, 49G; 34E.
13. See EN, 1140b.
14. HGA 19, 51G; 36E.
15. HGA 19, 51G; 36E.
16. HGA 19, 52G; 36–7E.
17. EN, 1141a (Ross).
18. EN, 1141a.
19. Met., 982b.
20. EN, 1177b.
21. HGA 19, 61G; 42E.
22. HGA 19, 123–24G; 85–86E.
23. See Met., 982b.
24. HGA 19, 166G; 114E.
25. HGA 19, 164G; 113E.
26. HGA 19, 178G; 122E.
27. SZ, 26; BT, 23.
28. SZ, 191; BT, 179.
29. Plato, *Sophist*, trans. Nicholas P. White, in *Plato's Complete Works*, 241d.
30. HGA 19, 207G; 143E.
31. HGA 19, 231G; 159–60E.
32. HGA 19, 17, 27G; 12, 19E.
33. HC, 27.
34. HC, 27.
35. EN, 1141b (Ross).
36. EN, 1140b (Ross).

37. EN, 1140b (Ross).
38. Plato, *Sophist*, trans. Nicholas P. White, in *Complete Works*, 233c.
39. HGA 19, 16G; 11E.
40. Aristotle, *Rhetoric*, trans. W. Rhys Roberts, 1354a, ebooks.adelaide.edu.au.
41. Aristotle, *Rhetoric*, 1354a.
42. HGA 19, 163G; 112E.
43. EN, 1143b (Ross).
44. EN, 1142a (Ross).
45. Jacques Taminiaux even translates Heidegger's *aneu logou* as "beyond speech." *The Thracian Maid*, 19.
46. EN, 1096a (Rackham).
47. EN, 1094b (Rackham).
48. EN, 1094b (Rackham).
49. EN, 1094b (Rackham).
50. HGA 19, 176G; 121E.
51. HGA 19, 176G; 121E.
52. HC, 196–97.
53. HC, 197.
54. HC, 198.
55. HC, 206.
56. *The History of Herodotus*, trans. George Rawlinson (New York: The Tandy-Thomas Company, 1909), 27, Archive.org.
57. Diogenes Laertius, *Lives of Eminent Philosophers*, 5.1, Greek and English, trans. R. D. Hicks (London: Heinemann, 1972), book 5, chapter 1: οὗτος γνησιώτατος τῶν Πλάτωνος μαθητῶν: "Aristotle was Plato's most genuine disciple."
58. See for instance Taminiaux, *The Thracian Maid*, 93.
59. Benhabib, *The Reluctant Modernism*, 117.
60. Benhabib, *The Reluctant Modernism*, 117.
61. Arendt, "The Tradition of Political Thought," 46.
62. Dana R. Villa, *Arendt and Heidegger: The Fate of the Political* (Princeton, NJ: Princeton University Press, 1996), 8–9.
63. Villa, *Arendt and Heidegger*, 114.
64. Villa, *Arendt and Heidegger*, 43.
65. Villa, *Arendt and Heidegger*, 18.
66. "Aristotle, therefore, without accepting Plato's doctrine of ideas, or even repudiating Plato's ideal state, still followed him in the main," Arendt, "What Is Authority?" 115.
67. Aristotle, *Politics*, trans. Benjamin Jowett (Oxford: Clarendon Press, 1885), 1252b, Archive.org.
68. Aristotle, *Politics*, 1252b.
69. Aristotle, *Politics*, 1253a.
70. Aristotle, *Physics*, trans. R. P. Hardie and R. K. Gaye, 261a (VIII, 7), classics.mit.edu.
71. Aristotle, *Politics*, 1253a.
72. Aristotle, *Politics*, 1323b/1324a.

73. Aristotle, *Politics*, 1326a.
74. HC, 196.
75. Arendt, *Denktagebuch*, 469.
76. HC, 301.
77. HGA 19, 270–71G; 186–87E.
78. Arendt, *Denktagebuch*, 375.
79. Arendt, *Denktagebuch*, 563.
80. Arendt, "What Is Freedom?" in *Between Past and Future*, 145.
81. Arendt, "What Is Freedom?" 150.
82. Arendt, "What Is Freedom?" 150.
83. HC, 205–06.
84. See *Denktagebuch*, 47.
85. HC, 77.
86. See Alasdair MacIntyre, *After Virtue: A Study in Moral Theory* (Notre Dame, IN: University of Notre Dame Press, 2007).
87. See Arendt, *Denktagebuch*, 47.

Chapter 6

Freedom and the World

Hannah Arendt's thought is constructed on dichotomies. One of the most important and constitutive ones is the dichotomy between life and the world, or between private and public spheres. On this opposition Arendt built her diagnosis of the modern world and without acknowledgment of this opposition her stance toward education is unintelligible. The main thesis of her essay on education is based on the belief that education is condemned to struggle with a paradox: It is a tension between the life of a child, which needs parental protection, and the endurance of the world, for which teachers and educators are responsible. The sphere of life, the private sphere, is connected with biological life. It is a sphere of darkness: "Everything that lives, not vegetative life alone, emerges from darkness and, however strong its natural tendency to thrust itself into the light, it nevertheless needs the security of darkness to grow at all."[1] The public sphere, in turn, is a realm of appearances, it is a sphere of light in which things can appear: "For us, appearance—something that is being seen and heard by others as well as by ourselves—constitutes reality."[2] What happens within the limits of the private sphere, "even the greatest forces of intimate life—the passions of the heart, the thoughts of the mind, the delights of the senses—lead an uncertain, shadowy kind of existence unless and until they are transformed, deprivatized and deindividualized, as it were, into a shape to fit them for public appearance."[3] The public sphere, the world, is not a sphere of darkness (or, more precisely, it is only in "dark times"). It is the space of brightness and the most intense reality, but it is fragile and needs constant protection. On the other hand, its light can be dangerous for life, whose natural environment is the dimness of privacy.

A human being functions in these two dimensions in a dichotomous way (Arendt did not care for an intermediate state: chiaroscuro). Education in her understanding is tantamount to "introducing the new-comers into the common world." However peaceful and harmonious associations this formulae can evoke, this "introduction" is far from being such, since it is pervaded by internal conflict: "The responsibility for the development of the child turns in a certain sense against the world: the child requires special protection and care so that nothing destructive may happen to him from the world. But the world, too, needs protection to keep it from being overrun and destroyed by the onslaught of the new that bursts upon it with each new generation."[4] The second part of this statement, where Arendt calls for the rights of the world so that education is not reduced to the so-called "interests of the child" and is able to also consider these "interests" with regard to the wider context of the public world, culture, in the twentieth century (which was supposed to be "the century of the child"), sounded controversial and evoked allegations of conservatism (as we will see in the third part, not fully justified).

Arendt's advocacy for the world means a special mission for educators: "The educators here stand in relation to the young as representatives of a world for which they must assume responsibility although they themselves did not make it, and even though they may, secretly or openly, wish it were other than it is."[5] Thus, it turns out that the concept of the world is central to pedagogical reflection. But we encounter a series of complex questions here: What does Arendt exactly advocate when she speaks for the world? What presuppositions lie behind this understanding of the world? Is a diagnosis of modernity, based on these presuppositions, accurate? Has modernity, especially modern philosophy, "distorted" the "original" concept of the world?

The understanding of the world in Arendt is at the same time indebted to Heidegger's concept of the world as it is a result of a polemics with this concept. In this chapter I will discuss this polemics, because it is essential for interpretation of the pedagogical chance present in Arendt's thought: the promise of freedom.

HEIDEGGER'S WORLD VERSUS DESCARTES

As we already know, Heidegger developed his fundamental understanding of the world in *Being and Time*. We also know the reasons why this ontological description of worldliness could not have been satisfactory for Arendt. Heideggerian worldliness, described in instrumental categories, did not leave space for human plurality. The world, as a structure of total relevance, could not constitute a factual space for speech and action, a space which at the same time connects and separates its inhabitants, being a natural site for the appearance of individuality. On the other hand, in these excerpts, where Heidegger went beyond private, instrumental categories, and described the world as a public space, this world revealed a different nature: It ceased to be the familiar world-workshop and manifested itself as a sinister realm of impersonal *das Man*, resembling the Platonic cave of illusion and semblance.

In this moment of the analysis it is important to avoid a certain misunderstanding: The fact that Heidegger characterized worldliness as a totality of tool-like relevance does not mean that his ontological sense of the world as a whole could be understood instrumentally. The world as a whole (contrary to inner-worldly entities) is not a tool, or a set of tools (as it is not a set of objects), but a meaningful structure, a totality of significations (*Bedeutsamkeit*) for *Dasein*. Being-in-the-world, *Dasein* opens up the world as a whole, which makes the world a meaningful being. This aspect Heidegger developed after his so-called turn.

I

Already in *Being and Time* the ontological understanding of the world is developed against the mathematical, Cartesian world as *res extensa* and against the derivative philosophical accounts of the world in neo-Kantianism and in Husserl's philosophy. Heidegger is looking for a more fundamental ontological access to the phenomenon of the world. The primary reality is *Dasein*, as being-in-the-world, and only on the basis of this indissoluble bond between man and the world does Heidegger build a phenomenological account of worldliness. In the phenomenological sense, the world is not a set of, or even an ontological structure of, objects, but a way of the being of *Dasein*: "'Worldliness' is an ontological concept and designates the structure of a constitutive factor of being-in-the-world [. . .]. When we inquire ontologically about the 'world,' we by no means abandon the thematic field of the analytic of Da-sein."[6] The world is not an entity, but a fundamental being of man. Human being in Heidegger *is* a way of revealing the world. Therefore, *Dasein*, concerned with the world, manifests a completely different way of being and completely different mode of seeing the world to that of a subject watching and analyzing an object. Heidegger's world is an existential definition of man. In a later text, *On the Essence of Ground*,[7] Heidegger underscores his belief that the ontological understanding of the world corresponds with the Greek understanding of the cosmos, which meant exactly being of the world as a whole, related to human existence.

Thus, Heidegger tries to overcome the modern understanding of the world as a Cartesian space. Since the subject-object relation is derived from everyday *dealing with* things (*Umgang*), the view of the world based on this secondary, cognitive relationship, also has a derivative character. An intentional effort of the cognizing subject is needed to transform the world as a sensible total relevance into three-dimensional space and to replace the locations of useful things into the points of this space. Ontologically, *res extensa* (as well as *res cogitans*) is a substance, that is, an entity that, being a separate thing, does not relate to other entities. An entity as a substance has to appear always in a specific mode, that is, as an intelligible mathematical entity. "Descartes does not allow the kind of being of innerwordly beings to present itself, but rather prescribes to the world, so to speak, its 'true' being on the basis of an idea of being (being = constant objective presence)."[8] Heidegger is concerned not so much with the mathematical aspect of this approach, but with the fact that "in this way Descartes explicitly switches over philosophically from the development of traditional ontology to modern mathematical physics and its transcendental foundations."[9] The Cartesian view of the world is not illegitimate, but it is not phenomenological; it misinterprets a derivative, *ontic* mode of access to entities as a fundamental ontological account of the being of these entities. Such a conception of the world reflects only a secondary, cognitive way of being-in-the-world. The reduction of the worldliness of the world to an objective presence not only conditions modern science, but also leads to what Heidegger calls "deworlding" of the world: "The 'world' as a totality of useful things at hand is spatialized to become a connection of extended things which are merely objectively present."[10] The world ceases to *be* for the sake of *Dasein*.

The Cartesian account of the world, although modified (e.g., in neo-Kantianism, through adding "values" to certain substances), remained untouched in its essence up to Husserl, who still considered the subject-object relationship to be the foundation of the phenomenological description of the world. It can be said that by overcoming the modern account of the world and recovering the ontological understanding of worldliness, Heidegger marks the end of modern thinking.

II

Being and Time is a fundamental point of reference for *The Human Condition*, where Arendt formulated a critical and affirmative understanding of the world concurrently with that of Heidegger's. But if we want to fully understand the meaning of Heidegger's concept of the world for Arendt, we also need to take into account some of his later works, which Arendt knew and which she certainly did not ignore.[11] In the second half of the 1930s, Heidegger abandons the transcendental and solipsistic methodology of *Being and Time* (not to mention again the nationalistic and collective relapse of the first half of the decade). Now, he describes the world "from a different direction," so to say, from the perspective of being as such, not from the perspective of *Dasein*; being is not regarded as a correlate of human existence any longer. Now, man becomes a "shepherd of being."[12] Nonetheless, the anti-Cartesian character of these analyses not only remained, but was also strengthened.

Already in *The Origins of the Work of Art* (1936) Heidegger undertakes the analysis from the point of view, so to speak, of the world itself; *the world* is connected here with a work of art, within which there is "a feud" with *the earth*. The basic characteristic of the world is not a totality of significations *for Dasein* anymore. A work of art, for example, a Greek temple, is a being that reveals a dual context: on the one hand, the belonging of a human being to the earth, and on the other, the human world, the sensible bond of nature and creation. The work is one of the possible sites of truth as *a-letheia*, unhiddenness or unconcealment: the dialectic of closure and disclosure, *physis* and *thesis*, a feud between the earth concealing the world and the world opening up the earth.

> World is not a mere collection of the things—countable and uncountable, known and unknown—that are present at hand. Neither is world a merely imaginary framework added by our representation to the sum of things that are present. World worlds, and is more fully in being than all those tangible and perceptible things in the midst of which we take ourselves to be at home. World is never an object that stands before us and can be looked at. World is that always-nonobjectual to which we are subject.[13]

When it comes to the ontological structure of the world, this description is basically congruent with *Being and Time*. Nevertheless, new accents appear here: In the work of art the world appears differently than in the total relevance of useful things. The work slinks from the structure of handiness, whose final relevance is always *Dasein*, for example, material ceases to be one of the useful things, hidden behind its handiness. Now, material is *the earth*. The work, such as a Greek temple, discloses the earth (e.g., the hardness of the rock), so *"The work lets the earth to be an earth."*[14] Here, the earth is the opposite to "the technological-scientific objectification of nature."[15] The earth and the world, in this understanding, are possible only in the mutual connection of closure and disclosure. "World and earth are essentially different and yet never separated from one another. World is grounded on earth, and earth rises up through world."[16] The work of art is a feud between the closure of the earth and the openness of the world; the earth tries to swallow up the world, the world overcomes the earth and prevails over it. "The earth cannot do without the openness of world if it is to appear in the liberating surge of its self-closedness. World, on the other hand, cannot float away from the earth."[17] The connection of worldliness with the work of art allows for a shift in the role of *Dasein*: "But it is not we who presuppose the unconcealment of beings. Rather, the unconcealment of beings (being) puts us into such an essence that all our representing remains set into, and in accordance with, unconcealment."[18]

Heidegger tackles the problem of the modern concept of the world in 1938 in *The Age of the World Picture*. Mathematical physics and the technology based on it (but also modern esthetics and culture) present the de-divined world, reduced to quantitative relations, where, in contrast to the worldliness of a Greek temple, or, according to another of Heidegger's examples, where a bridge *gathers* the earth as landscape around the stream, space and time are stripped of their world-references and become sets of identical points and moments. The cognition of nature is reshaped into research: "Projection and rigor, method and constant activity, each demanding the other, make up the essence of modern science, make it into research."[19] The metaphysical ground of modern science consists in research that precedes entities, "calculates" them: Nature and history "become objects of explanatory representation."[20] The modern understanding of the being of entities, although not self-aware, reduces being to objective presence, where the status of entities have only scientific objects. "We first arrive at science as research when the being of beings is sought in such objectness."[21] The objectifying of entities is their re-presentation in such a way that a calculation of being produces certainty. "Science as research first arrives when, and only when, truth has transformed itself into the certainty of representation,"[22] a transformation of which Descartes is the most characteristic example. Now the being of entities lies in their presentability; that is why the picture of the world, or world "coming to presence" as a picture, is possible only on the ground of modernity and its understanding of the being of entities, that is, as presentable objects. The counterpart to this process is a subjectification of man, making a *subiectum* of him, that is, medium, but also a master of re-presentations. "The fundamental event of modernity is the conquest of the world as picture."[23] Man struggles now to direct and to confer a measure on everything. This struggle, which is crowned in the metaphysics of the will to power in Nietzsche, is a proper metaphysics of the West: the attitude toward beings emerging from the understanding of being as objectivity and re-presentation.

Now the task of thinking lies in overcoming metaphysics, in reminding us of other ways of being, where the earth is dwelled in poetically and man is no longer a master of being. In *Building Dwelling Thinking* (1951) Heidegger describes the world in poetic terms of a "fourfold" of earth, skies, divinities, and mortals. The basic way of being of man is not a manipulation of useful things, but "dwelling." Dwelling connects here with building, which means not only transforming nature into a human world, but first of all, preservation of the world. Dwelling in the world gains its spatial sense in opposition to Cartesian space. The objective re-presentation of space as an extension of the set of points, let alone an algebraic space, are abstractions that resulted from the leveling of the world as a fourfold. Meanwhile, being close to, or far from something, has an original and different structure than objectively measurable distance. The world as a fourfold is a meaningful structure of locales, constituting "sites": spaces between earth and skies, divinities and mortals. The building of a bridge is not a construction of a useful thing (as it is in *Being and Time*). The bridge is not only an element of the handy structure of the world, but something that *gathers* the world as a fourfold, that is, organizes the space surrounding it: "The banks emerge as banks only as the bridge crosses the stream. The bridge expressly causes them to lie across from each other. One side is set off against the other by the bridge. [. . .] It brings stream and bank and land into each other's neighborhood. The bridge gathers the earth as landscape around the stream."[24] To dwell in or to preserve the world means "to look after the fourfold in its essence."[25]

The Heideggerian idea of dwelling in the world, as well as connecting worldliness with a work of art, will become relevant for Arendt; as will the attempt to "rescue" the world from the Cartesian view. At the same time, Arendt's thought is a disagreement with both the world-workshop and the closed world of the fourfold. For her, contrary to Heidegger, the world is, first of all, a public space with a fundamental feature of multispectrality, a result of being inhabited by *men*, their plurality being an ontological condition of this multispectrality. In Heidegger, no matter whether in *Being and Time*, or in the later works, we never find this plurality. In other words, neither the world as total relevance nor as a fourfold offers the space for action. While the instrumental structures in early Heidegger make people exchangeable, the community of mortals in later Heidegger defines man with a feature common to all. Mortality differentiates humans from divinities, but has no power to make people different from each other. Arendt's effort is directed at preservation of a multidimensional structure of the world and drawing out a new description of being-with.

ARENDT'S DOUBLED WORLD

Now, we will try to analyze how Arendt, on the one hand, constructs her concept of the world out of her polemics with Heidegger, and on the other, in her description of the alienation from the world, how she yields to certain Heideggerian assumptions concerning the "de-worlding" of the world.

I

The fundamental understanding of the world, characteristic for all her thought, Arendt developed in *The Human Condition*. It must be noticed that although in Arendt the world is an anthropological category, there is a certain duality in its understanding. This duality, which is by no means contradictory, stems from the fact that Arendt (no doubt under Heidegger's influence) searched for a fundamental understanding of the world in the Greeks. When in the "Prologue" to *The Human Condition* she outlines the task of her enterprise, which is "to trace back modern world alienation, its twofold flight from the earth into the universe and from the world into itself,"[26] she hints at a certain duality. The flight from the world into self is strictly connected with action, the most important aspect of the human condition, whereas the flight from the earth into the universe is a flight from the immediate contemplation of the order of nature, an abandonment of the Greek watching of the divine harmony, full of admiration.

For Arendt, the world, in its first and basic meaning, is an outcome of creation—shaping nature according to human needs (in the widest meaning of the word). We need now to remember the basic distinction between labor and work, which Arendt worked out in the polemics of Marx and Hegel. While, under "work," Marx and Hegel understood both creation or fabrication and a simple effort to survive, for example, gathering food, in Arendt we have an important conceptual distinction: The term "work" is reserved for creation or fabrication of endurable things, while an effort accompanying a relationship with nature that is non-creative and oriented toward survival she calls "labor." That is why, contrary to Hegel and Marx, Arendt does not understand labor as an activity emancipating humans from nature. In her view, labor is a function of biological life and, unlike work, is an exchange of matter and energy with nature. Its outcomes are never endurable results; its purpose is biological perseverance of humans both as individuals and as a species. The principle of labor is a natural necessity, which men as animals are under the yoke of—ontologically, labor is equal to instinctive activities, which animals undertake to secure continuity of their species. Therefore it is not labor, but work (fabrication) that is human *differentia specifica*. This seemingly purely verbal distinction enables a phenomenological account of an ontological differentiation of human activities. Work differs from labor ontologically by exceeding the circular workflow of nature and creates *objects*. Work, since it has the power of creating something endurable, that is, reshaping nature according to a supranatural pattern, and imprinting a human stigma on it, forms a foundation for a human world. Nature "furnished" with human artifacts (temples, bridges, towns, roads) is a human world indeed.

Out of all objects, the most individual are those that are least useful, for which the reason for existence is not profit of any sort, but beauty: works of art. Thus, within objects constituting human space, Arendt distinguishes two kinds: those with a practical usefulness, which undergo wear, and those that are potentially everlasting. A space organized solely according to the rules of utility could not be entirely human and would not deserve to be called the "world." *Eidos*, a blueprint for a work of art, surpasses the criterion of utility, for example, *eidos* of proportion or harmony. That is why artists are tradesmen in a special sense: Their acts are furthest from natural necessity. Works of art are the most "worldly" out of all material things. Their existence lies in independent appearance in the public sphere. The condition of their full existence is that they are watched, seen, or listened to and at the same time appreciated by many people taking different places in the common world. Their potential endurance makes them a good basis for the endurance of the human world. With relation to the metaphor of light, it can be said: beauty perishes in dimness when it becomes invisible. In order to remain what it is, it needs a well-lit place for its appearance.

The connection of a work of art with truth was one of the reasons why Heidegger could not see the multispectral character of work and the world. Truth, even if understood as unhiddenness (or, maybe exactly then), contains something compelling and indisputable. Either we experience beings in their being (as unhidden), or not. When truth is at stake, we cannot accept the plurality of opinions and appearances. Arendt disconnected art and beauty from truth and provided a different basis for the worldliness of the work of art than Heidegger. Works of art are not only the least useful, but also the least natural of all things. They are human artifacts, revealing human experiences and passions, not being as such. The human attitude toward the work of art is founded not on truth, but on freedom. Owing to the freedom from necessities that binds us with the functionality of other things, we gain distance, which is always a condition of disinterested contemplation. For Arendt, the measure of such contemplation is not truth but the Kantian power of judgment. The "letting the work be the work" is not "standing within the openness of beings that happens to the work,"[27] but letting the beauty of the work appear in a space constituted by plurality: of men and the perspectives they bring with themselves. The common, multispectral space is, so to say, the ontological condition of the possibility of the work of art. But it is also the other way round: Space does not exist without the works that can appear in it. The human world and art (beauty) condition each other.

That is why works of art, things furthest from biological life, are the most worldly creations of man. The world, understood as such, is a material basis of the political being-with-others (if we want to recall the world Arendt undoubtedly had in mind, we need to visualize Athens of the fifth century BCE). It can be said the world makes sense (creation has an *end* but not *sense*[28]), when inhabited by humans, not as *animal laborans* or *homo faber*, but as men of action.

The concept of action in Arendt is a complex, and at the same time, fundamental problem and its various revelations are the theme of this book. In the context of worldliness it suffices to say that the sense of the world is the multispectrality of its inhabitants. The meaning of "words and deeds," the main activities of humans among other humans, and the meaning of politics, is perseverance and renewal of the world (even if in the mode of revolutionary action) both in its synchronic and diachronic dimensions (protection of the past from being forgotten). The world is a space of appearance without which humans would be only animals; it is a prerequisite of humanity, which in Arendt expresses itself in the human faculty of "appearance," that is, being among others, talking to them, and persuading them of something, and attempts to see the world from a different perspective. This multispectrality exactly constitutes the basic ontological feature of the world; thus, acting people, "actors" as Arendt sometimes says, bestow the world of artifacts with worldliness: "The objectivity of the world [. . .] and the human condition supplement each other; because human existence is conditioned existence, it would be impossible without things, and things would be a heap of unrelated articles, a non-world, if they were not the conditioners of human existence."[29]

The second, and much less conspicuous aspect of the world in Arendt is that which follows from *vita contemplativa*. Since *The Human Condition* focuses on active life, we do not find a developed account of this second aspect. Nonetheless, as we will see, it is exactly the replacing of contemplation with the "active life" of scientific research that is for Arendt the turning point in human estrangement from the world in modernity. In her *Lectures on Kant's Philosophy* she cites *Oedipus at Colonus* by Sophocles and reminds us of Greek pessimism: "Not to be born prevails over all meaning uttered in words; by far the second-best thing is for life, once it has appeared, to go back as quickly as possible whence it came."[30] All the same, in *Thinking*, Arendt also recalls a Greek way of overcoming this pessimism:

> It is the distinctive mark of Greek philosophy that it broke entirely with this Periclean estimate of the highest and most divine way for mortals. To quote but one of his contemporaries, Anaxagoras, who was also his friend: when asked why one should choose rather to be born than not [. . .] he replied: "For the sake of viewing the heavens and the things there, stars and moon and sun," as though nothing else were worth his while.[31]

Regardless of the fact that the ideal of philosophical contemplation created a kind of immortality competing with political glory, and therefore was appreciated by philosophers seeking to flee from changeable human affairs, it seems that the ideal of watching the skies, always accompanying philosophy, was earlier than it.

In the following part we will see how Arendt's highly original concept of the world stems from her polemics with Heidegger and at the same time how she accepts certain premises of his account for her own struggles with modernity.

II

It seems that the description of the alienation of man from the world in modernity, the leitmotif of *The Human Condition*, refers primarily to the second, cosmological understanding of the world. For Arendt, the turning point in the modern concept of the world was Galileo, with his law of falling bodies, and Newton's laws of gravitation, which completed modern astrophysics, and thoroughly changed the human perception of the world. The unifying of terrestrial and heavenly laws, the undermining of the over two-thousand-year-old conviction of a fundamental difference between what happens on the earth or within its proximity and the divine rules for the celestial bodies, that is, the emergence of astrophysics and the unification of the cosmos, resulted in a mental shift of the earth onto the cosmic sphere on the one hand (the earth undergoes the same laws as other planets), and on the other, in making the cosmos "terrestrial" (the movements of celestial bodies lost their divine nature, once it was established that the apple falling on the earth and the orbit of Mars around the Sun are ruled by the same laws).

This not only means that the earth loses its old status, but also that man becomes a completely different observer of the cosmos; this fact had a fundamental impact on Arendt. "Without actually standing where Archimedes wished to stand [. . .], still bound to the earth through the human condition, we have found a way to act on the earth and within terrestrial nature as though we dispose of it from outside, from the Archimedean point."[32] The task of man ceased to lie in lifting up the head and contemplating the heavens *from the earth*. Now this task was different: with the power of the mind to rocket to a freely chosen point of observation of the cosmos and give up, first mentally, the bond with the earth. The renaissance love of the world and the Copernican desire for beauty and harmony, still Greek in their essence, were soon to "fall victim to the modern age's triumphal world alienation."[33] The alienation from the world, understood in this way, is in fact an alienation from the earth. The turning point was the development of algebra, which resulted in the subordination of the geometrical to an algebraic form, that is, in the homogenization of the space ("de-spacing") of the world and in "the modern ideal of reducing terrestrial sense data and movements to mathematical symbols."[34] In this way mathematics ceased to be a medium of truth for the intellect, and became its creation[35]; in short, in Arendt's view, mathematics stopped dealing with phenomena. Thus the alienation of man from the world in the modern age means, first of all, and here she echoes Heidegger, the loss of the Greek contemplation of the cosmos, the immediate watching of cosmic phenomena with awe and admiration, which excludes invasion or manipulation of the cosmic sphere.

Therefore, the most important aspect of modern alienation for Arendt is research by experiment: "In the experiment man realized his newly won freedom from the shackles of earth-bound experience; instead of observing natural phenomena as they were given to him, he placed nature under the conditions of his own mind."[36] Thus, the finding of the universal, Archimedean point for thought, paradoxically relativizes thinking, by making it dependent on the subject. An even more relevant consequence of the development of the experimental sciences was the belief, "that neither truth nor reality is given, that neither of them appears as it is, and that only interference with appearance, doing away with appearances, can hold out a hope for true knowledge."[37] Experiment introduces an element of fabrication into the observation of the world and the researcher becomes a *homo faber*, who uses tools to extract truth out of self-created phenomena.

In the philosophical dimension, this relativization of thinking and making cognition dependent on the actions of a researcher leads to the Cartesian doubt, which for Arendt has less of a methodic character and is more a symptom of the withdrawal of the human mind into its own depths. Descartes' desire for certainty is complementary to the premises of the new physics: If doubt once and for all severed our immediate relations with the world of appearances, man can attain certainty only within his own mind, or within what he creates himself. The hierarchy of *vita activa* and *vita contemplativa* was reversed; since then, not contemplation, but "action" would be the domain of true cognition. It is, of course, not action in the political sense, but "worldless" fabrication of the conditions of experiment.

As we can see, this account of alienation by no means considers the first concept of the world as a human space for speech and action. It refers rather to a less conspicuous, but present understanding of the world, derived from the ideal of contemplation, the world as it was revealed to the Greeks. This type of alienation was to prepare the conditions for a gradual estrangement from the human world. Modern science replaced the expectation that beings disclose themselves for humans with the bringing forth of repeatable phenomena, that is, it replaced the concept of being with the concept of process. This change, having an ontological character, also influenced human relations and the humanities.

The second reversal took place within the *vita activa* and lay in the disruption of the traditional hierarchy of active life: First, as in science, fabrication outbalanced action (the instrumentalization of human activities), and second, through the industrial revolution, labor (despised by the Greeks) gained the highest rank within the hierarchy of human activities, and therefore granted biological life priority over the world. But, before this process was completed, a human being, according to the assumptions of modern science, started "to consider himself part and parcel of the two superhuman, all-encompassing processes of nature and history."[38] This enabled the application of natural law to human affairs and the gradual subordination of man under the rules of scientific experiment (like psychological experiments, or in the statistical analysis of the behavior of human collectivities). The fundamental consequence of these transformations is the emergence of modern society, in Arendt understood as a blurring of the essential political difference between the public and the private spheres, which endangered the world understood as a space of free speech and action.

Thus, the measure for the "deworlding" of the world is for Arendt dual: On the one hand, it is a modern reduction of nature to quantitative relations, and on the other, as its consequence, the leveling of the public sphere and political realm to an instrumentally structured space, for example, the market. The most conspicuous symptom of this second type of alienation is stripping works of art of their worldly character: First, the instrumentalization of art by "society," using them for individual development, and later, their "consumption" by mass society.

ARENDT'S RELUCTANT MODERNISM AND THE QUESTION OF FREEDOM

In Arendt's attitude toward modernity there is a certain ambivalence, not to say instability. On the one hand, we know that Arendt was convinced of the irreversible break in the tradition; the big difference between her and such thinkers as Leo Strauss or Hans-Georg Gadamer is that she never believed in the attempts to return to the origins, or the peaceful dialogue with the past, and thought them to be doomed to failure.[39] At the same time, she tries to find lost treasures in the ruins of the tradition—the old meanings of words, which say something important about the human condition. For this purpose, Arendt had to deconstruct tradition, whose ruins could obscure the phenomenal content of the words and make us accept the "empty shells of concepts" in their place. Her effort is aimed at the intensification of the feeling of the gap between past and future, and at preventing any helpless attempt to reactivate tradition. One of the terms, perhaps the most important one, that Arendt desires to rescue from forgetfulness, is "the world." Not aiming at recovering tradition, which itself is to blame for certain ontological distortions of fundamental political categories, Arendt rummages through the ruins and digs in them to show us what "the world" could have meant for humans. This archeological effort is sometimes understood as a nostalgia for something long passed. The reason of this misunderstanding lies partly in Arendt's style: What on a theoretical level is a phenomenological deconstruction, on the level of words sounds like nostalgia, or a desire to revive a lost paradise. For instance, when Arendt describes the love of the world in renaissance astronomers, who momentarily appeared to yield to the new ideas of astrophysics, we have a feeling that she is describing the Greeks.

On the other hand, Arendt indeed wanted to "recover" something—she was convinced that in the human condition are inscribed certain ways of being, which were too fragile not to be swept away in history from time to time. But this "recovery" does not mean a return to the past, but such an understanding of the present that would facilitate conditions in which being-with-others could appear. When it comes to the concept of the world, we have a problem. As we remember, by the description of the alienation from the world, it was Arendt herself who shifted the accent from a description of the human political world to the cosmos. At the same time it needs to be kept in mind that Arendt's diagnosis of this alienation in modern science and philosophy does not emerge out of the typical anti-modern aversion to the new, scientific way of discovering the world. In fact, Arendt is not concerned about science and does not juxtapose it with other sources of truth (as did Heidegger). The analysis of the alienation of the modern mind from the world, understood as the cosmos, is only a preliminary stage to another form of alienation, that is, from the world as a public sphere of speech and action, constituted by the plurality of people. The concept of action in Arendt is strictly related to the problem of freedom.

I

To say that the problem of freedom is the pivotal theme of Arendt's struggles with modernity is to underestimate the role of freedom in all her thought. The concept of freedom is a prism through which we can see other concepts, more frequently occurring in her writings. Even if someone could rightly protest that Arendt could not appreciate the specifics of the new spirit of the sixteenth and seventeenth centuries,[40] or that she too easily found a common denominator of such diverse phenomena as Cartesian doubt and Galileo's astronomy,[41] these statements should be considered proportionately by showing them in the context of the problem of freedom.

The basic outline of the problem of freedom is present in the essay *What is Freedom?*, where Arendt situates the problem of freedom within the realm of politics. The purpose of her analysis is demonstrating that the, typical for philosophy, concept of freedom as an attribute of will (stemming from stoicism), or later, as an inner sphere of consciousness (in modern philosophy), is derivative, exactly speaking a modification of the primary concept of freedom, that is, its internalization. For Arendt, of fundamental importance is the phenomenological observation that "we first become aware of freedom or its opposite in our intercourse with others, not in the intercourse with ourselves."[42] Freedom is by no means simply a freedom of choice, but a freedom to begin something new, characteristic for action. Such an understanding of freedom coincides with the concept of the world: One can only begin something new in the public space, in the common world, which we inhabit with others. Outside these spaces, in the biological realm, there is no freedom but only natural necessity. Nonetheless, *natality*, the promise of a new beginning, stems from this realm. From this perspective, the paradox of education is clearer: education has to take care of life (biological and psychological) and protect it from the world, and at the same time (if it is not merely rearing of young), it has to risk the laws of life for the sake of the world. It is connected with a promise of freedom, different from philosophical freedom. By entering the world, man fulfills the prerequisites for the freedom of action.

Like many other categories fundamental for Arendt's thought, the concept of freedom also reveals her complicated relationship with Heidegger's philosophy.[43] Political freedom, as understood by Arendt, is Heideggerian ontological freedom, although reinterpreted in the opposite direction. In *Being and Time* Heidegger devotes to freedom no separate analysis. Nonetheless, the problem of freedom is present in the description of the ontological structures of existence. First of all, Heidegger corrects the traditional connotation of freedom in Western metaphysics, that is, its connection with the autonomy of subjects. In him freedom is a correlate neither of consciousness, nor of will. *Dasein*'s freedom consists in its openness and is based on the structure of care as a thrown project. Since thrownness and project are two intertwined structural moments of *Dasein*, freedom appears in both. As a result of *Dasein* being thrown in the world, always being-in-a-world can transcend this being thrown: Attunement reveals possibilities, on which it can project its own existence. This ontological structure of exceeding one's own *ontic* limitations, lying in being-toward-something, is an actual source of freedom: "In being ahead-of-oneself as the being toward one's ownmost potentiality-of-being lies the existential and ontological condition of the possibility of *being free for* authentic existential possibilities."[44] In a purely ontological sense, freedom in Heidegger is connected with detaching the human way of being from theological interpretations (like freedom of the will, given by God, or human nature created by Him). *Dasein* is free because of *negativity*, which is inscribed in its existence, that is, paradoxically speaking, through being (ontologically) what it is not (ontically): its own possibilities, the movement toward them. Heidegger says that *Dasein* "is a null ground of its nullity" (*Nichtigkeit*), which can be read also as negativity.[45] If so, human being has no external ground, is ground-less. Such a ground is no longer provided by God, reason, or consciousness. *Dasein*'s freedom lies not in a choice of pre-given options, but in transcending itself, in projecting itself onto its own possibilities. In *On the Essence of Ground* (1929), Heidegger develops this ontological aspect of the concept of freedom and makes it a condition of the possibility of the worldliness of the world: "Freedom alone can let a world prevail and let it world for *Dasein*."[46] Because the world is a human structure, *Dasein*, projecting itself onto its own possibilities, projects the ontological concept of the world as a whole, as a background in which individual entities can appear. By transcending its own entity toward being, *Dasein* approaches the world. This transcending and approaching is freedom itself.

So far, this ontological concept of freedom could be a basis for Arendt's political concept of freedom. But in *Being and Time* this ontological concept of freedom is inscribed in the rhetoric of authenticity, which made it unsuitable for Arendt. Although in Heidegger the ontological concept of freedom has an existential structure and is strictly related to the world, the public sphere falsifies the understanding of its own possibilities by *Dasein*. In everyday life *Dasein* is unable to recognize its own ontological possibilities because it is concerned with the world, undergoes certain ontological illusions, and it does not know itself to be a thrown project. That is why Heidegger puts some additional conditions on freedom, conditions exceeding the basic ontological structures of *Dasein*, which are their qualifications. It is only angst, which brings about a withdrawal from engagement in the world, that can reveal the nullity of all life-projects, and make *Dasein* face the problem of freedom: "*Angst* reveals in Da-sein its *being toward* its ownmost potentiality of being, that is, *being free for* the freedom of choosing and grasping itself."[47] Thus, freedom in Heidegger appears in conditions exactly opposite to the freedom in Arendt, that is, only in the moment of the withdrawal of man from worldly relations with other people and finding himself in the solitude of resolute being-toward-death. Freedom is a resolute decision for the ownmost possibility of being, the authentic being-toward-death.

Arendt accepted this basic structure of the thrown project as an ontological basis for human freedom. But placing freedom in the realm of the complete solitude of one's own relation to mortality meant for her that Heidegger, again, stopped halfway in the deconstruction of philosophical tradition. Having released freedom, through ontological analysis, from traditional relations with theology and from the modern account of an autonomous subject, Heidegger closed it up again in the *solus ipse* of *Dasein* related to its own finitude. Situating freedom in being-toward-death, on the one hand, shows rightly how human freedom is based on contingency and finitude, but on the other, it disables understanding of the fundamental (for Arendt) feature of freedom, which is revealed in being-with-others. It can be said that for Arendt freedom begins where for Heidegger it ends: in the public space of speech and action. Man is free not because he is-unto-death (at least, it is not the fundamental feature of human freedom), but because he can initiate something that did not exist in this world before. This, however, cannot be done without other people; this novelty is owed to them and for them. In Heidegger the collective subject (the they) veils the conditions of realization of human freedom; in Arendt the plurality of the people is an ontological condition of actualization of human freedom: the faculty of beginning, potentially given to us with the new beginning of our birth.

Therefore, freedom is connected foremostly with action in the public sphere and the right place for it is the common world. On freedom as beginning something new, Arendt puts difficult theoretical stipulations: Action, to be free, needs to be free both from a motive and from a goal (an echo of the Heideggerian anti-teleological analysis of existence from *Being and Time*[48]). Initially, such a stipulation can seem bizarre and unnecessarily detach action from the domain of rationality and purposefulness. But such a negative definition of action allows Arendt to distinguish political action from all other kinds of activities. Releasing free action from the biological sphere, in Arendt associated with labor, is nothing new in the philosophical tradition. But the most important allegation against the tradition of political thought was that it always, that is, since Plato, had a tendency to identify action with fabrication. Fabrication or creation cannot be free, since its goal is external and pre-given. As we already know from the previous chapter, Aristotelian *praxis* is also ultimately subordinated to instrumental categories connected with fabrication. Since then, the categories of political thought were established and passed forward up to Heidegger's times.

Nonetheless, in modernity a new phenomenon emerged. Freedom of action was challenged not only by the philosophical tradition, that is, a theory that excluded practical phenomena. The modern age began when man started to create things that earlier were not subordinated to instrumental categories at all, being either the domain of contemplation, or speech and action. Instrumental categories first felt at home in science and philosophy, replacing contemplation, and later moved into interhuman relations to replace free action, in turn. The whole genesis of the emergence of modern society in *The Human Condition* is an analysis of the gradual replacement of the old public spaces with their possibilities of action with a human collective (not yet a mass, though), which can be described by laws similar to those of natural sciences, although less precisely. A member of society does not act, but behaves, and the role of social sciences is a description and prediction of his/her behavior. It is exactly this direction of instrumentalization of all dimensions of the human condition that Arendt was concerned about. Fabrication or creation cannot be free. This is also the reason why Arendt was not especially appreciative of the new realms of freedom (like freedom of experimental intelligence, which enabled the human mind to release itself from pre-given natural conditions). For Arendt, this conquest of freedom of action by the rules of fabrication meant alienation from the world, and not only from the world understood as the cosmos, but first of all as the world of human coexistence. Alienation from nature was relevant insofar as it was an announcement and starting point for the later estrangement from the public sphere. However, all this does not mean that for Arendt modernity was only a process of decline.

II

Therefore, it is difficult to fully agree with Seyla Benhabib, who in her thesis of the "reluctant modernism" of Arendt, polarizes Arendt's attitude toward modernity. Benhabib's interpretation is based on the assumption that Arendt was a modernist insofar as she was not a Heideggerist: "Although Hannah Arendt, the stateless and persecuted Jew, is the philosophical and political modernist, Arendt, the student of Martin Heidegger, is the antimodernist Grecophile theorist of the *polis* and of its lost glory."[49] According to Benhabib, Arendt's modernism would appear when she abandons the phenomenological approach, which seeks original phenomena, and when she gets inspired by the fragmentary historiography of Walter Benjamin, for example, in the biography of Rahel Varnhagen, suggesting "the alternative genealogy of modernity."[50] However, as we have seen, Arendt's attitude toward modernity can hardly be assessed according to such a clear criterion. It is because (1) even Heidegger, particularly in his early writings, is not decisively antimodernist (being definitely anti-Cartesian, but not so much anti-Kantian, for instance); (2) Arendt reformulates Heidegger's presumptions toward the phenomenological description of the conditions of action, in order to take a step toward a truly political way of thinking and is aware that this step cannot be taken within Greek political thought. As we will see, it is a phenomenological approach, at the same time within and beyond Heideggerian influence.

Thus, it is modernity in which Arendt seeks earlier unknown glimmers of freedom and the public world. Such new experiences of action, for example modern revolutions, "are the only political events which confront us directly and inevitably with the problem of beginning."[51] At the same time, since revolutions were connected with the ability of man to begin something new, "what the revolutions brought to the fore was this experience of being free."[52] Arendt is not interested in the history or genesis of revolutions; instead, she strives to find out their essence: "If we want to learn what a revolution is—its general implications for man as a political being, its political significance for the world we live in, its role in modern history—we must turn to those historical moments when revolution made its full appearance."[53] Therefore, she searches for the very phenomenon, since it lets the faculty of beginning and freedom appear in a new way, and at the same time renews the public space. In *On Revolution* we come across a competitive diagnosis of the modern age to that delivered in *The Human Condition*. "The political spirit of modernity was born when men were no longer satisfied that empires would rise and fall in sempiternal change; it is as though men wished to establish a world which could be trusted to last forever."[54] The greatest political events of modernity, revolutions, were something so completely new and unexpected that the word "revolution" had to change its meaning; it ceased to refer to eternal celestial movements and began to mean something opposite: the establishment of a new order in human affairs. Thus, it is evident that to be able to discover revolutions as modern unprecedented phenomena of political freedom, Arendt had to refer to and apply not only the phenomenological, but also the hermeneutic, "approach" of Heidegger's Marburg lectures of the 1920s. It is true she used it in a highly original way and in a field alien to Heidegger, but all the same, had she not been Heidegger's student, however rebellious and innovative, she could not have written such a work as *On Revolution*. Even Arendt the "reluctant modernist" sometimes drew from her Heideggerian legacy; however, it also is true that her inspirations reached far beyond it.

Although Arendt connected freedom foremostly with action and found the model of free action in the political conditions of Greece, we come across the potential of a different, more modern understanding of freedom in her thought. It is a freedom connected with a certain type of thinking, concretely with the Kantian enlarged mentality. Free action always proceeds from the perspective of the actor, so that action can hardly be defined as unbiased. The freedom of action is actually based on something different: on the power of beginning and on independence from motive and goal. True impartiality is possible only when we withdraw from action and assume the perspective of a spectator. Then, a different kind of freedom opens up: It is the freedom from being confined to one's own place in the world, where we act. Only as spectators can we take into account the points of view of others, widen our perspective, or put ourselves into the place of other people, through our imagination. Such a detachment is possible only where we have a public sphere (e.g., readers) and where we are free in that we have "the public use of one's reason";[55] (by public use of reason Kant understands the freedom of communication of the results of critical thought to the public). This freedom means independence from a private place in the world (e.g., a position, function, or interest). If we understand freedom in such a way, its premise is also the public world. The changing of one's perspective in thought demands freeing oneself from "partiality": one's own interest, life needs, or even the limitations of action. Only then are we able to dare express an impartial judgment of what is happening. Thus, Arendt's thought contains at least two understandings of freedom: the more conspicuous freedom of political action and the less conspicuous freedom of judgment.

As we can see, Hannah Arendt's thought cannot be simply inscribed in the anti-modernist tendency. Arendt was a modernist insofar as in modern politics she saw glimmers of freedom and the common world. And through the modern thinkers she notices symptoms of the independence from the old metaphysical premises and prejudgments, which tended to subordinate action to fabrication, and later, life. To these thinkers, apart from Kant, belonged Machiavelli, Montesquieu, and Herder. Machiavelli refused the subordination of political action to morality, saving the autonomy of action. Montesquieu divided monolithic power into three elements and undermined the modern belief in sovereign, indivisible power. Herder, in his philosophy of history for the first time affirmed the plurality of people and the diversity of the world's perspectives. The greatest thinkers of the modern age were not philosophers per se (with the one exception of Kant): Their thought lacked the speculative depths of the German idealists. At the same time, they did not share the typical philosophical prejudices concerning politics, which enabled them, if only theoretically, to grasp the conditions for the specifically modern space of action.

The problem of the assessment of the modern age is far from being only a theoretical or historical one. The crux of the debate on modernity is our postmodern self-knowledge and, in this sense, this debate is deeply pedagogical. It is a question of what and who we are today, how the ontological conditions of being human have changed. Modernity, through the negation of transcendent orders, natural or political, evokes the question of human authorship of humanity, the question to what extent it is man himself who creates the conditions of humanity. The more positive the answer, the greater the role of education. Education then ceases to be a natural function of culture to secure its perseverance (*paideia*), or the mechanism naturally supporting providence, and becomes a description of the solitary human struggle for humanity (partly apparent already in *Bildung*). Arendt does not answer this question unequivocally either. Her care for the world and freedom has a conservative and at the same time revolutionary strain: Education is to protect the common world from the destruction emerging from the inflow of biological life. But this protection has one goal: the possibility of new free action.

By the description of biological life as a sphere of dimness, Arendt stays in accordance with the philosophical tradition. But while shifting the light, which traditionally was connected with contemplation and theoretical life (as we know, even Heidegger's resoluteness is combined with *Augenblick*, the moment of brightness) to the public sphere, Arendt turns against the prevailing pedagogical metaphor of the cave. Inner life, even a philosophical one, is for her, rather, a sphere of shadow: It is necessarily beyond the world, until it finds the means of public expression. In order to protect thinking from the dangers of the public sphere, philosophers from Plato to Heidegger tried to push the sphere of human affairs into shadow (situating them at the bottom of the cave, like Plato, or with a statement that the public sphere "obscures everything," like Heidegger). Education in Arendt leads from darkness to light. But it is not a release from the shadows of the public space and preparation for the bright light of contemplation; it is the preparation of man for transcending the line between necessity and freedom, to leave the dimness of life and take his place in the luminous common world.

NOTES

1. Arendt, "The Crisis in Education," 183.
2. HC, 50. Remarkable is the difference between such an understood appearance and the Heideggerian phenomenon: a phenomenon is hidden; the being of beings needs to be revealed. For Arendt, a phenomenon is the simple possibility of being seen, an appearance.
3. HC, 50.
4. Arendt, "The Crisis in Education," 182.
5. Arendt, "The Crisis in Education," 186.
6. SZ, 64; BT, 60.
7. Martin Heidegger, "On the Essence of Ground," trans. William McNeill, in *Pathmarks*, 111–12.
8. SZ, 96; BT, 89.
9. SZ, 96; BT, 89.
10. SZ, 112; BT, 104.
11. The first mention of *Off the Beaten Track* (published in 1950, comprising *The Origin of the Work of Art* and *The Age of the World Picture*) appears in the letters to Blücher during Arendt's first trip to Europe, even before her reunion with Heidegger, in January 1950. See Arendt to Blücher, January 3, and March 2, 1950 (see *Within Four Walls: The Correspondence between Hannah Arendt and Heinrich Blücher 1936–1968*, ed. Lotte Kohler, trans. Peter Constantine [Orlando: Harcourt, 2000]). The notes on *Letter on 'Humanism'* and *Building, Dwelling, Thinking* we find in her *Denktagebuch* in 1951, see Arendt, *Denktagebuch*, 118, 143f.
12. See Martin Heidegger, "Letter on 'Humanism,'" in *Pathmarks*, 260.
13. Martin Heidegger, "The Origin of the Work of Art," in Martin Heidegger, *Off the Beaten Track*, trans. Julian Young and Kenneth Haynes (New York: Cambridge University Press, 2002), 23.
14. Heidegger, "The Origin of the Work of Art," 24.
15. Heidegger, "The Origin of the Work of Art," 25.
16. Heidegger, "The Origin of the Work of Art," 26.
17. Heidegger, "The Origin of the Work of Art," 27.
18. Heidegger, "The Origin of the Work of Art," 29.
19. Martin Heidegger, "The Age of the World Picture," in *Off the Beaten Track*, 65.
20. Heidegger, "The Age of the World Picture," 65.
21. Heidegger, "The Age of the World Picture," 66.
22. Heidegger, "The Age of the World Picture," 66
23. Heidegger, "The Age of the World Picture," 71.

24. Martin Heidegger, "Building Dwelling Thinking," trans. Albert Hofstadter, in *Basic Writings*, ed. David Farell Krell (Auckland: HarperCollins, 2008), 354.
25. Heidegger, "Building Dwelling Thinking," 353.
26. HC, 6.
27. Heidegger, "The Origin of the Work of Art," 41.
28. See HC, 153–54.
29. HC, 9.
30. As cited in Hannah Arendt, *Lectures on Kant's Political Philosophy*, ed. Ronald Beiner (Chicago: The University of Chicago Press, 1992), 23. "Not to be born/ is far best scenario; but if a man appears/next best to go swiftly as he may/back down the path from whence he came," Sophocles, *Oedipus in Colonus*, 1224–26, trans. Robin Bond, https://ir.canterbury.ac.nz/bitstream/handle.
31. Hannah Arendt, *The Life of the Mind: Thinking* (New York: A Harvest Book, 1981), 133–34.
32. HC, 262.
33. HC, 264.
34. HC, 265.
35. Arendt's diagnosis is not entirely precise. Algebra is an Eastern discovery and functioned already in the Middle Ages independently from Western geometry. Descartes not so much subordinated algebra to geometry, but unified these two modes of mathematics, which enabled an enormous development of mathematics and natural sciences.
36. HC, 265.
37. HC, 274.
38. HC, 307.
39. See also Villa, *Arendt and Heidegger*, 8.
40. See Hans Blumenberg, *The Legitimacy of the Modern Age*, trans. Robert M. Wallace (Cambridge, MA: The MIT Press, 1983), 8–11.
41. See Colin Koopman, *Three Intellectual Histories of Modernity: Arendt, Blumenberg, Dewey*, presented at the Canadian Political Science Association, June 2006, York, Ontario.
42. Arendt, "What is Freedom?" 147.
43. See also Villa, *Arendt and Heidegger*, 125ff.
44. SZ, 193; BT, 180.
45. SZ, 306; BT, 283.
46. Heidegger, "On the Essence of Ground," 126.
47. SZ, 188; BT, 176.
48. See also, Villa, *Arendt and Heidegger*, 13.
49. Benhabib, *The Reluctant Modernism*, xxxvii–xxxix.
50. Benhabib, *The Reluctant Modernism*, 29.
51. Hannah Arendt, *On Revolution* (New York: Penguin Books, 2006), 11.
52. Arendt, *On Revolution*, 24.
53. Arendt, *On Revolution*, 34.
54. Arendt, *On Revolution*, 216.
55. See Arendt, *Lectures on Kant's Philosophy*, 39; Immanuel Kant, *An Answer to the Question: "What Is Enlightenment?"* Königsberg, Prussia, September 30, 1784.

Part III

THE PEDAGOGICAL PROMISE OF PHILOSOPHY

In the previous part of this book I analyzed Arendt's thesis of the break in tradition and the consequences of this break for our theme. Two intertwined motifs were of importance here: One was the attempt at understanding the philosophical dialogue between Arendt and Heidegger in the context of this break, showing both their common premises, and the places where Arendt revolted against the main stream of Heidegger's thought; the other motif was demonstrating that if we accept Arendt's thesis of the end of tradition, we need to question the traditional connections between pedagogy and philosophy, as outlined in the first part of this book, such as the promises of freedom, individuality, and authenticity, present in the projects of *paideia*, *Bildung*, and fundamental ontology. I also tried to sketch the ways in which Arendt transcended the limitations of classically understood philosophy, traditionally prejudiced against the themes most important for Arendt, such as political freedom, action, and the plurality of people.

In the third and last part of this book I will consider the consequences of these analyses. Now the accent will be shifted to searching the philosophical contexts for education in the situation where tradition no longer delivers classical solutions. Eventually, the relationship between education and philosophy will have to be reconsidered. We need to come back once again to the thesis of Antonia Grunenberg that, according to Arendt, "With the arrival of totalitarianism the educational mission of philosophy was discredited." We already know the philosophical reasons why this thesis was formulated and the historical background of its formulation (chapter 4). We know that the term "philosophy" refers here to the philosophical or metaphysical tradition (which, irrespective of its philosophical insightfulness and novelty, in Arendt's view does not grasp political matters adequately). We also know that the paradigm of such a philosophy for Arendt was Heidegger's thought.

Now we need to consider the question whether such an understanding of philosophy is the only possible understanding, that is, whether we can think about philosophy in less traditional ways and in this way let her still be somehow relevant for education. Thus, the third part of this book will be argumentation for a thesis contrary to that of Grunenberg's: With the arrival of totalitarianism the educational mission of philosophy is only just beginning.

Chapter 7

"The Educational Principle"
The Human Condition and the Power of Precedence

In this, the penultimate chapter of this book, I will permit myself two transgressions. First, in the analysis of Arendt's work I will go beyond the Heideggerian context. Secondly, I will also transcend the boundaries of Arendt's writing. It will allow us a glance at her work in a slightly different light and facilitate a resumption of the pedagogical promise of thinking, indicated in the previous chapter. In Johann Gottfried Herder's work, I will look for a counter-inspiration for Heidegger's prevailing influence on Arendt's thought. In Michel Foucault and Giorgio Agamben, I hope to find development of the traces Arendt left in her works. This will lead us, again, to the question of the pedagogical role of philosophy in the modern world.

"WHAT" AND "WHO": THE DIFFERENCE BETWEEN THE HUMAN CONDITION AND HUMAN NATURE

Heidegger, in *Being and Time*, looked at the question of the meaning of being in the perspective of being human. Regardless of the theoretical difficulties one can find in the stance of *Being and Time*, one cannot deny the novelty of the philosophical approach to humanity that Heidegger achieved. He did not put the traditional question: *What* is man? Instead, he asked: *Who* is *Dasein*? The being that transcends its own being, that is, exists, cannot be adequately grasped within the way of questioning reserved for other entities. The question of *what* man is suggests, namely, a pre-understanding of man as an entity amongst other entities. It also suggests an answer situating man in a structure or hierarchy of entities. Such were the traditional philosophical answers on this question: man as *what* turned out to be an *ens creatum*, put in between animals and angels, or, a rational animal, a combination of body and soul, a substance, *ego cogito*. Contrarily, when we ask *who man is*, these traditional answers occur as irrelevant, and at the same time, a space for answers of another kind opens up: It is no longer a placing of humankind in a structure of entities, but grasping the actual way of being of man and, only on this basis, capturing the way of being of entities other than *Dasein*.[1] Such is the direction of the analyses of *Being and Time*: They are not an answer to the question of *what* is man is, but, rather, what it actually *means* that man *is*.

I

The project of *Being and Time* can be succinctly summed up as a search for *Dasein*'s identity in the solitude of being-toward-death and in liberation from the public sphere, whereas Arendt's effort strives exactly at liberating the Heideggerian *Dasein* from this philosophical solitude, and the reinstatement of being-with-others and speech as inalienable conditions for humanity. Arendt's ambition is a description of the specifically human ways of being, but not a description of the meaning of being as such. Her question therefore, unlike Heidegger's, is deliberately anthropological. All the same, the premise of her anthropology is the Heideggerian question of *who Dasein* is.

The distinction between *human condition* and *human nature* is one of the fundamental demarcations of Hannah Arendt. When writing *The Human Condition*, Arendt did not desire to deliver the essence of man, that is, the constitutive features without which one is no longer human. She is convinced that such attempts, undertaken on and off by metaphysics, "almost invariably end with some construction of a deity" and that "the fact that attempts to define the nature of man lead so easily into an idea which definitely strikes us as 'superhuman' and therefore as identified with the divine may cast suspicion upon the very concept of 'human nature.'"[2] Arendt did not want to construct an idea of man, but to describe the fragile and changeable conditions of humanity. She desired to understand man independently from metaphysical structures and at the same time from any form of theology and teleology. The account of the human condition is an account of being human in human terms only, in other words: the account of the fragile circumstances in which man appears human. Since these circumstances are not constitutive features, it is impossible to list them fully. Clearly, certain aspects, with which we are already familiar, belong to them: life, worldliness, speech, and action, but also mortality and natality.

In *The Human Condition*, Arendt consistently avoided referring to Heidegger and this is the reason why her distinction between *human condition* and *human nature* is supported by St. Augustine's, rather than Heidegger's, authority: "The question of the nature of man is no less a theological question than the question about the nature of God; both can be settled only within the framework of a divinely revealed answer."[3] Nonetheless, Arendt's questioning is beyond a shadow of a doubt inspired by Heidegger's *Who* of *Dasein*. Arendt, like Heidegger, quests for a phenomenological description of humanity directed against metaphysics, but unlike Heidegger, has a different goal in mind: She does not want to give a foundation for ontology. She does not so much want to remind us of being as such, but, instead, strives at remembering the specifically *human* ways of being. Her phenomenology is anthropology and, at the same time, more directly than Heidegger's phenomenology, has a *pedagogical* sense; when examining concepts and the phenomena underlying them, she strives at excavating them from under the ruins of dead tradition. For instance, when distinguishing freedom from will, authority from tyranny, action from fabrication, or thinking from reasoning, she untangles the knots of meanings and by doing so she rescues concepts and saves them from becoming "empty shells," whose content would be long forgotten. This rescuing of concepts is by no means a mere philosophical or philological endeavor; it is also a recovery of certain ways of life, which had been partially forgotten or obscured. As Julia Kristeva puts it, Arendt's "concerns about the 'who'" can be integrated "with a pedagogical, even educational, reflection."[4] In other words, the deconstruction of metaphysics is relevant not only in the context of thinking, but it is also the prerequisite of action. The choice of *human condition* over *human nature* is by no means a purely conceptual gesture. The basic assumption of Arendt in her analyses of modernity is a conviction that the human condition can undergo changes and that events such as totalitarianism can annihilate its basic dimensions: human plurality, freedom, and the world. The desire to understand these phenomena is derived from the care for their durability, even if in "dark times" the only place they can find sanctuary is in thinking.

II

In the Western metaphysical tradition, man had to be an element of a superstructure. The first, although incomplete, attempt to set man free from metaphysical structures was undertaken by the Enlightenment. Its crowning achievement was the Kantian man living in two dimensions: as a determined phenomenon and free *noumenon*, the unknowable "thing-in-itself." Only the latter could pretend to be really human. Along with the inscription of humanity in the realm of *noumena*, the hope of grasping human nature like we grasp the essences of other entities turns out to be futile. Kant still formulated his question in terms of *what* man is, but his questioning was not aimed at grasping man within the great chain of entities, and was, instead, a milestone toward an understanding of the human condition. Kant was no longer interested in a substance (*ens creatum*, *res cogitans*, *animal rationale*), but only in the *conditions of possibility* of humanity, of which the freedom of rational creatures is a prerequisite. That is why Kant became a great ally of Arendt. Nietzsche, taking a step forward from Kant, undermined the autonomy of reason and ultimately frustrated the conceptual framework of Western philosophy and anthropology. Heidegger, in turn, deconstructed metaphysics and introduced different rules of description for anthropology. But it is only Arendt, who, by questioning some of Heidegger's assumptions, poses a question of the human condition.

The change of formulae of the anthropological quest was possible only after the break in the thread of philosophical tradition. In the context of education, it is at the same time a loss and a chance. On the one hand, questioning of the human condition abandons hope for situating man in a stable structure of the universal order, while also undermining consistent, positive, and conservative theories of education (which often sum up to edifying man to a higher stage in the hierarchy of beings). On the other hand, that questioning of the changeable and fragile circumstances of being human is a chance for pedagogy. It ceases to be a function of a more or less closed metaphysical system and becomes an open space for questions. It does not mean that the attitude of man toward transcendence (God, Idea, Reason) becomes automatically irrelevant. But the answer for this question can no longer rely on dogma, it needs to derive from experience. The expression "cannot" is not a restriction or logical impossibility. "Cannot" means here "is not worth." Arendt showed that sticking to old concepts in circumstances where they lose their meaning is a manifestation of helplessness. Clinging to "unchangeable human nature" or "eternal values" where the basic conditions of freedom are negated is surely harmless, but it does not contribute to saving these conditions. In order to do so one has to find an adequate language for the description of these phenomena. The whole work of Arendt can be defined as a search for such a language: By giving an account of loss and by attempting to understand the essence of it, Arendt changed people's awareness of human affairs. That is why such texts as *The Origins of Totalitarianism* or *The Human Condition* have strong pedagogical potential, perhaps even stronger than her scarce direct contributions to education. This is how Aaron Schutz underscores the performative function of Arendt's work: "As important as her writings ask us to think, is who they encourage us to be."[5]

With the exception of Kant (Kant was for Arendt an exceptional figure, since his thinking was a very rare combination of features that in the tradition tended to exclude one another: a deeply philosophical insight and at the same time a true acknowledgment of what Arendt called "human affairs"), it can be said that Arendt looked for allies for her thinking on the margins of philosophical thought. She found some glimmers of authentic descriptions of "human affairs," that is, the conditions of the political, beyond the philosophical mainstream. As already seen, she found support for her analyses of action and public affairs in such thinkers as Montesquieu, Machiavelli, and Herder. Not being philosophers in the strict sense of the term, they never reached such heights of philosophical speculation as did the German idealists, for example. At the same time they were free from purely philosophical or metaphysical assumptions, which compelled philosophers and made them look upon human affairs from the point of view of theoretical life. Thus, for Arendt, their works could become sources of fresh insights into the political as an autonomous sphere, free from the traditional paradigm of "political philosophy," as launched by Plato.

If we are interested in the relationships between political thought and pedagogy based on the question of the human condition, we need, first of all, to reconstruct the reasons why Arendt studied Herder. While we can say that Machiavelli liberated politics from heterogeneous moral rules, and Montesquieu from quasi-theological dogma of indivisible and sovereign power, it was Herder who set it free from the real philosophical nightmare: thinking of humanity always in terms of singularity.

HERDER AND "THE EDUCATIONAL PRINCIPLE"

Elisabeth Young-Bruehl in her excellent intellectual biography of Arendt writes: "The aspect of Herder's thought that Arendt never abandoned was the educational principle."[6] The biography is not a literary form where such statements can be thoroughly explained, let alone analyzed, and "the educational principle" remains in Young-Bruehl a somewhat mysterious expression. Thus, it will be our task to solve this mystery. Therefore, we now need to ask what "the educational principle" could mean and why it was Herder who introduced it into Arendt's sensitivity.

Arendt got interested in Herder very early. At the beginning of the 1930s she began a study of German Romanticism, crowned by Rahel Varnhagen's biography.[7] Already then she had found motifs in Herder that influenced the general context of her later thought. But what is even more important here is that the study of Herder facilitated a discovery that allowed Arendt to enter a polemics with the premises of *Being and Time* and had an enormous impact on her political theory. The essence of this discovery can be found in the quote from *Outlines of the Philosophy of History*, which would accompany Arendt her whole life: "Did man receive every thing from himself, and develope every thing independently of external circumstances, we might have a history of an individual indeed, but not of the species."[8] This means that for Arendt, Herder was the first to notice that "not one man but men in the plural inhabit the earth."[9] Nonetheless, although he seems to have delivered such an important impulse for Arendt's mature thinking, he is certainly not expressively over-present in her works (the reasons will be clarified in what follows). Therefore I will try, using the scarce references present in her writings, to draw out these aspects of the Herderian description of the *condition humaine*, which disclose the importance of this inspiration.

Firstly, Herder is not a Platonic philosopher. He does not believe in the clear sky of ideas beyond the cave of human affairs and even less in its accessibility for the finite human mind. Man educates himself in human, not divine, conditions and has to use human, limited powers. The most relevant knowledge of himself he can learn by studying human affairs in their complexity and multifariousness, without an attempt to create an idea of human nature, independent from terrestrial, provisional, and contingent conditions: "Has the human being ever been so, then, except, in philosophers' abstractions and hence in their heads?"[10] asks Herder. He is also mistrustful of academic philosophy. Pure speculation, which does not get challenged by experience is a game of the mind, which brings nothing to an understanding of reality. His remarks on philosophers of his age are full of irony: "If there is a *business* in the world that you wish to have poorly looked after, just hand it over to the *philosopher*! On paper, how pure, how gentle, how beautiful and great, but hopeless in *execution*—at every step, *marveling* and *bristling* with unseen obstacles and consequences!"[11] Herder wants philosophers to come back from the kingdom of thought and abandon the self-constructed idea of humanity as an isolated individual, whose development proceeds independently from other people and external circumstances: "The philosopher [. . .] must [. . .] soon quit his ideal world, in which he feels himself alone and all-sufficient, for our world of realities."[12]

Secondly, for Herder, humanity is a phenomenon that cannot be reduced to nonhuman orders: "If the question were, whether a human being could and should become more than a human being, a superhuman or non-human, each verse written on the topics would be redundant"[13]—we read in the beginning of "Letters for the Advancement of Humanity." Herder clearly distinguishes philosophical comparative anthropology (to which he devoted his life), from both theology and naturalistic, Rousseauian anthropology. In his *Treatise on the Origin of Language* (1770), he defends, against the mainstream dispute of the time, the thesis of the purely human origins of language and develops arguments against both naturalism and the divine genesis of speech: "The goal of truth is only a point! But, set down on it, we see on all sides: why no animal can invent language, why no God must invent language and why the human being as a human being can and must invent language."[14] Language is a human phenomenon and its genesis cannot be attributed to natural sounds or the organic component of the human body, and Herder believes that no language can come into being according to the law of nature and without the influence of reason. Language is not a donation from God, either. Men create languages as they go along, through millennia. But the creation of language is possible only due to the fact that a human being is not alone on the earth: "I cannot think the first human thought, cannot set up the first aware judgment in a sequence, without engaging in dialogue, or striving to engage in dialogue, in my soul."[15] Language is also a proof that man is able to gain a distance from reality: "The human being, put in the condition of awareness which is his very own, with this awareness (reflection) operating freely for the first time, invented language."[16] For language and thinking are both essentially and genetically inseparable: *"There is also no condition in the human soul which does not turn out to be* [werde] *susceptible of words."*[17] Thus, speech and language emancipate humanity both in the order of creation and in the order of nature. Language is an element in which men create their humanity on an autonomous basis. Plurality is inevitably inscribed in the sheer possibility of speech; it is known neither in the animal kingdom nor in the divinities. In other words: Herder's man is *zoon logon echon.*

Thirdly, language connects men with each other and enables mutual understanding regardless of distance in space or time. The understanding of the character of a people or of a culture means for Herder a comparison of details, omitted by philosophical abstraction: "No one in the world feels the *weakness of general characterization* more than I."[18] That is why in his comparative studies he looked for the documents of a real life, the differences between people and nations. But in particular he avoided the assessment of the past with Enlightenmental universals (as did Michel Foucault many years later). He did not want to decide which people in history were closest to happiness, since he understands that "even the image of human happiness changes with every condition and location."[19] He avoided reckoning one epoch with the measures of another, or one people with another: He did not accept scolding Egyptians for not being Greeks. Even less acceptable for him was the short-sighted taking of the contingent ideals of his own time for the universal measures of history; he did not understand how some contemporaries could despise the ideas of medieval monks for not being inspired by Voltaire and Hume.[20]

What is more, for Herder, the timeless, unconditioned, and universal truth of reason does not exist. It is difficult to speak on truth in the singular; the unity of truth requires an a-historic, transcendent medium, which is lacking in Herder's thought. The medium of truth is not pure reason but history, which is a carrier of many fragmentary and conditional truths. The individual is unable to fathom all the truths dispersed in tradition. Pure reason, clear truth, and Good appear in many different guises and are dependent on external circumstances. Reason is not a trans-historic, transcendent being, or the ultimate end of history, but is transformative like Proteus, and dispersed all over the earth. It is a provisional outcome of the totality of human experiences and can never be completed. "Reason is an aggregate of the experiences and observations of the mind, the sum of the education of man."[21] Humanity is not an abstract idea, and "the whole species lives solely in the chains of individuals."[22] External conditions and circumstances educate different people from the same stem of humanity. In Arendt's view it meant that for Herder, not the pure Enlightenment possibility of humanity is important, but, rather, the reality of each human existence. The actual difference between people is more relevant than their potential identity.

Additionally, in Herder, the dualism between philosophy and history, cherished by the Enlightenment, was overcome. Truth is dependent not only on reason, but also on numerous conditions outside human beings, just as reason is the result of human total experience. "For Herder [...] reason is subject to history."[23] Thus, he historicized reason and, by the same token, the idea of education. In Arendt's view, it enabled him to establish an intellectual distance from reality, very different from philosophical speculation: "This distance of understanding and, in general, its corresponding idea of understanding as an entirely new possibility of gaining access to the world and to reality, has become extraordinarily effective not only for the principle of *Bildung* but also for the intellectual elite."[24] The distance Arendt discovered in Herder allows for judging reality in terms of what really happened, "without pedagogical goals and connivances."[25] Herder's thesis of the intersubjective character of education, that "no one of us became man of himself,"[26] is an exact opposition to the idea of education in the Enlightenment, which underscored self-sufficiency, independence, and rationalism. Thus, according to Arendt, it was Herder who initiated the transformation of the German historical consciousness. This made him capable of a new definition of education in opposition to the rationalistic ideas of the Enlightenment. Education "is never anything other than a *work of Fortune:* the result of a thousand *coexisting causes*, the product, as it were, of the *entire element within which [a nation] lives*. And is this—what *child's play!*—a mere matter of recasting this education with and according to a few *more luminous ideas* [. . .]?"[27] Therefore, it is not the universal historical or natural law, but a constellation of contingent events that at the end of the day is decisive for the process of the development of humanity.

Here we approach the crucial phenomenon of this analysis: the power of precedence in Herder's thought and its relevance for Arendt. Precedence is an event that cannot be traced back to earlier events and at the same time is an emergence that initiates a new beginning: It brings forth something that did not exist earlier. The understanding of the discreet nature of a precedential event is a prerequisite of an understanding of reality, for which the subscription of events under one universal idea is deeply unsatisfactory. It is how Arendt sums up the Herderian idea of education: "The 'backwards step' of formation—of true formation which forms, re-forms, and constitutes to form—is governed by the past, 'the silent, eternal power of precedence, of a series of precedents.' The Enlightenment cannot preserve this past."[28]

These motifs in Herder's thought turned out to be of relevance for Arendt. This somehow schematic presentation allows us to identify one of the important impulses that directed Arendt's thinking on new paths and was one of the many sources of her intellectual originality. The "educational principle" of Herder, which Arendt never abandoned, can be summed up in two mottos: the plurality of people and the need to understand. In the next steps of this analysis we need to come closer to an understanding of this "educational principle." Herder will serve here as a figure or metaphor of such thinking that is driven by these two postulates. Now we need to develop this Herderian motif of the power of precedence as an alternative rationality to that of Heidegger's, starting with the sources of Arendt's thought and proceeding toward newer philosophies where we find the developments of the traces present in her work.

UNDERSTANDING THE POWER OF PRECEDENCE: ARENDT, FOUCAULT, AGAMBEN

Herder was one of Arendt's allies in her political way of thinking. Nevertheless, apart from his innovative insights, he was a thinker from the depths of tradition. That is why for Arendt, even more important than his positive beliefs on history and humanity was his new *way* of thinking on these matters. Herder was still convinced of the pedagogical role of external circumstances whose multifarious influences facilitate the development of humankind toward a fulfillment. Arendt, as a witness and a victim of the totalitarian regimes of the twentieth century, could not believe in an entirely positive pedagogical meaning of historical events. On the contrary, as we know, she feared that as a result of these events, the human condition could be endangered by a degeneration to its animalistic level. This is also the reason why in Arendt's thought Herder functions more as a methodological figure than an outright positive point of reference and why he is not an over-present reference in her works. The understanding of what *really* happened in its whole individuality and uniqueness is a heroic intellectual contribution to the effort of preservation of endangered human plurality. As we will see, such a way of thinking will find its continuators in following generations, in Michel Foucault and Giorgio Agamben.

I

The Origins of Totalitarianism and the report of Eichmann's trial are perhaps the most expressive testimonies of an uncompromised attempt at understanding historical events. *The Origins* can be defined as a quasi-Herderian quest for a description of a series of precedents that led to the catastrophe of totalitarianism. Arendt does her best to avoid the trap of philosophers: the reduction of new phenomena to old categories and known terms (for her, totalitarianism is *not* simply a form of gnosis, the result of Enlightenmental reason, or a new version of paganism). She also tries to avoid Heidegger's mistake at all costs: seeing all the modern phenomena as an actualization of an inauthentic understanding of being. In the postwar addresses of Heidegger, the being as will-to-power, and later the technological mastering of being ("en-framing") are an ontological common denominator of all worldly events and the universal pattern for their description: "Today everything stands in this historical reality—says Heidegger in 1945—no matter whether it is called communism, or fascism, or world democracy."[29] Arendt will try to understand the uniqueness of phenomena that in the light of the history of being are indistinguishable.

The Origins of Totalitarianism constitutes a complex account of a weave of circumstances and events that led to the emergence of the Third Reich and Soviet Russia. Their genesis cannot be attributed to one factor or one idea, since it is comprised of many motifs, stemming from different dimensions of reality, like economic facts, historical events, ideas shared by groups of men, etc. However, from the point of view of thinking in the categories of the human condition, a tendency can be distinguished, which, when coming to the extreme, constitutes the unprecedential character of totalitarian rule. This tendency consists in the gradual but consistent leveling of every form of human plurality.

First of all, totalitarian rule is impossible without mass society. Mass society is the opposite pole of political plurality, which presupposed the appearance of unique individuals in the public sphere. Mass society also differs from modern class society, whose principle is the desire to distinguish through establishing groups, for example, groups of interest. Mass society is a bulk in which the differences between people are politically irrelevant. Important is not what an individual or a group of people does, but the behavior of the collective, which can be described with statistical laws. One of the features of totalitarianism is that a mass becomes a political *body*: By bestowing the regime with a legitimization, it becomes a subject of total organization. "The masses grew out of the fragments of a highly atomized society whose competitive structure and concomitant loneliness of the individual had been held in check only through membership in a class. The chief characteristic of the mass man is not brutality and backwardness, but his isolation and lack of normal social relationships."[30] However, the mass society that emerges on its own accord as a result of historical events, is never fully atomized, is never completely homogenized, and one can never count on its total loyalty. Therefore, the establishment of totalitarian rule (Arendt gives examples from Soviet Russia in the 1930s) is based on the annihilation of all societal and family bonds, which could outweigh the atomization and be an obstacle for their total subordination.

Control over the masses, which is based on the leveling of "worldly" differences between people, has two stages: the totalitarian movement, with its main tool of propaganda, and totalitarianism in power, with its main tool of terror. The first stage precedes the seizing of power by the totalitarian movement. Propaganda aims at the creation of a coherent, yet imaginary, world, as far as possible isolated from the reality of the external world. It is a world in which "uprooted masses can feel at home."[31] The denser the isolation of individuals from the criteria of verification of ideology that could be provided by the external world, the more perfect the consistency of the imaginary world. Since ideology, the prerequisite of propaganda, excludes the plurality of opinion that emerges from a confrontation with the outside world, "the true goal of totalitarian propaganda is not persuasion but organization."[32]

Along with the seizure of power by totalitarianism, that is, along with the transition from the stage of movement to the stage of government, the situation changes. When a movement, which always has global political aspirations and needs support of international organization, gains power, such power is necessarily limited to a territory. Now, the external world is a real threat to the coherent imaginary "reality": "Power means a direct confrontation with reality, and totalitarianism in power is constantly concerned with overcoming this challenge."[33] Propaganda and organization become too weak to stop the challenge of the external reality: "The struggle for total domination of the total population of the earth, the elimination of every competing nontotalitarian reality, is inherent in the totalitarian regimes themselves [. . .]. Even a single individual can be absolutely and reliably dominated only under global totalitarian conditions."[34] That is why totalitarianism in power, by using the methods of terror, creates a poor substitute for global exclusivity, a *laboratory*, where it experimentally researches modes of total control over people and reality; the extreme examples of such laboratories are concentration camps and gulags.

The development of a totalitarian system is staged: Before the seizure of power, the enemies of the system are actual adversaries and potential dissidents. At the next stage, this category of enemies is replaced by the so-called objective enemy, referring to certain groups, (like Jews or communists in Nazi Germany, or rich peasants or counterrevolutionaries in Soviet Russia), to which one attributes the potential danger for revolution. The final stage of totalitarianism replaces the collective category of the "objective enemy" with a new category of superfluous people. These groups are not faced with even absurd allegations of potential crimes. Instead, they are marked as "unfit to live." The actions of the terror apparatus against them cannot be grasped in terms of punishment or even murders. Even the most unjust punishments and political crimes are still directed toward a man whose disappearance leaves an empty spot in the world, like the memory of his next of kin, sometimes the glory of a hero. The victims of fully-fledged totalitarian regimes disappear without a trace and memory concerning their existence is systematically effaced: "In totalitarian countries all places of detention ruled by the police are made to be veritable holes of oblivion into which people stumble by accident and without leaving behind them such ordinary traces of former existence as a body and grave."[35]

The concentration camp is for Arendt a laboratory, where experiments of the perfect reduction of the human condition to the purely biological dimension are performed; these are places where people become one sick organism. "Total domination, which strives to organize infinite plurality and differentiation of human beings as if all of humanity were just one individual, is possible only if each and every person can be reduced to a never-changing identity of reactions."[36] Arendt shows mechanisms that preclude camps being regarded only in terms of the extreme physical cruelty they inflicted. The reality of the suffering is here combined with the gradual derealization of the artificial camp reality and the beings within it: "The human masses sealed off in them are treated as if they no longer existed, as if what happened to them were no longer of any interest to anybody, as if they were already dead."[37]

The first step in the path to total control over human beings is the killing of their juridical personalities: The prisoner of a camp is not a criminal, but a person put outside the law and stripped of his bonds with the world, such as citizenship. The most characteristic feature of a prisoner is his complete innocence. The second step is the murder of the moral person in man: The unreality of the camp space makes any attempt to sacrifice one's life in a protest futile; the lack of witnesses would make such a protest meaningless. Victims are made to be accomplices, which levels the choice between good and evil, and the line between tormentors and the tormented is blurred (e.g., the prisoners' contribution to the camp administration or organization). The final step to the total domination over man is annihilation of uniqueness and identity: It is abolishing the conditions of possibility of any spontaneous action. What victims do, is at the end of the day reducible to predictable reactions and the simplest impulses: "The society of the dying established in the camps is the only form of society in which it is possible to dominate man entirely."[38] Thus, camps are epitomes of total domination:

Totalitarianism strives not toward despotic rule over man, but toward a system in which men are superfluous. Total power can be achieved and safeguarded only in a world of conditioned reflexes, of marionettes without the slightest trace of spontaneity. Precisely because man's resources are so great, he can be fully dominated only when he becomes a specimen of the animal-species man.[39]

The Origins of Totalitarianism is the most historical of Arendt's works. But the rules of description applied here go far beyond the goal of an account of the past. It is a basis of philosophical ideas, developed later in *The Human Condition* and the essays of the 1950s. When analyzing the mechanisms of the total liquidation of the fragile conditions of humanity, Arendt refers to the future: "Totalitarian solutions may well survive the fall of totalitarian regimes in the form of strong temptations which will come up whenever it seems impossible to alleviate political, social, or economic misery in a manner worthy of man."[40]

As we already know, the philosophical categories familiar to us from *The Human Condition*, such as labor, work, and action, and the distinctions between the world and life, the public and the private spheres, are a response to a philosophical description of humanity, especially to the ontological anthropology of Heidegger. Now we can see that this feud with philosophy by no means was limited to a conceptual level, let alone a speculative one. The philosophical categories of Hannah Arendt were coined in a phenomenological-empirical way; they were meaningful generalizations of authentic experiences. Arendt notices that the newest history delivered unprecedented possibilities of amalgamating people into a mass, wrapped in an iron band of terror, which "holds them so tightly together that it is as though their plurality had disappeared into One Man of gigantic dimensions."[41] Arendt discovered, by the generalization of this experience, that the transformations of the human condition are possible when the hierarchy of human activities is turned upside down, or when some of them are abandoned and replaced with others.

Not all of these processes are connected immediately to totalitarianism. In *The Human Condition* Arendt develops an account of experiences that create prerequisites for a total annihilation of plurality. Such are the principles of being-together in contemporary societies, which are not based on action anymore, or even fabrication, but on labor and consumption, that is, on the principles of biological life. The public sphere disappears under the inflow of life and ceases to be a common place to be shared by people. That is why massification, by making the life process a political issue, and isolation of people are not contradictory. "What prepares men for totalitarian domination in the non-totalitarian world is the fact that loneliness [. . .] has become an everyday experience of the evergrowing masses of our century."[42] The society of workers is the most "worldless" form of humanity. The principle of a mass is not action or fabrication, but labor and accompanying consumption: a member of the masses is *animal laborans*. Within the perspective of biological life the plurality of people is only a numeric one.

Arendt protected politics, free action, from the philosophy of politics, which grasped action in the idiom of making, that is, described it in instrumental categories. But now, the model of public life is not the instrumental relations of preindustrial society, but the biological cycle of life, whose anthropological expression is labor. Totalitarian rule consists in leading this process to the extreme, avoided in the normal, mass society of laborers. But contemporary humanity, such is the lesson of history, is constantly endangered with a reduction to biological life, where people would be amalgamated into One.

II

Arendt's research on the nature of totalitarianism was focused on the problem of domination: The unprecedented nature of totalitarianism was based on the, inexistent in the earlier forms of government, thoroughness of the control over people. It was possible only by reducing people to their common denominator of biological life. In her way of thinking of power, Arendt had an unknown ally: Michel Foucault. As we will see, he was also a protagonist of the possibility of a new, post-Heideggerian description of the pedagogical promise of philosophy: Philosophical thinking, though understood not as traditional metaphysics, or, in Foucault's language, the official philosophical discourse, becomes a chance for resistance against power, especially a biopower.

The fundamental achievements of Foucault in the genealogy of power were worked out in the 1970s within the series of lectures at the Collège de France. The most interesting in our context is the problem of the relationship between power and the sphere of biology, the problem of biopolitics, which was developed soon after Arendt's death, in the years 1976–1978. The problem of biopolitics emerged for the first time in 1976 within the first volume of *The History of Sexuality*. Foucault shows there, how the scientific discourse of sexuality, gradually intensified since the eighteenth century, on the one hand generates the mechanisms of control over individuals (disciplinary power), and on the other, how within this discourse something new appears: a global discourse of the management of a population with control of the health of humankind at its center. This discourse "in the name of a biological and historical urgency, justified the racisms of the state, which at the time were on the horizon."[43] Toward the end of *Will to Know* (the title of the first volume of *The History of Sexuality*), Foucault generalizes his considerations in order to reveal a paradox of modern power, which will become his main theme in later years: power, constituted in the nineteenth century, whose purpose (contrary to the sovereign power to take life) is an amplification and enhancement of life, yet and leads to unprecedented genocide.

The historical mechanism of this paradox Foucault describes minutely in the series of lectures of 1976, *Society Must Be Defended*.[44] When depicting the basic assumptions of his methodology, Foucault underscores the need for attributing primacy to knowledge situated beyond "the tyranny of global discourses," knowledge disqualified, illegitimate, not fitting in the continuum of official knowledge, inscribed in the mechanisms of power and its disciplinary techniques. Indeed, Foucault searches history for precedence, invisible when traditional, philosophical-legal political categories are applied. The invisibility of precedence does not diminish its impact, in fact it intensifies it. That is why his lectures were constructed in accordance with the conviction, uttered a few years later, that "the history of various forms of rationality is sometimes more effective in unsettling our certitudes and dogmatism than is abstract criticism."[45] The stake of the lectures of 1976 was finding the moment in which by means of military discourse a genealogy of racism and power over life begins to emerge. Foucault finds the moment of a transition in understanding political matters in the seventeenth-century history of England and the seventeenth- and eighteenth-century history of France. It is a moment of a clash of two different types of historical discourse.

The official political-legal discourse, connected with sovereign power and the legitimacy of monarchy is for the first time challenged by a historical-political discourse, for which, for the first time, war, not law, will be the principle of rule. Official political-legal discourse was based on the linear history of sovereignty since Roman times and served for the legitimization of absolute monarchy. Its presuppositions were, first, the identification of the people with the sovereign, and second, the identification of truth with peace; this type of discourse regards war as a borderline event, sometimes unavoidable, but generally marginal for politics. The history of sovereign power begins with compromising the necessity of war and it was a history of brilliance and glory since Antiquity (the model of Livy). But, on the basis of the opposition of nobility against absolutism, a new reading of history appears (the biblical model), in which sovereign power is depicted not as a universal history of the progress of legitimate power, but a particular story of usurpation and intrigue, used by the king with the purpose of enslavement of the nation (nobility). This alternative, historical-political model, brings new content, alien to the official history of sovereignty.

First, it regards war as a primary power-relation and a paradigm of politics. It is an anticipation and an inversion of the famous Clausewitz statement of war being a continuation of politics by other means: Now it is politics that is the continuation of war by other means (Foucault asks: "Who had the idea of inverting Clausewitz's principle?"[46]). It is not war that is an extension of politics, but politics that is a form of war. War is an extension of social relations. Secondly, it connects with a radical tear in the subject of history. Since war is permanent, society has a bipolar structure. This means, thirdly, a foregoing of neutrality. Since there is no universal subject of history (as was the sovereign and the people in the discourse of sovereignty), history becomes a narration of one of the parties at war. In this way history polarizes and stratifies: The story of triumph of one group is challenged by the story of enslavement of another. Instead of a linear process of glory, we have a narration of misery and exclusion of the antecedents of one group; in other words, the Roman model is challenged by a biblical one. History narrated from the point of view of the excluded becomes a discourse of a demystification of the official power; at the same time it is a discourse of dissent. Along with this, lastly, the status of law undergoes a transition: It is not the basis of power and political relations anymore, but a secondary outcome of military actions and the domination of one group over another.

From our point of view, the most important here are two things. First of all, the political-historical discourse makes a radical cut within the homogenous political body: The response of the nobility to the absolute monarchy establishes "the nation" as a group (in this case the nobility) in juxtaposition to the "non-nation" of the sovereign and the people supporting him (this explains the hostility of the nobility to the third estate). Only in association with the political paradigm of war can the discourse of the war of races and classes emerge. Second, of relevance is the connection of these contrary histories with knowledge. The political-historical discourse will also be a discourse of dissent against the knowledge administered by the official discourse. It strives at a system of counter-knowledge, with an alternative history as well as an alternative to the royal economy and science of law. In this way the official, political-legal discourse, which "until then, had been inferior to the State's discourse about itself; its function was to demonstrate the State's right, to establish its sovereignty, to recount its uninterrupted genealogy, and to use heroes, exploits, and dynasties,"[47] is split.

Modern society begins to shape itself not in the very moment of the emergence of the oppositional discourse, but only when this discourse undergoes a generalization and is included in the discourse of official power, that is, in the moment when the opposition of power and counter-power, knowledge and counter-knowledge is transformed into a dialectical relationship. This process of transformation began, according to Foucault, in the eighteenth century, when state institutions tried to dominate knowledge (through archives and, later, universities). Thus, the counter-discursive practice of anti-monarchist reaction is generalized and statized. In other words, the counter-discourse of war is universalized and gradually swallowed by power. In this way, counter-knowledge is disciplined and begins to serve a description of a social conflict: Philology accounts for differences between peoples, while the political economy accounts for differences between classes; last, but not least, what is most relevant from our point of view, biology and medicine become official knowledge of man, grasped in racial categories.

The historical-political discourse, which emerged as an opposition against the bourgeoisie, was gradually tamed by it. Subsequently, the status of war changes and it ceases to be a principle of the intelligibility of social relations and becomes an element preserving society. In this moment we have an important transition, "a great retreat from the historical to the biological, from the constituent to the medical."[48] It is impossible to overestimate the meaning of this occurrence: The historical-political discourse of dissent becomes in the nineteenth century an official discourse, that is, a discourse of the bourgeoisie, but at the price of its biologization and medicalization; it begins to describe the conditions of the hygiene of a social organism. The bourgeoisie transforms the concept of nation and establishes its relationship with the state. The essence of the function and the historical role of a nation is not a domination over other nations anymore, but the "ability to administer itself, to manage, govern, and guarantee the constitution and workings of the figure of the State and of State power. Not domination, but State control."[49] As a result, the historical discourse becomes, paradoxically, a totalizing and statist discourse in which sovereignty regains its privileged position, but this time as sovereignty of the people or the nation.

In this way it turns out that modern society is a cross section of three different models of power. First, we have the model of sovereign power, reshaped into a democratic sovereignty (where the sovereign is a collective, not an individual). Second, we have the model of disciplinary power, initiated in the seventeenth and eighteenth centuries, as an economic organization of individual bodies (management, organization, and bureaucracy). Third, we have the historically newest, but in cooperation with the previous ones, model of systematic power over life, biopower. The extension of state power over life, not so much over an individual body, but as control over the life of the mass, when "the biological comes under State control," as Foucault put it,[50] is ultimately a product of the nineteenth century. This newest form of power, biological power, has something in common with disciplinary power: Both are based on a "natural" norm as defined by clinical knowledge and biological theory, while the model of sovereignty is based on a legal principle, where individuals are subjects of law. The fundamental difference lies in the modes of subjectivity. Whereas disciplinary power controls man as an individual, biopower refers to men as a biological species: the plurality addressed here is not the plurality of bodies, but that "they form, on the contrary, a global mass that is affected by overall processes characteristic of birth, death, production, illness, and so on."⁵¹ Biopower does not discipline individuals, but regulates the life process of a collective; its mechanism works not by taming individuals, but by securing the safety of the mass.

We are approaching the point where Foucault's analyses become very congenial with those of Arendt. Nazism, says Foucault, developed as a paroxysm of an amalgam of the three above-described forms of power: sovereignty combined with an extremely disciplined society (terror) on the one hand, and with extremely developed mechanisms of safety (regulation of the purity of race) on the other. Racism, inscribed in state mechanisms and connected with techniques of biopower lets us solve the paradox: power, whose purpose is securing life, regains the old sovereign legitimization to kill, this time in the name of life. "Once the state functions in the biopower mode, racism alone can justify the murderous function of the State."⁵² Racism brings about a cut in the biological continuum of power and, using the state, it leads to the "healing" of the race through killing: "The enemies that have to be done away with are not adversaries in the political sense of the term; they are threats, either external or internal, to the population and for the population"⁵³ (in Arendt: life unfit to live). The discourse of race struggle, which previously was a discourse of those stripped of power, is centralized and becomes a discourse of combat that has to be pursued in the name of the race and against those who endanger it (in this way it becomes a discourse of a society that must be defended from external dangers). Nazism was a monstrous combination of the sovereign power of killing, disciplinary techniques, and biopower, enhanced with the authority of "scientific" discourse (Arendt also underscored the "scientific" character of the "iron laws" of biology and history, underlying the newest ideologies).

The lecture course of 1978, titled *Security, Territory, Population*,⁵⁴ is, on the one hand, a development of the analyses of *Society Must Be Defended*, but on the other, opens up a new perspective. Foucault delivers a kind of definition of biopower, closely corresponding with Arendt's diagnosis: "A number of phenomena that seem to me to be quite significant, namely, the set of mechanisms through which the basic biological features of the human species became the object of a political strategy"⁵⁵ (while in Arendt it was: "Through society it is the life process itself which in one form or another has been channeled into the public realm";⁵⁶ and: "Society is the form in which the fact of mutual dependence for the sake of life and nothing else assumes public significance"⁵⁷). In these lectures Foucault goes deeper into a genealogy of biopower and at the same time approaches it from a wider perspective, which makes it penetrable in the history of the West. Here, the analysis shifts from the level of historical discourse to the level of political subjectivity. Foucault traces back the elements constituting the new collective subject of population. He reaches back to the precedence of the Christian pastorate, which "organized a type of power that I think was unknown to any other civilization."[58] Along with Christianity, a new model of politics emerges, the model of "pastoral power," where power is created as a result of a tension between the absolute responsibility of a shepherd for the salvation of the whole flock and every single sheep, and the precept of absolute obedience on the part of the members of the flock. It allows Foucault to derive the elements of biopower from pastoral power and to connect the genealogy of biopower with the emergence and development of Christianity, and ultimately, to connect these two things with the establishment of the modern state. On the level of the relations between power and knowledge, the most relevant turn out to be the economy and statistics. According to Foucault, the modern political economy emerged from the Christian *oikonomia psychon*, the economy of souls, a term used by Gregory of Nazianzus for pastoral techniques. The application of the term "economy" to the rule over souls shifts the connotation of the term from the private sphere of the household to the whole of humanity. It overturns the Aristotelian definition of the economy, which referred solely to the administration of a house (*oikos*, the private sphere of a household), and casts the administrative and managerial techniques into the public sphere. Arendt, in *The Human Condition*, traces the connection between modern society and the emergence of the political economy and comes to the analogical conclusion: "According to ancient thought on these matters, the very term 'political economy' would have been a contradiction in terms."[59] Although Arendt uses a different language than Foucault, in both thinkers the new forms of knowledge, related to modern scientific rationality, enable the new modes of rule: administration of masses (Arendt) or techniques of "governmentality" (governmental reason) for the safety of the population (Foucault). These new forms consist basically in the regulation of a human collective, that is, the foreseeing of natural phenomena and steering them. Thus, it is a reduction of this collective to nature, and the knowledge of humanity to natural science.

It is not my intention to downplay the differences in the accounts of Arendt and Foucault. They are the results of different methodologies and different points of departure. Whereas for Arendt, it is the essence of the political in relation to the human condition, for Foucault it is a problem of power, which determines understanding of humanity in a secondary way. And, certainly, the problem of the political and the problem of power are not the same. Whereas for Arendt, politics is basically independent from power, for Foucault, power functions primarily and independently from politics. Out of these two stances, different conceptions of humanity also emerge (if one can speak of "humanity" in Foucault at all[60]). Nonetheless, without underrating these oppositions, an astonishing affinity must be noticed: For both thinkers late modernity is a moment of an unprecedented inflow of life into politics. For both, Nazism and Communism are outcomes of an extreme radicalization of this process, which turned out to be destructive for both politics and life. For both, the realization of the newest form of power leads to a leveling of human plurality in the name of a homogeneous political body.

In the lectures analyzed above, we find the emancipatory intention as well as the potential of Foucault's thought. The phenomenological description of power in its "how" is aimed not so much at cognition as it is at a "rebellion of knowledge," "against the centralizing power-effects that are bound up with the institutionalization and workings of any scientific discourse."[61] This is an idea of a new approach to the role of philosophy, which could also become a pedagogical role, although far from the traditional meaning of pedagogy: "Maybe philosophy can still play a role on the side of counterpower, on condition that, in facing power, this role no longer consists in laying down the law of philosophy, on condition that philosophy stops thinking of itself as prophecy, pedagogy, or legislation."[62]

III

Giorgio Agamben, in the series titled *Homo Sacer*, took a step further by outlining the very up-to-date implications of Arendt's and Foucault's insights. Agamben undertakes considerations on the relationship between politics and biological life, initiated by Arendt and Foucault. In doing so, he turns Arendt's thesis upside down and radicalizes the meaning of precedence described by her. He maintains that it is not life that invaded politics but, rather, the other way round: It is politics that conquered life. Moreover, the concentration camp is not an extreme event of the past, which is always looming over humanity, but a paradigm, a blueprint of contemporary politics.

In order to characterize the modern relationship between politics and life, Agamben applies the figure of "sacred man," *homo sacer*, referring to an outlaw, stemming from Roman antiquity. The "sanctity of life" primarily referred to a situation where life is no longer protected by law and has a meaning contradictory to modern associations of life's protection. The possibility to become an outlaw is strictly correlated with the possibility of making an exception within the legal sphere, an attribute of sovereign power.[63] In this way the sovereign and *homo sacer* are, on the one hand, exact oppositions, but on the other, they have something in common. Both are situated in a spot, a "threshold": both are beyond the legal order and at the same time within it, although in different ways—the sovereign through his power to take life or not,[64] which makes him "the point of indistinction between violence and law";[65] "sacred man," because he can be killed without it being a crime (neither in terms of execution or sacrifice, which makes him an outcast from both law and the sacred). In this way the sovereign and *homo sacer* are on a threshold, between them the sphere of a normal legal order, for which they are exceptions, one by virtue of power of exclusion, the other by virtue of being excluded.

In Agamben's analysis, the most relevant is exactly this motif of a threshold, the dialectics of inclusion and exclusion, analyzed minutely in *Homo Sacer*. It is decisive because it enables the mode of life we encounter on the edges of the law, and which, according to him, is at the same time a fundamentally political category. On this border, on the threshold, we have to make do with "bare life," for Agamben a basic category of modern biopolitics. Exclusion and exception do not mean exemption from the political order and a return to a natural state. Bare life is not simply outside the legal or political order, it is at the same time within and beyond, a paradoxical relation between exception and rule. Neither the sovereign (bare power) nor *homo sacer* (bare life) are simply in a state of nature; indeed, they are in between nature and the political order in the classical meaning as a legal order. In this way the triad of the sovereign, state of exception, and bare life constitutes the primary political structure, the essence of politics. Only on this basis is "normal" politics founded with such concepts as action, contracts, citizenship. But this order can always be suspended and reduced to the primary political structure.

This is, outlined roughly, Agamben's qualification of Arendt and Foucault: "What characterizes modern politics is not so much the inclusion of *zoe* in the *polis*—which is, in itself, absolutely ancient—nor simply the fact that life as such becomes a principal object of the projections and calculations of State power."[66] Thus, for Agamben, it is not the inclusion of life into the political sphere that determines the power of precedence in modern history. What fuels this power is the extension of the fine line of the threshold into a sizeable territory, the colonization of bare life by politics, that is, the conditions of the state of exception which loses its exceptionality and becomes a rule: "The decisive fact is that, together with the process by which the exception everywhere becomes the rule, the realm of bare life—which is originally situated at the margins of the political order—gradually begins to coincide with the political realm."[67]

This leads Agamben to the provocative thesis of the concentration camp being a paradigm of modern politics (of course, in the structural, not historical sense). In this sense, the camp is a territory in which bare life becomes the basic political criterion. In this respect, modern democracies and totalitarianism, apart from all the flagrant differences, are based on a common premise: Both function in the space where the legal frameworks of the nation states were shattered, which made the exception state a norm of politics:

> And only because biological life and its needs had become the politically decisive fact is it possible to understand the otherwise incomprehensible rapidity with which twentieth-century parliamentary democracies were able to turn into

totalitarian states and with which this century's totalitarian states were able to be converted, almost without interruption, into parliamentary democracies.[68]

Arendt convincingly demonstrated, how so-called inalienable human rights all too easily turned out to be illusions in the moment of the demise of nation states. Along with nation states, the legal framework for establishment of human rights was shattered, these rights lost their legal basis and fell into a legal void.[69] In the situation where they were not accompanied by civil rights anymore, that is, in the situation, to translate it into Agamben's language, where they were to function in the sphere of bare life to protect it, they turned out to be empty abstracts. The twentieth century was a time when it came to light that when one was "simply a human being," as displaced persons and refugees, but not a citizen of a state, one dropped out of the social order and fell into "the space of this absolute impossibility of deciding between fact and law, rule and application, exception and rule."[70] This space, as a space of bare life, is potentially and structurally a camp, a sphere of biopower. It can take many different moral forms, from physical extermination to humanitarian aid, but in political terms, it always has a premise of being excluded from state law. The history of the twentieth century showed that people without a passport can always be gathered in a stadium, held in an airport, separated with wire, transported to another place, only by virtue of a sovereign decision, not limited by law, and that then anything can happen to them. The history of the twenty-first century has also shown that statelessness is not a limit for biopower. As Agamben puts it, in the contemporary political sphere, "we are all virtually *homines sacri*."[71] Our civil rights can always be suspended in the name of public safety. One does not have to find oneself in such an extreme situation as Guantanamo to experience this. It suffices to apply for a passport or visit an airport.

However, the strict connection of biopower with sovereignty leads to some theoretical difficulties. While certain forms of modern biopower can surely be associated with a sovereign decision (for instance, U.S. president George W. Bush's political actions after 2001[72]), when we consider humanitarian aid or medical control over bodies, pursued by physicians and scientists, the model of sovereignty loses its interpretative impact. How then could the sovereign source of the decision to switch off a patient's ventilator or using biometrical data to identify a citizen be identified? It seems to be the anonymous rule of nobody, so perceptively described by Arendt in Eichmann, or Foucauldian dispersed power, independent from a political decision par excellence, being an amalgam of administration, bureaucracy, and modern technology. Moreover, even when the model of sovereignty describes a source of power accurately, it turns out to be insufficient when it comes to the account of its mechanism (e.g., Hitler can be regarded as a sovereign by virtue of having suspended the constitution and introduced a state of emergency that became the rule and by identification of his order with law. But the rule of his administrators, like Eichmann, was often the complete opposite to sovereign power).

In *The Kingdom and the Glory*, Agamben extends his genealogy of bio-power and exceeds the strict model of sovereignty (and, in this way, frees himself, at least to some extent, from the common premises with Carl Schmitt). He undertakes and deepens the motif initiated by Foucault: the theological background for the "political economy." Agamben researches the theological context of the emergence of modern forms of power. Even on the level of theology, power turns out to have a non-homogenous character. It is the result of a tension within theology: pure theology as a description of the divine substance in the writings of Church Fathers supplemented with an account of a "political economy." The Greek concept of economy, which referred to managing households, gets through to theology as a metaphor with a rhetorical function. The "economy" in theology is not an accidental term, but comes along "with the attempt to articulate in a single semantic sphere [. . .] a series of levels whose reconciliation became problematic."[73] The concept of the economy in theology does not refer, like in Foucault, to pastoral power, but has a more fundamental basis: It refers to such a dimension in theology that does not analyze the very nature of God, but, rather, His heavenly and terrestrial activity. The Greek concept of economy, applied in theology, functions as a descriptive term for the double mechanism of divine influence: On the one hand, it describes the relationship between the Persons of the Trinity, allowing for an overcoming of dogmatic difficulties, particularly the unity and the multitude of the Persons of the Trinity (Trinitarian economy), and on the other, it describes divine intervention in the world (Providential economy). The function of the concept of economy consists not so much in the solving of the paradox, but in the adroit management of it: the combinations of God's transcendence with his interventions into the order of creation, monotheism with the plurality of divine Persons, and ontology with history, Providence with freedom. In an analogical way, the modern political economy defines a complicated circuit of power: both in the mutual relations of ruling subjects (king and government) and in the relations between authorities and the people.

Whereas political theology generates the political problem of sovereignty, theological economy is, according to Agamben, an original paradigm of modern administration. In this way the relations typical for *oikos*, the household, based on subordination and domination, become, through Christianity, a model of modern politics. By the same token, free action in the public sphere (*polis*) loses its primacy for the sake of life, dominant in the economic sphere. The conclusion of Agamben's analyses are compatible with Arendt's, who in *The Human Condition* pointed to a tendency, stemming from the Middle Ages, to model "all human relationships upon the example of the household"[74] and who wrote on modern society: "Society always demands that its members act as though they were members of one enormous family which has only one opinion and one interest."[75] Although the analysis from *The Kingdom* shifts on a theological context, leaving the problem of biopower in the background and as an indirect implication, from our point of view the most important is that along with the supplementation of the paradigm of sovereignty with the model of economic and administrative power, Agamben's thought opens up a way to overcome the impasse of *Homo Sacer*: Biopower ceases to be exclusively a function of sovereignty and begins to function in a bipolar political-administrative structure. The mechanisms of economy and management are extensions and complementations of sovereign decisions, constituting the precise machinery of modern power over life.

In the cogs of this machinery the human condition undergoes an irreversible transformation. In this way Agamben takes a step further than the outcomes of Foucault's and Arendt's analyses: The extreme form of bare life is not a human being reduced to an animal, but to merely vegetative functioning. That is why the paradigm of bare life—this is another of Agamben's provocations—is, equally, the existence of a camp "Muselmann" and the life of an unconscious patient, hooked up to machines: "Biopower's supreme ambition is to produce, in a human body, the absolute separation of the living being and the speaking being, *zoe* and *bios*, the inhuman and the human—survival."[76] *Homo sacer*, our potential being, also constitutes a space of indistinctiveness between individuals, where bare life floods our political identity. In this way *homo sacer* becomes a new and the most actual dimension of the human condition, apart from the forms described by Arendt (*animal laborans*, *homo faber*, *zoon politicon logon*). The contemporary political sphere, the space of the camp structure, is the exact opposite of political space in Arendt's understanding. Once again it turns out that in the conditions of modern politics we become one man, one body, one biological species, bare life.

We need to again face the question of the role of philosophy. If, as Agamben maintains, "there is no return from the camps to classical politics,"[77] it points to the critical impact of philosophical analysis. The meaning of the Agambenian critique is close to Foucault's; while Foucault is trying to enlarge the capacities of counter-power, Agamben's appeal is "ceaselessly to try to interrupt the working of the machine that is leading the West toward global civil war."[78] On the other hand, the role of their philosophies is very close to Arendt's plea for understanding as remembrance of what really happened: Philosophy (and literature) is a witness of what cannot speak for itself. At the end of the day, its role is existential: to save bare life from muteness and forgetfulness, to give it its voice back and secure its place in the narration.

CONCLUDING REMARKS

As we have seen, thinking in terms of the human condition is rather alien to Foucault, but the Herderian precedence gains an enormous power, even more than in Arendt. In turn, Agamben undertakes the problem of the human condition anew, while precedence and contingency are somehow weakened in his thought. At any rate, both thinkers, although in different ways, cherish the elements of the "educational principle": thinking of the human condition in pluralistic categories and with the weight of historical precedence. "Herder's figure" (not being a historical figure, but appearing where Arendt finds in the tradition an element of counterbalance for metaphysics and Heidegger's impact) supplements the great Heideggerian inspiration in Arendt, while at the same time creating a tension in her thought. The aim of this chapter was to demonstrate, how thinking in terms of the human condition, which undoubtedly stems from Heidegger, connects with other streams, alien to Heidegger, whose sources we found in Herder. Thinking in terms of understanding particular historical phenomena cannot be reconciled with thinking in terms of the history of being. The history of being has to be accounted for from a universal ontological perspective, whereas the Herderian understanding of the power of precedence undermines this perspective. In the above-analyzed authors, both perspectives are present, which means that they remained philosophers *par excellence*, that is, not having lost the ability to universalize and describe ontological frameworks of reality, they were capable of working out new philosophical methodologies that allowed them to minutely observe concrete events to start with, to begin with particularities and differences instead of universals and still not to limit themselves to the register of facts, but to use them as materials to understand reality. This endows their philosophies with a particular critical power.

Of course, the pedagogical scope of these authors is much wider than the interpretative path outlined here. In this work I limited myself to one motif only, the motif of biopolitics, in order to disclose a line that leads from Arendt to the newest philosophies. My goal was dual: firstly, sketching the path which, on the one hand, shows the ingenious actuality of Arendt, and on the other, opens up the possibility of a step further, beyond a strict attachment to her conceptual framework; secondly, I wanted to demonstrate (counter to Antonia Grunenberg) that the pedagogical role of philosophy is not only not completed along with metaphysics, but becomes more and more relevant. This relevance is different from the classical promise of philosophy as described in the first part of this book. For the pedagogical role of philosophy today is rather a function of critique than of constructing conceptual frameworks for education. While Heidegger's thought can be regarded as a border between metaphysical construction and critique, tradition and its break, Arendt, Foucault, and Agamben are on the side of discontinuity and critique.

Philosophy does not change reality. But if it is committed to its understanding, it fractures its solid structure, and this fracture can become a space of freedom, a space where pedagogy can feel at home. Thinking in the sense given by Arendt, thinking as an attempt at understanding the changing conditions of humanity (which, as we will see in the next chapter, can protect us from the banality of evil), Foucauldian philosophy, situated on the side of counter-power, the philosophical provocations of Agamben, are just a few out of a multitude of possibilities of creating the critical power of philosophy and a philosophy of education. All of them are connected with a Herderian postulate of preservation of human plurality, which played such a great role in Arendt, and which the (bio)political tendencies of the present constantly challenge.

In this sense the pedagogical promise of philosophy consists in the opening up of the possibilities of the critical philosophy of education rather than in delivering a positive framework for systematic pedagogical knowledge. The educational power of philosophy is based on the premise that even mere thinking about reality, inaccessible without concepts, is powerful. Not undermining the practical meaning of theory as an intervention into the world, the importance of working out the language of critique on the border between philosophy and education must be emphasized. In the last chapter, I will focus on demonstrating that thinking has an immanent educational and ethical power, even if it does not have an immediate impact on social reality.

NOTES

1. See SZ, 44–45; BT, 41–42.
2. HC, 11.
3. HC, 11 (footnote).
4. Julia Kristeva, *Hannah Arendt*, trans. Ross Guberman (New York: Columbia University Press, 2001), 186.
5. Aaron Schutz, "Theory as Performative Pedagogy: Three Masks of Hannah Arendt," *Educational Theory*, 2, no. 51 (2001): 127.
6. Young-Bruehl, *Hannah Arendt*, 94.
7. Arendt's interest in Herder was revealed in 1931 on the occasion of reviewing Hans Weil's, *Die Entstehung des deutschen Bildungsprinzips* for *Archiv für Sozialwissenschaft und Sozialpolitik*; see Hannah Arendt, "Review of Hans Weil, The Emergence of the German Principle of Bildung," in Hannah Arendt, *Reflections on Literature and Culture*, ed. Susannah Young-ah Gottlieb (Palo Alto, CA: Stanford University Press, 2007), 24–31.
8. Johann Gottfried Herder, *Outlines of the Philosophy of the History of Man*, trans. T. Churchill (New York: Bergman Publishers, 1800), 226.

9. Hannah Arendt, "On the Nature of Totalitarianism," in *Essays in Understanding*, 360.

10. Johann Gottfried Herder, "Treatise on the Origin of Language," in Johann Gottfried Herder, *Philosophical Writings*, trans. Michael N. Forster (New York: Cambridge University Press, 2002), 146.

11. Johann Gottlfried Herder, "Another Philosophy of History for the Education of Mankind," in Johann Gottfried Herder, *Another Philosophy of History and Selected Political Writings*, trans. Ioannis D. Evrigenis and Daniel Pellerin (Indianapolis: Hackett Publishing Company, 2004), 50.

12. Herder, *Outlines of the Philosophy*, 225.

13. Johann Gottfried Herder, *Briefe zur Beförderung der Humanität*, in Johann Gottfried Herder, *Werke in fünf Bänden*, Band 5 (Berlin und Weimar: Aufbau Verlag, 1959), 93.

14. Herder, "Treatise on the Origin of Language," 96.
15. Herder, "Treatise on the Origin of Language," 97.
16. Herder, "Treatise on the Origin of Language," 87.
17. Herder, "Treatise on the Origin of Language," 132.
18. Herder, "Another Philosophy of History," 23.
19. Herder, "Another Philosophy of History," 28.
20. See, Herder, "Another Philosophy of History," 39–45.
21. Herder, *Outlines of the Philosophy*, 226.
22. Herder, *Outlines of the Philosophy*, 226.
23. Arendt, "The Enlightenment and the Jewish Question," in Arendt, *Jewish Writings*, 12.
24. Arendt, "Review of Hans Weil," 27.
25. Arendt, "Review of Hans Weil," 27.
26. Herder, *Outlines of the Philosophy*, 227.
27. Herder, "Another Philosophy of History," 53.
28. Arendt, "The Enlightenment and the Jewish Question," 13.
29. Heidegger, "The Rectorate 1933/34," 485.
30. Arendt, *The Origins*, 317.
31. Arendt, *The Origins*, 353.
32. Arendt, *The Origins*, 361.
33. Arendt, *The Origins*, 392.
34. Arendt, *The Origins*, 392.
35. Arendt, *The Origins*, 434.
36. Arendt, *The Origins*, 438.
37. Arendt, *The Origins*, 445.
38. Arendt, *The Origins*, 456.
39. Arendt, *The Origins*, 457.
40. Arendt, *The Origins*, 459.
41. Arendt, *The Origins*, 465–66.
42. Arendt, *The Origins*, 478.
43. Michel Foucault, *The History of Sexuality*, vol. 1, trans. Robert Hurley (New York: Pantheon Books, 1978), 54.

44. Michel Foucault, *Society Must Be Defended*, Lectures at the Collège de France 1975–1976, trans. David Macey (New York: Picador, 2003).

45. Michel Foucault, *Omnes et Singulatium: Towards a Criticism of 'Political Reason'*, 253, https://tannerlectures.utah.edu/_documents/a-to-z/f/foucault81.pdf.

46. Foucault, *Society Must Be Defended*, 47.

47. Foucault, *Society Must Be Defended*, 139.

48. Foucault, *Society Must Be Defended*, 216.

49. Foucault, *Society Must Be Defended*, 223.

50. Foucault, *Society Must Be Defended*, 239.

51. Foucault, *Society Must Be Defended*, 242–43.

52. Foucault, *Society Must Be Defended*, 256.

53. Foucault, *Society Must Be Defended*, 256.

54. Michel Foucault, *Security, Territory, Population*, Lectures at the Collège de France, 1977–1978, trans. Graham Burchell (New York: Pelgrave, 2007).

55. Foucault, *Security, Territory, Population*, 16.

56. HC, 45.

57. HC, 46.

58. Foucault, *Security, Territory, Population*, 174.

59. HC, 29.

60. Obviously, strictly speaking, one cannot. Man in Foucault is not a primary phenomenon, or a universal point of departure from philosophy (like it is in Arendt). Man is a secondary reality, emerging out of the knowledge/power knot. In this sense, on the basis of the archaeology of knowledge, man is an outcome of eighteenth-century episteme of humanities, on the basis of the genealogy of power, it is a relation coming out of the mechanisms of power and the discourses attached to them (such as the subject of the king or an individual subordinated to discipline).

61. Foucault, *Society Must Be Defended*, 9.

62. Michel Foucault, "La philosophie analytique du povoir," in *Dits et écrits*, vol. 3, eds. Daniel Defert and François Ewald (Paris: Gallimard, 1994), 540. As cited in Michael Senellart, "Course Context," in Foucault, *Security, Territory, Population*, 484.

63. According to the famous definition of Carl Schmitt: "Sovereign is the one who decides on exception." Carl Schmitt, *Political Theology: Four Chapters on the Concept of Sovereignty*, trans. George Schwah (Chicago: The University of Chicago Press, 2005), 5.

64. This is, in turn, Foucault's definition of sovereignty, see *Society Must Be Defended*, 241.

65. Giorgio Agamben, *Homo Sacer: Sovereign Power and Bare Life*, trans. Daniel Heller-Roazen (Palo Alto, CA: Stanford University Press, 1998), 25.

66. Agamben, *Homo Sacer*, 12.

67. Agamben, *Homo Sacer*, 12.

68. Agamben, *Homo Sacer*, 72.

69. See Arendt, *The Origins*, 290–302.

70. Agamben, *Homo Sacer*, 98.

71. Agamben, *Homo Sacer*, 68.

72. See Giorgio Agamben, *State of Exception*, trans. Kevin Attell (Chicago: The University of Chicago Press, 2005), 3–4.

73. Giorgio Agamben, *The Kingdom and the Glory. For a Theological Genealogy of Economy and Government (Homo sacer I, 2)*, trans. Lorenzo Chiesa and Matteo Mandarini (Palo Alto, CA: Stanford University Press, 2011), 51.

74. HC, 35.

75. HC, 39.

76. Giorgio Agamben, *Remnants of Auschwitz: The Witness and the Archive*, trans. Daniel Heller-Roazen (New York: Zone Books, 1999), 156.

77. Agamben, *Homo Sacer*, 105.

78. Agamben, *State of Exception*, 87.

Chapter 8

The Promise of Thinking

"I have come back to philosophy, a little," wrote Arendt in 1970 to Joachim Fest.[1] This statement contrasts with the vehement protest Arendt uttered six years earlier (1964) in a television interview with Günter Gaus, when he addressed her as a philosopher: "I have said good-bye to philosophy once and for all."[2] In this context the later statement sounds a little guilt-ridden or, at least, as if owning up to an inconsistency. The reasons why Arendt, up to the last years of her life, did not want to be considered a philosopher are clear and have already been described in this book. On the theoretical level it is the inability of philosophy to give an adequate account of human affairs, like human plurality and action, and a stubborn negation by philosophers of the specifics of the political and public spheres. On the biographical level it is strictly connected with her disappointment with the political demeanor of Heidegger. It is the latter that led Arendt to a belief that philosophical thinking, even of the highest quality, not only does not protect us from committing grave political mistakes, but even facilitates them by a *deformation professionelle*, the weakness of philosophers for "tyrants and Führers,"[3] resulting from the fact that the true philosopher dwells in the "kingdom of thought," a place too far away from human affairs to provide the opportunity of clear insight.

In Arendt's view, between philosophy and politics we have a tension, as there is a tension between thinking and action. This explains why Arendt after World War II consistently denied being a philosopher and claimed to be rather a representative of "political theory." She did not want to consider human affairs from the heights of theoretical contemplation, or from a point of view of the truth of being. She wrote books which, in different proportions, were historical analyses, sociology, political science, and which were shaped in various forms from *feuilleton* through scientific dissertation up to reportage. Nonetheless, Gaus' obstinacy in addressing Arendt as a philosopher is for Arendt's reader understandable. Political, historical, or sociological analyses function in her like masks: beginning with *The Origins of Totalitarianism* and ending with *Willing* we cannot find a book by Arendt which does not have a deeply philosophical character. Philosophy, so to say, always emerges from under other layers. Even when Arendt describes political or historical events, they are never left as they are; they always refer to more general insights, anthropological and ontological.

It was Heidegger, otherwise never a very diligent reader of Arendt, who emphasized this in one of his letters: "I think that, despite your numerous publications directed elsewhere, you have also always remained in philosophy."[4] Arendt's fascination with philosophy has something tragic about it. Great love of philosophy ("I can either study philosophy or I can drown myself"—Arendt said recalling her youthful attitude to philosophy[5]), magnified by love for a philosopher, are interrupted by fate and history. Both philosophy and the philosopher turn out to be helpless against events. Arendt desires to understand what really happened and knows that classically practiced philosophy will be of no help (let alone that for some time she lost the life conditions for such practice). Thus, she looks for other rules of description. This is why her books do not much resemble academic research written according to rules of German universities. But her love of philosophy, against Arendt's own declarations, would always express itself, sometimes in different disguises. Toward the end of her life, Arendt, eventually, dropped the mystification and admitted returning to her old love, from which she, in truth, never departed.

This comeback means that Arendt deals with a theme whose pure philosophical character cannot be masked (or, perhaps it could, as psychology, but Arendt preferred a "return to philosophy" over becoming a psychologist), namely with the problems of thinking, willing, and judging, in *The Life of the Mind*. Her intellectual biography came full circle in this way. The return to philosophy however, was by no means a return to metaphysics. Arendt drew conclusions from her diagnosis of the end of tradition: "I have clearly joined the ranks of those who for some time now have been attempting to dismantle metaphysics [. . .]. Such dismantling is possible only on the assumption that the thread of tradition is broken and that we shall not be able to renew it [. . .]. What you then are left with is still the past, but a *fragmented* past, which has lost its certainty of evaluation."[6] In the ruins of tradition she sought exactly these fragments, which facilitated her attempt to deliver an answer for the question "What is called thinking?," and discern the activity of thinking from the discipline of "professional thinkers." Nevertheless, if we desire to understand the reasons why Arendt toward the end of her life returned to Ithaca, a place of thinking, and what's more, strived at a description of this place, we cannot limit our analysis to the paradox of Heidegger. For the problem of thinking attacked Arendt from a different direction: the discovery of the connection between non-thinking and the banality of evil.

THE SCANDAL OF NON-THINKING

The famous, controversial thesis of the banality of evil, formulated in the report on Eichmann's trial, was a retort on a widespread tendency to mythologize the crime and the criminal. One wanted to see in Eichmann a monster, a man stripped of conscience, the embodiment of dark powers. It happened also in the legal context. Gideon Hausner, the attorney general of Israel, pointed at Eichmann, sitting in a bulletproof cabin, with an accusatory finger and said: "And there sits the monster responsible for all this."[7] Arendt herself did not expect to see a monster, but awaited a figure with a demonic trait of the "great" criminal from the past. Instead, what she saw was a mediocre figure with a runny nose, a functionary in a suit, a hundred of whom one sees daily in offices and city streets. Eichmann's looks and his demeanor, not betraying any demonic features, in a sense completely "normal," were in flagrant contrast with the vastness of his crimes (which, by the way, Arendt never denied; on the contrary, she claimed that banal evil can be extreme). Arendt's diagnosis, that "it was sheer thoughtlessness [. . .] that predisposed him to become one of the greatest criminals of that period,"[8] was a solution to this paradox. It was so disturbing that many years had to pass before outrage made place for the will to understand her analysis of the nature of evil.

For us the most important now is the question of what it means that Eichmann did not think. It will lead us to a more general problem: What is thinking for Arendt and how is it connected with morality.

The best testimony of what Arendt had in mind when speaking of Eichmann's thoughtlessness was delivered by himself during the trial when he described his feelings accompanying the end of war and the demise of the Third Reich: "I would have to live a leaderless and difficult individual life, I would receive no directives from anybody, no orders and commands would any longer be issued to me, no pertinent ordinances would be there to consult."[9] What in any other context would be read as an ironic expression of relief, was uttered with deadly seriousness. Eichmann's identity, from early youth shaped by membership of an organization (YMCA, Wandervogel, masonry, and eventually the SS), fell apart when an organizing structure vanished. The ideological content represented by an organization was of secondary importance: it did not really matter whether it was a Christian organization, freemasonry, or the Nazis. The structure and the clear rules of conduct of an organization imposed on its members turned out to be more important than the ideology offered. Eichmann did not have to manifest a pathological hatred toward Jews with fanatic anti-Semitism in order to play a prominent role in the organization of the extermination of Jews. Moreover, he did not seem to be completely stripped of conscience, but his conscience functioned in a specific mode: indeed, he recoiled at the extermination (at least when it came to German Jews), but only up to the moment when during the Wannsee conference he saw that the project of the Final Solution met with the full acceptance not only of the Reich's leaders, but also the SS-men of ranks higher than Eichmann himself: "At that moment, I sensed a kind of Pontius Pilate feeling, for I felt free of all guilt."[10] Eichmann, and here was the main problem, did not feel entitled "to have [his] own thoughts in this matter."[11] Thus, he not so much lost his conscience, but placed it within the organization and it would torment him had he failed in his duties connected with his function. His conscience, which up to 1942 spoke with the traditional Christian voice of "thou shall not kill," astonishingly easily and quickly started to speak with the voice of Himmler and Heydrich, uttering the exact opposite order. With a similar ease he accepted the new role of being the main war criminal during the trial: "He knew that what he had once considered his duty was now called a crime, and he accepted this new code of judgment as though it were nothing but another language rule."[12]

Language is a clue to the second issue. Eichmann's inability to think is, according to Arendt, strictly connected with his inability to speak. Arendt comments on the interrogations during the investigation as "Eichmann's heroic fight with the German language, which invariably defeats him."[13] Eichmann's inability to speak, in Arendt's view, not a symptom of standard incapacity or lack of intelligence, was compensated by him with a set of ready stock phrases, fixed expressions, and slogans he could use regardless of the circumstances as banisters any time his language failed him: "Officialese [Amtsprache] is my only language"[14]—said Eichmann quite earnestly. Indeed, in the organizational structure which completely protected him against reality, he did not need any other language. Accused of genocide, he simply accepted new language rules. But because he was unable to think them over, he was unable to work out a new individual language and remained by the idiom of "officialese." Arendt describes a situation that illustrates it excellently:

> When Captain Less asked his opinion on some damning and possibly lying evidence given by a former colonel of the S.S., he exclaimed, suddenly stuttering with rage: "I am very much surprised that this man could ever have been an S.S. *Standartenführer*, that surprises me very much indeed. It is altogether, altogether unthinkable. I don't know what to say." He never said these things in the spirit of defiance, as though he wanted, even now, to defend the standards by which he had lived in the past. The very words "S.S.," or "career,"

or "Himmler" [. . .] triggered in him a mechanism that had become completely unalterable. The presence of Captain Less, a Jew from Germany and unlikely in any case to think that members of the S.S. advanced in their careers through the exercise of high moral qualities, did not for a moment throw this mechanism out of gear.[15]

Thus, what exactly does Arendt accuse Eichmann of when she speaks of his inability to think? From the above characteristics two problems emerge which will later be crucial for the phenomenon of thinking in Arendt: First, Eichmann's identity, based on an organizational structure and hierarchy, indicates an inability to to interrogate oneself, to engage in an inner dialogue which enables us to think over what happens and, on the basis of these considerations, come to an aesthetic or moral judgment. Arendt's thesis would be as follows: had Eichmann been able to engage in such an inner dialogue, the mechanism of acquisition of subsequent sets of organizational rules would have been unsettled. A traditional moral code confronted by an order to kill should have at least elicited an inner conflict. The excellent efficiency of Eichmann in the organization of the mass crime relied on the complete unity of his person: no considerations impaired his great bureaucratic task.

Secondly, the case of "officialese" indicates another aspect of non-thinking. Eichmann was not only unable to engage in an inner dialogue, he was also incapable of acquiring, even for a moment, the perspective of another human being (e.g., Captain Less), of looking on matters from a different point of view, of imaginatively departing from his place in the world. In other words, he was unable to step back from reality, which is a condition of understanding and judging events. Eichmann could see the world from one perspective only, which let him remain in perfect harmony with reality, no matter what happened. However paradoxically it might sound, it was this perfect personal unity and ideal harmony with the external world (as it appeared to him) that made him an excellent cog in the Nazi apparatus of power. This inability to engage in an inner dialogue and to see the world from any perspective other than his own, by no means the same thing, was complementary and in Arendt's eyes constituted "outrageous stupidity," the inability to think with horrible consequences. The problem consisted in the fact that Eichmann, although an extreme case, was not an isolated one: The "German society of eighty million people had been shielded against reality and factuality by exactly the same means"[16]—says Arendt. Regardless of the fact that this statement is certainly touched with exaggeration (not uncommon in Arendt), one thing remains disturbing: Eichmann was a caricature, but he reflected and augmented features of "respectable society" in which it was only a marginal minority "who were fully aware of the fact that their own shocked reaction was no longer shared by their neighbors."[17]

But how to deal with the problematic fact that the greatest twentieth-century German philosopher, who brilliantly described the mechanisms of an anonymous "the they," himself had fallen prey to these mechanisms and, at least for a time, suffered from the same paralysis of thinking and judging? How someone, of whom Arendt said thought passionately, the extreme opposite of the thoughtless and mute Eichmann, could have become a member of that "respectable society" of Eichmanns on a smaller scale? How come, as Dana Villa put it, "the two extremes of Eichmann's extraordinary shallowness and Heidegger's extraordinary thinking meet at this zero point"?[18] In chapter 4 I tried to describe two things independently: the real reasons of how it could have happened and the way Arendt intellectually dealt with this problem. As we remember, according to her, Heidegger's mistake did not stem from thoughtlessness but from his philosophical detachment from human affairs, which resembled Plato's mistake. Arendt saved Heidegger's reputation at the price of inconsistency: she inscribed him into the traditional conflict between philosophy and politics, as started by Plato, although she basically regarded Heidegger as the philosopher who ended the philosophical tradition and opened up new paths of thinking. But Arendt's answer to Heidegger's paradox, insufficient as it is, lets us understand why she, when looking for paradigms of thinking, a counterbalance to Eichmann's thoughtlessness, could not rely solely on Heidegger's authority, but found her points of reference in Socrates and Kant. Thus, if we want to understand the problem of thinking in Arendt, we need to return to the problem of the difference between philosophy and thinking, or, to the question of different modes of thinking.

WHAT IS CALLED THINKING?

In order to answer this question, we need to look closely at three figures who in Arendt's eyes were living hypostases of thinking, each in his own mode: Heidegger, Socrates and Kant.

I

Although the political commitment of Heidegger cannot be regarded solely in the context of the classical, Platonic mistake, it seems that in the question of thinking Heidegger shows more affinity with the Platonic ideal of contemplation than he himself would have been ready to admit: "There are, then, two kinds of thinking, each justified and needed in its own way: calculative thinking and meditative thinking."[19] When "later" Heidegger is trying to characterize the essence of thinking, he always does so in opposition to "calculative thinking" or "calculative-representational thinking." Calculative-representational thinking is the only kind of thinking known to the West since Plato. It is also a principle of the two major realms of the Western world: philosophy (metaphysics) and science, being the consequence of metaphysics. Metaphysics began, according to Heidegger, along with Plato, who identified truth with the presence of *idea* and launched forgetting truth as *aletheia*. It was Plato who made the first step toward the correspondence theory of truth underlying metaphysics and science. It came to its full appearance and at the same time ended with Nietzsche's will to power and his "reversal of Platonism." Heidegger's earlier deconstructional works exposed this tradition as a "metaphysics of objective presence," which enabled modern philosophy to objectify entities. The end of metaphysics does not mean the end of its essence: it is fulfilled in modern science and technology. Calculative thinking in science is an implication of metaphysical representational thinking: "The end of philosophy proves to be the triumph of the manipulable arrangement of a scientific-technological world and so of the social order proper to this world."[20]

Thus, philosophy since Plato had forgotten about thinking of being, and identified it with the objective (timeless) presence of entities. Science takes advantage of this objectification and additionally calculates entities and subjects them to technological processing. Western philosophy and technology stem from one root: it is the forgetfulness of being, forgetfulness of the truth as *aletheia*, forgetfulness of thinking which does not re-present, en-frame, and calculate, which does not work at the service of enframing and will-to-power. Therefore, the famous dictum of Heidegger: "science itself does not think,"[21] refers also to metaphysics, although Heidegger puts it mildly: "Philosophy knows nothing of the clearing."[22]

That is why Heidegger sought traces of non-calculative thinking beyond the Western intellectual tradition, beyond science and beyond philosophy. He sought "a *first* possibility of thinking"[23] that can be neither metaphysics nor science. The testimonies of this "first possibility" are in thinkers beyond the influence of the Western intellectual tradition: the Pre-Socratics and poets. It is they who bestowed us with traces of thinking of being. In other words, Heidegger strives at returning to true thinking from before the era of calculative thinking launched by Plato, that is, before the intellectual act of expelling poets from the ideal *polis*.

In *What Is Called Thinking?* Heidegger detects these testimonies in Hölderlin and Parmenides. With the quote of Hölderlin (*We are a sign that is not read*) Heidegger tries to grasp the elusive and evasive character of thinking: "As he [man] draws toward what withdraws [thinking], man is a sign. But since this sign points toward what draws away, it points not so much at what draws away as into the withdrawal. The sign stays without interpretation."[24] Man is haunted by thinking even when he does not think, it is he who opens access to being. Nevertheless, Heidegger never shows the factual boundary between thinking and poetry. This knowledge is restricted to those who already think and Heidegger states authoritatively: "we are still not thinking."[25] "But the question to what end and with what right, upon what ground and within what limits our attempt to think allows itself to get involved in a dialogue with poesy, let alone with the poetry of this poet—this question, which is inescapable, we can discuss only after we ourselves have taken the path of thinking."[26] Since we do not think yet, we are not entitled to demand an answer to the question of the bond between thinking and poetry, *noesis* and *poiesis*. It is knowledge restricted to the initiated. That is why Heidegger de facto does not analyze Hölderlin, but uses Hölderlin's line now and again like a chorus.

An excerpt from Parmenides: *It is necessary to say and to think Being (for there is Being, but nothing is not)* functions differently. Here Heidegger analyzes the sentence thoroughly, tracking back the original meanings of the words and recovering sense from the traditional interpretations. He shows the dynamics of the formula "being is" referring to the ontological difference; he demonstrates the relationship between thinking and speaking, and the identity between thinking and being. He shows how philosophy from Plato to Kant is actually a reformulation of Parmenides' saying. But doing so, he comes back to the traditional themes of his earlier philosophy: the ontological difference and the deconstruction of metaphysics. But the basic question of thinking of being beyond the tradition of thought remains unanswered.

And here, I believe, is the problem of the Heideggerian description: as long as he is trying to say negatively what thinking *is not*, he delivers controversial, yet very interesting insights into science, technology, and philosophy ("Thinking does not bring knowledge as do the sciences; Thinking does not produce usable practical wisdom; Thinking solves no cosmic riddles; Thinking does not endow us directly with the power to act"[27]). The problem with Heidegger's description begins when Heidegger tries to say positively what thinking *is*. Then, instead of a description of a phenomenon, we encounter sentences like these: "Only when we are so inclined toward what in itself is to be thought about, only then are we capable of thinking." Or: "Whenever man is properly drawing that way, he is thinking"; Thinking is "the essential telling";[28] Reflection "is calm, self-possessed surrender to that which is worthy of questioning";[29] "Socrates did nothing else than place himself into this draft, this current, and maintain himself in it."[30]

Looking for thinking outside the borders of the accessible intellectual world brings about the result that thinking has to be condemned to the elusiveness of being, which has no support in concrete reality any more. If we want to learn from Heidegger what is called thinking, we get the best answer not when he is trying to grasp thinking itself, but when he testifies to his own thinking: in the analyses of understanding of Being in philosophy and metaphysics. But when Heidegger is trying to escape from philosophy and detach thinking from the familiar world of thought, then the description of thinking turns into incantations. It is not accidental, that in these contexts thinking relapses into mystical-religious language. In this way Heidegger avoids the positive question (later put by Arendt) of the meaning of thinking for our lives, replacing it with the question of the mysterious and elusive power we need to obey: "What calls on us to think?"[31] Thinking, along with being, is detached from human experience and the human world.

Heidegger had good reasons to try to overcome the modern philosophy of subjectivity. Already in *Being and Time*, where the phenomenon of the transcendental self is still present, *Dasein*'s identity is situated not in the subject, but in the relation with the world and temporality, which decentralizes subjectivity. In later Heidegger, this tendency radicalizes itself, which is also understandable when we take into account that Heidegger's agenda was to overcome the solipsism and transcendentalism of his early work. But when trying to overcome the modern philosophy of subject, Heidegger dissolved the phenomenon of self in impersonal powers: it is not *me* who speaks, it is language that speaks through me, it is not *me* who thinks Being, it is Being that thinks *me*. By abolishing the intentionality of thinking, Heidegger wanted to abolish the last residue of modern subjectivity in phenomenology. However, he managed to do this at a certain price: along with shifting thinking beyond the boundaries of the self, he abolished the conscious responsibility for thinking. Thinking that we do not think, but that thinks *us*, becomes at the same time very elitist: "The involvement with thought is in itself a rare thing, reserved for few people."[32] From the point of view of the meaning of thinking for human beings and the world, Heidegger's alternative turns out to be problematic: Either I am called for thinking or I am not, either I am in the clearing or I am not. Being appears in thinking as an epiphany.

It seems that classifying Heidegger as a Platonic philosopher is, paradoxically, more to the point when Heidegger departs from the philosophical tradition and turns to "true" thinking beyond that tradition. Heidegger, interpreting Western thought hermeneutically and phenomenologically, is at the same time within this tradition and beyond it. His deconstructive work, such as searching for different modes of understanding Being, unconsciously acquired by the Western tradition, is a dynamic struggle, a dialogue and a feud with the giants of this tradition. It is a never-ending movement of thought, which finds support in the concreteness of the analyzed text. But in the moment when Heidegger, after the so-called turn, tries to move thinking out beyond the struggles with the tradition, this movement, so to say, congeals in contemplation.

Certain confirmation of such an interpretation can also be found in Arendt: Heidegger, when trying to locate the meaning of the word "thinking," refers to, according to his customary method, etymology: he connects thinking (*Denken*) with thanking (*Danken*).[33] Arendt, in *Thinking*, shows this connection to be an echo of Plato's situation of the origin of philosophy in wondering: The Heideggerian thinking as thanking is "closer to Plato's wondering admiration than any of the answers discussed."[34] Heidegger himself, in his early Marburg lectures, maintained that the goal of thinking, pursued in dialogue, is simply seeing. Plato, according to him, failed in overcoming dialectics and did not reach this seeing.[35] The Heideggerian gesture of turning to Being itself can be interpreted as an attempt at overcoming Platonic dialectics toward contemplation. In this sense, Heidegger's struggles with tradition can be read as a moment of *dialegesthai*, leading to *noein*. But the problem with sheer contemplation is that—contrary to dialectics—it is incommunicable. That is why Heidegger, who earlier delivered many testimonies of discursive thinking, when describing contemplation, has to refer to quasi-religious terms.

Philosophical contemplation, being a privilege of few chosen people, is not what interested Arendt the most. Arendt was not fascinated with the religious, contemplative dimension of thinking (or, she was, but only in a negative sense, insofar as philosophers tried to apply the results of contemplation in the *polis*). She was interested mostly in thinking "from this world," thinking as a phenomenon of everydayness. Therefore, she tried to answer the questions of the experience of thinking: How is it related to the world of appearances? What is its role in our lives? How is it connected to action? What makes us think? What are the effects of non-thinking? She did not look into thinking for the moment of release (*Gelassenheit*) from reality, but a way to find a place in this world, such as it is, even if we "wish it were other than it is."[36] That is why the Heideggerian answer for the question, what is called thinking, had to be insufficient for Arendt. In order to describe thinking as a phenomenon connected with human affairs, Arendt referred to those for whom thinking was not a festivity of initiation for the chosen ones, but an acute problem of the everyday life of each human being: Socrates and Kant.

II

Arendt valued Socrates' testimony of what thinking is because Socrates embodied a combination of two features: he spent his life on thinking, but he was not a "professional philosopher": "The question, when asked by the professional, does not arise out of his own experiences while engaged in thinking."[37] In order to describe thinking, one has to put aside philosophical doctrines and gain an insight into the experience of thinking itself. In the first chapter of this book, devoted to Plato, I showed the different ways in which, according to Arendt, Plato and Socrates related themselves to politics. While Plato tried to work out the transcendent philosophical standards to be imposed on the world of the *polis*, Socrates only desired conversations with his fellow-citizens, which would help them in finding out whether they knew what they were talking about when using words like "justice," "courage," or "friendship." These dialogues were not aimed at final definitions of these concepts. The specific inconclusiveness of the Socratic dialogues, in contrast with the ultimate solutions given by Plato, indicates a crucial feature of thinking which Arendt discovered in Socrates.

When trying to account for thinking, Socrates used the metaphor of wind. As we remember, in Arendt's view, Socrates believed that a mere conversation on what is good and just, can make people better, even (or, perhaps, especially) if it is not crowned with knowledge of good and justice. The invisible wind of thought airs out our concepts and intellectual habits and sets them in motion. This motion never stops: "The trouble is that this same wind, whenever it is roused, has the peculiarity of doing away with its own previous manifestations."[38] Since we cannot reach the tangible and ultimate results in thinking, once one has started to think, he will have to think again and again. Whoever once sets in motion stable customs and rules, is stripped of "frozen thoughts": "These frozen thoughts, Socrates seems to say, come so handily that you can use them in your sleep."[39] Whoever once wakes up, will never sleep peacefully again. Otherwise he would be prone to act like Alcibiades and Critias, who "changed the non-results of the Socratic thinking examination into negative results."[40] In thinking there is indeed certain danger: whoever starts to think, but does not release himself from "the desire to find results that would make further thinking unnecessary,"[41] will be tempted to satisfy himself with the destruction of inherited concepts. In this way conventionalism is replaced by nihilism, but both have one common feature, that is, they emerge from a reluctance to think. The danger of thinking does not originate in the destructive power of thought (as most conservatives seem to believe), but in the desire to make thinking redundant. The difficulty of Socrates' way is that once we enter it, once we start to think, we have to do it for the rest of our life. "The need to think can be satisfied only through thinking, and the thoughts which I had yesterday will satisfy this need today only to the extent that I can think them anew."[42] Thinking is like Penelope's veil: "it undoes every morning what it had finished the night before."[43] Thinking as the wind and as Penelope's veil—these two metaphors describe one of the most important features of thinking, which Arendt found in Socrates: one cannot expect tangible results, moral codes, directions for action. Whoever starts truly to think, will have to start again and again. This leads us to the second important feature of Socrates' thinking.

In the testimony of the role of thinking for Socrates, Arendt found in one of his statements from Plato's *Gorgias*: "It would be better for me that my lyre or a chorus I directed should be out of tune and loud with discord, and that multitudes of men should disagree with me rather than I, *being one*, should be out of harmony with myself and contradict me" (482c).[44] From the point of view of the world, when we are with others, out identity is intact: "Certainly when I appear and am seen by others, I am one; otherwise I would be unrecognizable."[45] The withdrawal from the world of appearances, from being-with-others, which always precedes thinking, actualizes a difference in the identity of an individual. Only when I am with myself, can I be my own interlocutor. The inner, silent dialogue splits the monolithic identity of the self and makes it dual: me and myself. Between me and myself (Arendt calls it "two-in-one") a real space for thinking opens up. The condition of possibility of inner harmony (or disharmony) is the existence of this duality; in thinking we are in company with (or adversaries of) ourselves. In other words, the condition of thinking is self-awareness. "What thinking actualizes in its unending process is difference, given as a mere raw fact (*factum brutum*) in consciousness [. . .]. Socratic two-in-one heals the solitariness of thought; its inherent duality points to the infinite plurality which is the law of the earth."[46]

The sheer possibility of leading the inner dialogue does not yet explain the role of thinking in moral questions. We need an additional assumption here: the doubling of the self, that comes to voice in thinking, should lead to an agreement between me and myself. "To Socrates, the duality of the two-in-one meant no more than that if you want to think, you must see to it that the two who carry on the dialogue be in good shape, that the partners be *friends*."[47] Since I am the only person I cannot escape from, it is better that everybody disagrees with me than if I, being one, can't reconcile with myself. On this assumption the only positive thesis of Socrates on morality is based: "It is better to be wronged than to do wrong" (474b).[48] It is not because it is written in a code or a set of commandments. It is better not to do wrong because then we have to lead an inner dialogue with a villain with whom it is impossible to reconcile. Arendt illustrated this with the inner dialogue of Richard III and showed how this dialogue becomes a nightmare when it is impossible to stay a friend to oneself: "I rather hate myself for hateful deeds committed by myself. I am a villain."[49]

The example of Shakespearean figures shows that the sheer ability to have an inner dialogue does not ultimately protect us from committing a crime. But the essential difference between Richard (or, to use a different source, Raskolnikov) and Eichmann is that the latter never undertook this dialogue, in other words, never encountered his conscience which would "fill a man full of obstacles." Richard and Raskolnikov rescue themselves from the ordeal of the night conversations with an escape from thinking: the painful duality disappears in the daylight, among company. But it caught them once and made them aware of what they had done, even if only for a moment. The problem of Eichmann was, according to Arendt, that he never entered into this inner dialogue. His crime is not committed against his inner friend. That is why he wouldn't "mind committing any crime, since he can be sure that it will be forgotten the next moment."[50] The difference between the protagonists of Dostoyevsky or Shakespeare and a functionary of Eichmann's type is essential: a crime committed of passion or greed, though awful, is something individual and is automatically followed by punishment. A crime committed out of thoughtlessness never meets limitations of this sort. If the inner split does not endanger the unity of the self, as in the case of Eichmann, "he never meets his midnight disaster,"[51] he can send thousands of people to death for years and never realize what he really did. That is why Arendt could have said that extreme evil can be banal and that the anonymous subject of such a crime, just because he has no deeper passions or motives, is capable of evil to a scale unimaginable for Shakespeare or Dostoyevsky. Thinking does not protect man from any evil per se, it instead protects him or her from the banality of evil.

III

Apart from Socrates, Kant was for Arendt a second important witness of the phenomenon of thinking. She saw many similarities between them, for example, she regarded the categorical imperative to be a modern formula for the Socratic postulate of inner consistency.[52] But the affinity between Socrates and Kant is not limited to the realm of practical reason. An even more important field of congeniality of the two thinkers is the power of judgment, at the same time being a new mode of thinking, developed by Kant. When in chapter 1 I accounted for the contrasting way in which Arendt juxtaposed Socrates and Plato, I underscored the importance of the egalitarian style of Socrates. Socrates chatted with everybody and was truly interested in what his fellow-citizens thought of problems such as good or justice. He did not challenge many different opinions with any absolute truths from beyond the realm of the *polis*. The philosophical method of his conversations, dialogues, was not reserved for an elite group of professional philosophers. Socrates conversed with anybody who was ready to answer his questions. For Socrates, contrary to Plato, a conflict between philosophy and politics did not yet exist.

In Kant's times this conflict had had a long tradition already. But it was Kant himself who challenged this tradition. Arendt emphasizes that contrary to Plato, Aristotle, or Spinoza, Kant did not attempt to project politics to be "the best condition for the life of the philosopher."[53] He abandoned the elitist and "sectarian" self-knowledge of philosophers; the task of a philosopher is to understand the conditions of the possibility of morality, cognition and judgment and to present them in a way accessible to every reasonable human being. Kant "does not claim that the philosopher can leave the Platonic Cave or join in Parmenides' journey to the heavens, nor does he think that he should become a member of a sect."[54] Kant, similarly to Socrates, appreciated the meaning of philosophy for public affairs. Therefore, and again in accordance with Socrates, he believed that thinking cannot be reserved for the few: "Philosophizing, or the thinking of reason, which transcends the limitations of what can be known, the boundaries of human cognition, is for Kant a general human 'need,' the need of reason as a human faculty. It does not oppose the few to the many."[55]

Socrates chatted with people in the agora of the city. Kant's agora was to be a community of interested readers (that is why he deplored the hermetic style of *The Critique of Pure Reason* and "never gave up hope that it would be possible to popularize his thought"[56]). Since Kant did not write a separate work on the philosophy of politics which could match the three *Critiques*, Arendt sought for the premises of the political in the whole of the Kantian oeuvre. The answer to the question of the relationship between plurality, the basic prerequisite of politics, and thinking she found in the first part of *The Critique of Judgement* and in *What Is Enlightenment?*. The connection between plurality and thinking is present in what Kant called the "enlarged mentality." This concept refers to two things, closely related to each other: critical thinking (being the result of the public use of reason) and judgments of taste, that is, aesthetic judgments, independent of subjective fancies and partialities.

The enlarged mentality has much to do with what Kant called the "public use of reason." The public use of reason is in Kant juxtaposed with private use. The private use of reason is the result of a private place in the world, for example, a function or a profession, and, therefore, is limited. The public use of reason requires from a man an "unlimited freedom to use his own reason."[57] Kant delivers a definition of the public use of reason: "I understand the public use of one's reason, to anyone as a scholar makes of reason before the entire literate world."[58] The basic prerequisite of the public use of reason, or, in other words, of critical thinking, is freedom, and freedom in a dual sense: on the one hand, it is freedom understood as a liberty of public speech and publishing. On the other hand, there is more to it than that: freedom of speech would be futile had we not been able to detach ourselves from our private situation in the world (such as a function or an interest) and to see things from a universal point of view. As Arendt says: "Critical thinking is possible only where the standpoints of all others are open to inspection [. . .]. by the force of imagination it makes the others present and thus moves in a space that is potentially public, open to all sides [. . .]; To think with an enlarged mentality means that one trains one's imagination to go visiting."[59]

The obvious premise of both critical thinking and judgments of taste is their communicability, their ability to be transmitted to others and understood by them. The condition of the possibility of communication is a community of people one can address as listeners or readers, an inter-human space, independent from set social relations and roles. Thinking requires, even if only potentially, a forum, a transparency, a space of transmission. This plurality is a transcendental condition of the possibility of thinking, that is, in thinking we always presume the presence of others, even if they are physically absent. Although Kant did not deal with action, the essence of politics for Arendt, his prerequisites for thinking turn out to be concurrent to the prerequisites for action in Arendt. They are: the plurality of people and the public space. This explains why Arendt read Kant so intensively: thinking, and particularly the judging emerging from it, becomes a chance to mitigate the opposition between thinking and action: the faculty of judgment is, so to say, a bridge between the inner dialogue and the world of appearances. The complete reconciliation of thinking and action is thought to be impossible; action always proceeds from the particular perspective of an actor. The freedom of action does not consist in a distance, but in spontaneity (freedom from motive and goal). Thinking, instead, requires impartiality, that is, taking into consideration the points of view of others, the enlarging of one's view with other perspectives, putting oneself, by virtue of imagination, in the places of others.

That is why critical thinking is so much related to the faculty of judgment. Judging also requires detachment from individual partiality (this time it is subjective pleasure connected with an object) and working out an independent stance, based on what Kant called "common sense": But "under the *sensus communis* we must include the Idea of a sense *common to all, i.e.*, of a faculty of judgment, which in its reflection takes into account (a priori) of the mode of representation of all other men in thought."[60] But, unlike scientific or moral judgments, aesthetic judgment cannot be based on universal concepts, it always concerns a concrete object.[61]

Nevertheless, aesthetic judgment also has to aspire to universal validity. It is because it is not based on private individual senses but on common sense, *sensus communis*, which is closely related to the postulate of the enlarged mentality: "to put ourselves in thought in the place of everyone else."[62] *Sensus communis*, or enlarged thinking allows us to avoid partiality in our judgments, "to abstract from charm or emotion if we are seeking a judgment that is to serve as a universal rule."[63] The concept of *sensus communis* and enlarged mentality allows Kant to detach the judgments of taste from the incommunicable sphere of private feeling, with whom they have always been identified and bestow them with public significance. Aesthetic taste in Kant is not an inner feeling (like physical sensations, for example, pain), but "taste is the faculty of judging a priori of the communicability of feelings that are bound up with a given representation."[64] In this way a judgment of taste can expect the agreement of everyone and "he who describes anything as beautiful claims that everyone *ought* to give his approval to the object in question and also describe it as a beautiful."[65] In other words: one can dispute beauty and ugliness as well as other things. It is significant for the political sphere; the question how the common world is to look cannot or should not be the outcome of a set of private fancies, but should be a result of a public debate on taste.

For the connection between thinking and moral questions the most important is Arendt's extrapolation of the aesthetic faculty of judgment in the sphere of morality. The taste of judgment can help us not only to distinguish beauty from ugliness (like in Kant), but also good from evil. Indeed, the judgment "this is wrong" has for Arendt something of an aesthetic element. For instance, betrayal is wrong not only in the individual perspective, since it makes me live with a traitor (which becomes clear in inner dialogue), but also because, irrespective of this individual perspective, it disfigures the common world. In Arendt's view, the two basic features of the faculty of judgment make them relevant for moral considerations: First, judgment requires "thinking without banisters" of the established general rules and norms, because it always concerns one concrete matter or object. It means that it can also be practiced in "dark times," when all norms and rules are in ruins; secondly, judgment, not being based on private individual feeling, but engaging the enlarged mentality, could claim universal validity, or, to put it in Arendt's language, could be related to the common world. Thus, Kant discovered a new dimension of thinking: to the Socratic postulate of inner consistency he added the postulate of the enlarged mentality, of putting oneself in another's position, which for Arendt "is the greatest step in philosophy since Socrates."[66]

In the situation of totalitarian rule, when the conditions of political action are destroyed completely, when the multi-spectrality of the public world and human plurality are abolished, the necessary space for the public use of reason or critical thinking is lacking. But the basic gesture of the enlarged mentality, assuming the perspectives of others is still possible. Arendt despised Eichmann (and the majority of German society) not for being unable to comprehend public use of reason in the conditions of the Third Reich and not criticizing the rulers, but because he was unable to make this elementary gesture of freedom, which is distancing from himself and looking on things with another's eyes.[67] When the multi-spectrality of the world disappears and plurality is condensed to a mass, the rescue for judging is the duality of the inner Socratic dialogue: "the faculty of judging particulars [. . .], the ability to say 'this is wrong,' 'this is beautiful,' and so on, is not the same as the faculty of thinking [. . .]. But the two are interrelated, as are consciousness and conscience."[68] The faculty of judgment unifies the duality of the inner dialogue and allows the self, now being one again, to re-enter the world and understand what is really going on. This faculty "realizes thinking, makes it manifest in the world of appearances."[69] "The manifestation of the wind of thought is not knowledge; it is the ability to tell right from wrong, beautiful from ugly. And this, at the rare moments when the stakes are on the table, may indeed prevent catastrophes, at least for the self."[70]

UNIVERSITY BETWEEN PAST AND FUTURE

Twentieth-century totalitarianism and its aftermath sealed the end of tradition. It is a situation when non-thinking does not mean simply non-reflexive acceptance of the traditional norms, but much worse: the acceptance of any rules actually offered by society. The activity of thinking, at least when we have in mind an inner dialogue, always disturbs the daily basis of life and action; the thinking self withdraws from the world of appearances and everyday activities. This means that time and space of everyday life is suspended: "The thinking ego [. . .] is, strictly speaking, *nowhere*."[71] Thinking also destroys linear time and creates a gap between past and future; especially, the influence of the past is suspended, while its message is being questioned. At times deprived of the influence of tradition, this experience becomes common: "When the thread of tradition finally broke, the gap between past and future ceased to be a condition peculiar only to the activity of thought and restricted as an experience to those few who made thinking their primary business. It became a tangible reality and perplexity for all; that is, it became a fact of political relevance."[72] The gap in time ceased to be strictly connected with the elusive experience of thinking and became something tangible. Since tradition does not tell us what to do and think, thinking becomes a challenge for everybody, and, in extreme situations, it can be the only rescue from committing banal evils. In such a situation the attitudes of Socrates and Kant become public good: "the self as the ultimate criterion of moral conduct is politically a kind of emergency measure."[73] In critical situations—such is Arendt's lesson—non-thinking is really dangerous. This danger emerges from the situation when the lack of thinking is replaced by the attachment to having rules of conduct, no matter *what* these rules are: "The faster men held to the old code, the more eager will they be to assimilate themselves to the new one; the ease with which such reversals can take place under certain circumstances suggests indeed that everybody is asleep when they occur."[74]

Just as thinking is not a privilege of the few, non-thinking is a temptation for everyone, irrespective of the level of education and intelligence.

If we accept Arendt's argumentation that thinking has the power to protect human beings from the possibility of "banal evil," it gains enormous pedagogical relevance. This relevance is even stronger if we accept the thesis of the broken thread of tradition. In this situation the sense of thinking is not only what it used to be for Socrates: to make one's own life worth living. There is more to it than that, that is, a real influence on the amount of evil in the world. Arendt's considerations imply a strong thesis: had people been really able to lead an inner dialogue and to put oneself in another's position, the extreme evil of the twentieth century would have been impossible. This, of course, does not mean it would have been a century of general happiness and harmony. Arendt was anybody but an utopist. But, perhaps, the evil done in this century would not have been of the sort of guilt which "anger could not revenge, love could not endure, friendship could not forgive."[75]

We encounter a paradox here: situating the pedagogical promise of philosophy in thinking evokes justified, to some extent, expectations for an answer of a pragmatic nature, that is, what to do to make people think, or, how to educate people for thinking. On the other hand, the elusive nature of thinking makes it always risky to place it in scholarship; it is the risk that under didactic rules it becomes something else. The two basic features of thinking, that it does not bring tangible results and that it requires a withdrawal from the world of appearances, make it unfit for a "teaching outcome" and for being designed "in the classroom."[76] Even Socrates did not claim to be able to teach thinking. The question would then be: Can we, not trying to design thinking or subjugate it under technical didactic rules, try to create conditions in which it *could* thrive?

Nowadays, when we think of worldly spaces, not so much for teaching how to think, but for attempts to simply practice it, it seems after all that such a place is the university. This "after all" is important here: thinking in a contemporary university, subordinated to a free-market economy and the bureaucracy supporting it, becomes doubtful. Thinking cannot be taught, even less can a method of such teaching be formulated.[77] But it does not mean that we are completely helpless in the matter of thinking: we can always create the conditions for thinking. One can, for instance, show why non-thinking is dangerous; one can, through analysis and interpretation of texts, learn to see the world from many different perspectives. One can also, through an education of philosophy and history, try to understand the genesis of the modern world, and, by the same token, face its non-obviousness through dialogue with the authors of the past. All these are not thinking yet, but they create a good atmosphere for inner dialogue and critical reflection. The problem is that all these activities, one could say, only natural for such a place as a university, are similar to subversive and underground actions. That is why the protection of the small isles of academic freedom, without which even exercises in thinking are impossible, requires the strong virtue of non-conformism.

It seems that the most important problem nowadays is the demand of the state that university education be subjugated to market rules and the university itself becomes an enterprise with a corporate structure. This demand is additionally sanctioned by a massive bureaucratic machine, which impedes the emergence of the spaces of free thought at modern universities. The tension between the university and the state does not seem to be a special feature of our times. It is, so to say, a modern version of the conflict between a philosopher and the *polis*. On Socrates, Arendt said: "Nobody can doubt that such a teaching was and always will be in a certain conflict with the *polis*."[78] As we remember, even Humboldt's university found itself pressed by limitations from state machinery. The ideals of this university, freedom and individualism, which were the ideal conditions for thinking, were subordinated to state goals at every stage: the difference was that then it was not the market but the national identity of the Prussian state. But the modern state is also in conflict with the claims for freedom in academia. This time the state limitations of this freedom do not rely on the limitations of the freedom of speech. It is more serious: the university is legitimized by the state, which now means: by the market economy. The problem is that market mechanisms automatically exclude the possibility of discussion of their principles. They claim to be an obvious premise, an axiom. That is why for contemporary students and many scholars it is obvious that the purpose of the university is to "find yourself in the labor market" and "acquire social competence." The mere attempt at questioning such clichéd expressions is strenuous and endangers the person who dares to do this with the label of backward scholar.

To avoid misunderstandings; the goal of this critique is by no means a plea for coming back to the good old days of "true education," or to enliven the ideal of *Bildung*. Also any attempt to mend the broken thread of tradition with, for example, a canon of "Great Books," seems to miss the point (and contradict academic freedom). It is always easier to create a canon than to let the voices of the tradition to speak now. If thinking cannot be the prerogative of the few, and the university is (was?) one of the places of the modern world which sets down the basic conditions for thinking, the ideal of elitist education for higher ranks of society, usually associated with the old universities, is unacceptable. First of all, it is impossible factually: it would require a return to the past, the reestablishing of the old order of the division between the educated and uneducated, that is, the reestablishment of the class-society. Second, it is also controversial if we take into account Arendt's arguments, confirmed by the history of Germany: neither the high level of education nor the membership of an intellectual elite is a guarantee that one can really *think*.

Alas, graduation from today's mass universities guarantees it even less because academia is gradually forfeiting presentation of material worth thinking over and is replacing it with training of practical competences (or, even more commonly, with what *passes for* them in the neoliberal rhetoric). The contemporary university faces a truly deep dilemma: how to reconcile free access to higher education with quality of learning. (Open access to education does not mean that everybody can study anything. It seems that the massification of universities is not an outcome of equal opportunities, but rather of market rules; it stems from the conviction that a university education is a sort of contract and that a student-client can buy a higher rank in society and in the marketplace). On the other hand, at least to some extent, how universities can be made independent from the claims of state patronage.

Any attempt at finding a remedy for these antinomies would be intellectual *hybris* and out of place here. Instead, I recall the specific case in Arendt's biography, which is telling in our context. *Eichmann in Jerusalem* was a book which caused a storm on both sides of the Atlantic. I will not describe the nuances of this controversy. It suffices to say that the book crossed the current standards of judgment (the two most important flash points were Arendt's accusation that the Jewish councils had contributed to the Nazi administration and her de-demonization of Eichmann), which evoked a wave of public persecution, fuelled additionally with administrative tools by the Jewish establishment. The matter-of-fact arguments were interwoven with personal attacks, invective and slander. Years had to pass before the wave of outrage subsided and the report underwent a matter-of-fact critical analysis.[79] Nevertheless, already during the first months of the storm Arendt found a harbor free of the rules of mystified public discourse and where true attempts of understanding were possible.

In 1964 Arendt wrote to Jaspers: "As far as I am concerned, the universities have saved me."[80] What happened at the American universities that the debate, which had become stuck in a dead point, fettered with emotions, clichés and pre-judgments, could be revived again? The counterbalance to the excommunication that Arendt had suffered from her own generation, were the students who crowded her public lectures (at Yale, Columbia, and Chicago). The precedence was the organization, by a courageous rabbi, of a meeting with Jewish students at Columbia, when, in the middle of the summer, the audience was three times bigger than the capacity of the hall. After a short speech by Arendt there was a long discussion, during which she received sheets with questions: "And none of them contained a single provocation [. . .] some of the questions were questions excellent"—she reported with relief and astonishment to Jaspers.[81] The situation was repeated at other academies, despite a strong reaction from Jewish organizations, striving at taking control of the debate. The reaction of the younger generation had an impact exceeding the territory of universities. During the following years the public debate was re-opened and the organizations which had earlier attacked Arendt, started to invite her for lectures and discussions. Universities made possible what was impossible anywhere else: seeing matters from the general point of view, going beyond the bi-polar perspective of "us versus them" (Jews-Gentiles), where nationality defined one's presumed stance in advance. Of course, it is only a *casus*, but an important *casus* that requires a generalization.

Arendt did not deal with the idea or theory of university. Nonetheless, after the Eichmann controversy, as well as in the context of 1968, in her texts and interviews appear sparse, but telling, remarks. She was rather disappointed with the German academic tradition and did not share the view, widespread in this tradition, that the university should be detached from political and social life. Arendt believed that the university had an important public role to fulfill. And she was convinced that "the historical sciences and the humanities, which are supposed to find out, stand guard over, and interpret factual truth and human documents, are politically of greater relevance"[82] than natural, or even social, sciences (which she associated more with engineering than with freedom). Nevertheless, she believed in the university as an exterritorial site, independent not only of actual political power, but also from social divisions. A student's freedom she conceived as *"standing outside all social groups* and obligations."[83] It is exactly this social independence that became a condition of the possibility of an enlarged mentality after the publication of *Eichmann*: in this case it meant considering the controversy, against the Jewish establishment, not as a problem limited to the Jewish community or a political problem of the state of Israel, but as a public one (in Arendt's understanding), which concerned the public world and all people inhabiting it. Universities (and courts) should be protected from political and social power, because

> very unwelcome truths have emerged from the universities [. . .]. Yet the chances for truth to prevail in public are, of course, greatly improved by the mere existence of such places and by the organization of independent, supposedly disinterested scholars associated with them. And it can hardly be denied that, at least in constitutionally ruled countries, the political realm has recognized, even in the event of conflict, that it has a stake in the existence of men and institutions over which it has no power.[84]

It seems that what is happening at universities today is going exactly in the opposite direction: toward subordination to social pressure and state power, as the two instances connect in the claims of the market. In the 1970s Michel Foucault excellently described this mechanism by analysis of Ludwig Erhardt's speech of 1948, especially one sentence, at the same time being a performative act of the foundation of post-war Germany: "Only a state that establishes both the freedom and responsibility of the citizens can legitimately speak in the name of the people."[85] The marketplace has to be freed from state regulations, otherwise the state does not represent the people. The meaning of this statement is not only the banal fact that a state that exceeds its power in the economic order violates some primary rights. There's more to it than that: the economy, development, and growth *produce* sovereignty and political legitimacy. The economy produces sovereign political power that supports the economy, that is, the economy bestows the state with legitimacy that, in turn, becomes a guarantee for the economy. By the same token, public law has to respect and include the laws of the market economy. In other words: the economy becomes a source of public law.[86] Thus, this almost tautologically sounding statement of Erhardt becomes a universal manifesto of neoliberalism: a system guaranteeing not so much the freedom of the market, but rather making it the source of the legitimization of the state and source of public law. In this way the state and the economy are caught in a cycle of mutual legitimization: the state has to defend the market, because the market, especially in the moment when the old foundation myths are not valid any more, is the source if its existence. At the same time, the market refers to the state as a guarantor of its own functioning. Therefore Foucault could say: "The economy produces legitimacy for the state that is its guarantor,"[87] and "The economy produces political signs that enable the structures, mechanisms, and justifications of power to function."[88]

Now we can better understand why the university, still a state institution, is being harnessed in the cycle of legitimization. And why it is the state that uses the power apparatus of administration and bureaucracy in order to make academia subordinate under the rules of the market economy.[89] For instance, the marketization of the university is becoming a sort of indirect instance of censorship; one can theoretically write and say anything, but the bureaucratic machine makes sure that only utterances fitting into the paradigm of utility are acknowledged and financially supported. Under the pressure of state control, the representatives of academia (also the humanities) take over a new logic and new language of entrepreneurialism. Henry Giroux showed the consequences of such semantic changes for the role of universities in public spaces where scholars transform from independent intellectuals, whose role is to spread theoretical analyses and critical thinking, to a "cheap army of reserve labor."[90] The market logic of the university "suppresses dissent by keeping them in a state of fear over losing their jobs."[91] We have here another example of how the Agambenian "bare life" supersedes public discourse; the fear of existence, accompanying the uncertainty of employment is not a factor facilitating non-conformism and independence.

The critiques of the reform of university teaching turn our attention, and rightly so, to the fact that the demise of education leads to a crisis in culture, erosion of language, annihilation of the intellectual elite, in short, to functional illiteracy and a new barbarism. It seems however that there is even more to it: along with the subordination of the conditions of free thinking under instrumental rules not only the conditions of individual development and cultural memory are destroyed; the very habit of reflection (on an individual level) and the centers of inconvenient thoughts, potentially subversive against the status quo are destroyed as well. The economic paradigm requires obedience and is automatically set to exclude the conditions of inner dialogue and critical thinking. The danger arises that the intellectual activities hampering the automatic nature of bureaucratic machinery and instrumental control will be silenced. And this fertilizes the subsoil for the growth of lesser or bigger evils, emerging from thoughtlessness.

NOTES

1. Hannah Arendt and Joachim Fest, *Eichmann war von empörender Dummheit. Gespräche und Briefe* (München-Zürich: Piper, 2011), 94.
2. "What Remains? The Language Remains: A Conversation with Günter Gaus," 2.
3. Arendt, "Martin Heidegger at Eighty," 54.
4. Martin Heidegger to Hannah Arendt, April 13, 1965, *Letters*, 124. A similar thought was expressed by Jaspers at the same time, completely independently from Heidegger: "Your wonderful political books are philosophy," Karl Jaspers to Hannah Arendt, June 27, 1966, *Correspondence*, 642.
5. "What Remains? The Language Remains," 8.
6. Arendt, *Thinking*, 212.
7. Hannah Arendt, *Eichmann in Jerusalem: A Report on the Banality of Evil* (New York: Penguin, 2006), 8.
8. Arendt, *Eichmann in Jerusalem*, 287–88.
9. Arendt, *Eichmann in Jerusalem*, 32.
10. Arendt, *Eichmann in Jerusalem*, 114.
11. Arendt, *Eichmann in Jerusalem*, 114.
12. Arendt, "Thinking and Moral Considerations," 159.
13. Arendt, *Eichmann in Jerusalem*, 48.
14. Arendt, *Eichmann in Jerusalem*, 48.
15. Arendt, *Eichmann in Jerusalem*, 50.
16. Arendt, *Eichmann in Jerusalem*, 52.
17. Arendt, *Eichmann in Jerusalem*, 110.
18. Dana R. Villa, "The Banality of Philosophy," in *Hannah Arendt Twenty Years Later*, eds. Larry May and Jerome Kohn (Cambridge, MA: The MIT Press, 1997), 92.
19. Martin Heidegger, *Discourse on Thinking: A Translation of Gelassenheit*, trans. John M. Anderson and E. Hans Freund (New York: Harper & Row Publishers, 1966), 46.

20. Martin Heidegger, "The End of Philosophy and the Task of Thinking," trans. Joan Stambaugh, in *Basic Writings*, 435.
21. Martin Heidegger, *What Is Called Thinking?. A Translation of Was heisst Denken?* trans. J. G. Gray (New York: Harper Perennial, 2004), 8.
22. Heidegger, "The End of Philosophy and the Task of Thinking," 443.
23. Heidegger, "The End of Philosophy and the Task of Thinking," 435.
24. Heidegger, *What Is Called Thinking?* 9–10.
25. Heidegger, *What Is Called Thinking?* 6.
26. Heidegger, *What Is Called Thinking?* 18.
27. Heidegger, *What Is Called Thinking?* 159.
28. Heidegger, *What Is Called Thinking?* resp. 4, 17, 128.
29. Heidegger Martin, "Science and Reflection," in *Question Concerning Technology and Other Essays*, trans. William Lovitt (New York: Garland Publishing, 1977), 180.
30. Heidegger, *What Is Called Thinking?* 17. See also Arendt, *Thinking*, 174.
31. Heidegger, *What Is Called Thinking?* 115.
32. Heidegger, *What Is Called Thinking?* 126.
33. See Heidegger, *What Is Called Thinking?* 139.
34. Arendt, *Thinking*, 150.
35. See HGA, 197G; 142E; also Arendt, *Thinking*, 118.
36. Arendt, "Crisis in Education," 186.
37. Arendt, *Thinking*, 166.
38. Arendt, *Thinking*, 174.
39. Arendt, *Thinking*, 175.
40. Arendt, *Thinking*, 175.
41. Arendt, *Thinking*, 176.
42. Arendt, "Thinking and Moral Considerations," 163.
43. Arendt, "Thinking and Moral Considerations," 166.
44. As quoted in Arendt, *Thinking*, 181.
45. Arendt, *Thinking*, 183.
46. Arendt, *Thinking*, 187.
47. Arendt, *Thinking*, 187–88.
48. As quoted in Arendt, *Thinking*, 181.
49. As quoted in Arendt, *Thinking*, 189; William Shakespeare, *Richard III*, V/3.
50. Arendt, "Thinking and Moral Considerations," 187.
51. Arendt, "Thinking and Moral Considerations," 188.
52. See Arendt, *Thinking*, 188.
53. Arendt, *Lectures on Kant's Political Philosophy*, 21.
54. Arendt, *Lectures on Kant's Political Philosophy*, 28.
55. Arendt, *Lectures on Kant's Political Philosophy*, 29.
56. Arendt, *Lectures on Kant's Political Philosophy*, 38.
57. Immanuel Kant, *Answer the Question: What Is Enlightenment?* trans. Daniel F. Ferrer, 2013, 6, Archive.org.
58. Kant, *What Is Enlightenment?* 4.
59. Arendt, *Lectures on Kant's Political Philosophy*, 43.

60. Immanuel Kant, *Kritik of Judgment*, trans. J. H. Bernard (New York: Macmillan, 1892), 170, Archive.org.
61. Strictly speaking, it applies to judgments which Kant calls reflexive.
62. Kant, *Kritik of Judgment*, 171.
63. Kant, *Kritik of Judgment*, 171.
64. Kant, *Kritik of Judgment*, 173.
65. Kant, *Kritik of Judgment*, 92.
66. Arendt, *Denktagebuch*, 570.
67. More telling is the passage from *What Is Called Thinking?* in which Heidegger, seven years after World War II (his first lecture after regaining his *venia legendi*) sees only "fearful consequences for my country, cut in two," Heidegger, *What Is Called Thinking?* 66.
68. Arendt, *Thinking*, 193.
69. Arendt, *Thinking*, 193.
70. Arendt, *Thinking*, 193.
71. Arendt, *Thinking*, 199.
72. Arendt, "Preface: Between Past and Future," in *Between Past and Future*, 13.
73. Arendt, "Some Questions of Moral Philosophy," in *Responsibility and Judgment*, 104.
74. Arendt, "Thinking and Moral Considerations," 178.
75. Arendt, *Origins of Totalitarianism*, 459.
76. It seems that Mathew Lipman yielded to this very temptation with his *Philosophy in the Classroom*, (see Matthew Lipman, Ann Margaret Sharp, and Frederick S. Oscanyan, *Philosophy in the Classroom* [Philadelphia: Temple University Press, 1980]). "Free" discussions of children are performed in a paradigm planned in detail by adults. The basis for these discussions are, prepared particularly for this purpose, didactic stories, whose premise is the affirmation of a (rather postulated by the authors than factual) canon of values of American society. I do not exclude the practical relevance of such activities, like an ability to take part in discussion, for instance. But they have nothing to do with *thinking*. As Peter Euben notices: "Thinking can be a part of political action only in result, not in aim. If it is instrumental, it undermines both the integrity of thinking itself and its status as an emergency resource when law and morality are complicit with criminality." Peter Euben, "Politicizing the University and Other Clichés," in *Hannah Arendt and Education: Renewing our Common World*, ed. Mordechai Gordon (Boulder, CO: Westview Press, 2001), 192; see also Eduardo Duarte, "The Eclipse of Thinking: An Arendtian Critique of Cooperative Learning," in *Hannah Arendt an Education*, 207–8.
77. "When thinking comes to an end by slipping out of its element it replaces this loss by procuring a validity for itself as τέχνη, as an instrument of education and therefore as a classroom matter," Heidegger, "Letter on 'Humanism,'" 242. Arendt herself, when teaching, did not use innovative didactic tools. Apart from this, her lectures were attended always by more people than predicted, and long before she became a public person in connection with Eichmann's case. "What made Hannah Arendt a great teacher? She seemed to violate many of the canons that make for effective teaching. She had no special pedagogical methods and no set doctrines. She

made no attempt to attract students through polemics or flattery, and she did not try to entertain them. In fact, the format of her lectures probably sound quite dull; for the first hour or so she would read from a fully written set of notes; then, for the remaining forty minutes, she would answer questions," Peter Stern and Jean Yarbrough, "Teaching: Hannah Arendt," *The American Scholar*, 3, no. 47 (1978): 371.

78. Arendt, "Socrates," 24.

79. However, in relatively new literature we also come across the condemnation of Arendt's theses with argumentation ad hominem. A good example here can be the account of Richard Wolin who mixes up the arguments with insinuations. He repeats the old misunderstanding that Arendt equated victims with their torturers. The thesis of banality of evil he rejects on the basis of the fact that Eichmann was very high in the Nazi hierarchy, "second only to Himmler and Heydrich." Wolin's allegations concern not so much theoretical shortcomings, but Arendt's personal features: lack of empathy and taste. According to Wolin only one reason of these failures is thinkable: it is Arendt's love for Heidegger, the representative of the German *Geist* and *Kultur*, that made her "purvey such calumnies about the Jews," see Richard Wolin, *Heidegger's Children. Hannah Arendt, Karl Löwith, Hans Jonas and Herbert Marcuse* (Princeton, NJ: Princeton University Press, 2001), 52–57.

80. Hannah Arendt to Karl Jaspers, February 19, 1964, *Correspondence*, 546.

81. Hannah Arendt to Karl Jaspers, August 9, 1963, *Correspondence*, 516.

82. Arendt, "Truth and Politics," in *Between Past and Future*, 256–57.

83. Hannah Arendt, "Thoughts on Politics and Revolution: A Commentary" (Interview by Adelbert Reif), trans. Denver Lindley, in Hannah Arendt, *The Last Interview and Other Conversations* (Brooklyn: Melville House, 2013), 77.

84. Arendt, "Truth and Politics," 256.

85. Michel Foucault, *The Birth of Biopolitics*, Lectures at the Collège de France 1978–1979, trans. Graham Burchell (New York: Picador, 2008), 81.

86. See Foucault, *The Birth of Biopolitics*, 84.

87. Foucault, *The Birth of Biopolitics*, 84.

88. Foucault, *The Birth of Biopolitics*, 85.

89. And, sometimes even the means of physical violence. For instance, Giroux described the brutal attacks of police on the students in Quebec, who protested against rising tuition fees and the debt machinery that increases the profits of banks, see Henry A. Giroux, *Neoliberalism's War on Higher Education* (Chicago: Haymarket Books, 2014), 164–65.

90. Giroux, *Neoliberalism's War*, 137.

91. Giroux, *Neoliberalism's War*, 26.

Afterword

I.

"The premier demand upon all education is that Auschwitz not happen again."[1] This postulate of Adorno, although formulated over fifty years ago, has not lost its relevance and acuteness, for the conditions that lead to "banal" evil continue to exist in the Western world, as Hannah Arendt first, and later Michel Foucault, Giorgio Agamben, and others demonstrated. Henry A. Giroux reminded us of this postulate in the face of the human rights controversies of Abu Ghraib and Guantanamo Bay.[2] It seems that the instrumentalized logic of neoliberalism, especially when combined with nationalistic ideology (astonishingly, these two ideologies, although contradictory, turn out not to be impossible to reconcile in the modern world), destroys the conditions of critical thinking in the public space, paving the way for more or less banal evil. The purpose of this book was to deliver a humble intellectual contribution to this demand by attempting to understand these conditions.

II.

This book is an academic work and from the very beginning was planned as such. Nonetheless, my intention was to reconcile the requirements of academic discipline with a desire to present the outcomes of my research as a narrative. The choice of the intellectual relationship between Hannah Arendt and Martin Heidegger as a leitmotif of this narrative was not accidental. This relationship reflects the most important turns of the newest philosophies and history of the West. Thus, this book is a story of the intellectual relationship between two of the most important thinkers in twentieth-century Western thought. At the same time it is intertwined with another story: with a critical analysis of the cultural, historical, and philosophical context of the categories which in the tradition reconciled education with philosophy; it is also a story of the disintegration of these categories along with the end of the tradition of European metaphysics and the tragedy of European totalitarianism; and, last but not least, it is a narrative about a search for the conditions of thinking anew about the connection between education and philosophy in times stripped of clear and universal philosophical-pedagogical categories, and about the chance emerging from this lack. That is why in the final part of this book I attempted to overcome Antonia Grunenberg's claim that according to Arendt, "The educational mission of philosophy was discredited." To fulfill this purpose, I followed the trail of Arendt's thought, sometimes against her own intentions, and reinterpreted the tensions and ambiguities present in her oeuvre toward a pedagogical or educational promise intrinsic in thinking, as a new philosophical chance of communication between philosophy and education. Communication, but not reconciliation, for the intention of this book was entirely free from the desire to revive or reinstate the old categories that used to unify education and philosophy, and free from any illusion that it would be possible or even welcome.

III.

Although the perspective of this book far exceeds the individual dimension of the intellectual relationship between Arendt and Heidegger (and practically ignores purely biographical aspects), it seems that the motif of faithfulness and unfaithfulness, by means of which Arendt succinctly described her attitude toward Heidegger, is at the same time the essence of the opposition or even the dialectics of the master-student relationship. This particular relationship goes against the common belief that the sense of the master-student relation is fulfilled only when the student outgrows the master. Arendt did not outgrow Heidegger: but not because she was unable to exceed his level. She simply went another way, which makes an attempt to find the criterion, according to which one could measure and compare their achievements, futile. At the same time, Arendt's way would be impossible without Heidegger's signposts or "pathmarks" (*Wegmarken*). Were Arendt not "faithful" to Heidegger, we would miss her original thought, which emerged out of a constant struggle with the Heideggerian *opus*. But so would we miss it, paradoxically, had she not also been "unfaithful" and simply followed his directions (such as "listen and try to *follow along*"). In each of these two possibilities we would lose not only a distinguished philosophy, but also one of the most interesting contexts for the philosophy of education.

To Heidegger's attempt at overcoming Western metaphysics Arendt responded with a consistent struggle with the residue of Western political thought. Both offered a new language, each a different one, adequate for description of new cultural phenomena, which grew out of the ruins of the old orders. For this reason, Heidegger's language, and even more Arendt's, are not simply instruments of narrowly thought academic philosophy, but became very promising tools for interpretation of modern reality, and also the reality of education. These languages must not be simply acquired but critically reworked, which is exactly what I intended to do in this book.

NOTES

1. Theodor W. Adorno, "Education after Auschwitz," Critical Models: Interventions and Catchwords, trans. Henry W. Pickford (New York: Columbia University Press, 2005), 191.

2. Henry A. Giroux, "What Might Education Mean after Abu Ghraib: Revisiting Adorno's Politics of Education," *Comparative Studies of South Asia, Africa and the Middle East*, 24 (2004): 5.

Bibliography

Abensour, Miguel. "Against the Sovereignty of Philosophy Over Politics: Arendt's Reading of Plato's Cave Allegory." Translated by Martin Breaugh. *Social Research* 4, no. 74 (2007): 955–82.

Adorno, Theodor W. *Critical Models: Interventions and Catchwords.* Translated by Henry W. Pickford. New York: Columbia University Press, 2005.

Agamben, Giorgio. *Homo Sacer: Sovereign Power and Bare Life.* Translated by Daniel Heller-Roazen. Palo Alto, CA: Stanford University Press, 1998.

———. *Remnants of Auschwitz: The Witness and the Archive.* Translated by Daniel Heller-Roazen. New York: Zone Books, 1999.

———. *State of Exception.* Translated by Kevin Attell. Chicago: The University of Chicago Press, 2005.

———. *The Kingdom and the Glory: For a Theological Genealogy of Economy and Government (Homo Sacer I, 2).* Translated by Lorenzo Chiesa and Matteo Mandarini. Palo Alto, CA: Stanford University Press, 2011.

Arendt, Hannah. *Rahel Varnhagen: The Life of a Jewish Woman.* New York: A Harvest/HBJ, 1974.

———. "Martin Heidegger at Eighty." Translated by Albert Hofstadter. *The New York Review of Books* 17, no. 6 (1971): 50–54.

———. *Between Past and Future: Eight Exercises in Political Thought.* New York: Penguin Books, 2006.

———. *Denktagebuch 1950–1973.* Edited by Urula Ludz and Ingeborg Nordmann. München-Zürich: Piper, 2003.

———. *Eichmann in Jerusalem: A Report on the Banality of Evil.* New York: Penguin, 2006.

———. *Essays in Understanding 1930–1954: Formation, Exile and Totalitarianism.* New York: Schocken Books, 2005.

———. *Lectures on Kant's Political Philosophy.* Edited by Ronald Beiner. Chicago: The University of Chicago Press, 1992.

———. *Love and Saint Augustine.* Translated by Joanna V. Scott and Judith Ch. Stark. Chicago: The University of Chicago Press, 1996.

———. *Men in Dark Times*. New York: A Harvest Book, Harcourt Brace, 1995.
———. *On Revolution*. New York: Penguin Books, 2006.
———. *Reflections on Literature and Culture*. Edited by Susannah Young-ah Gottlieb. Palo Alto, CA: Stanford University Press, 2007.
———. *Responsibility and Judgment*. New York: Schocken, 2003.
———. *The Human Condition*. Chicago: The University of Chicago Press, 1998.
———. *The Jewish Writings*. Edited by Jerome Kohn and Ron H. Feldman. New York: Schocken, 2007.
———. *The Last Interview and Other Conversations*. Translated by Joan Stambaugh et al. Brooklyn: Melville House, 2013.
———. *The Life of the Mind: Thinking*. New York: A Harvest Book, 1981.
———. *The Origins of Totalitarianism*. New York: A Harvest Book, Harcourt, 1985.
———. *The Promise of Politics*. New York: Schocken, 2005.
Arendt, Hannah, and Heinrich Blücher. *Within Four Walls: The Correspondence between Hannah Arendt and Heinrich Blücher, 1936–1968*. Edited by Lotte Kohler. Translated by Peter Constantine. New York: Harcourt, 2000.
Arendt, Hannah, and Joachim Fest. *Eichmann war von empörender Dummheit. Gespräche und Briefe*. München-Zürich: Piper, 2011.
Arendt, Hannah, and Karl Jaspers. *Correspondence 1926–1969*. Edited by Lotte Kohler and Hans Saner. Translated by Robert and Rita Kimber. New York: A Harvest Book, 1992.
Arendt, Hannah, and Martin Heidegger. *Letters 1925–1976*. Edited by Ursula Ludz. Translated by Andrew Shields. New York: Harcourt, 2004.
Aristotle. *Metaphysics*. Translated by W. D. Ross. classics.mit.edu.
———. *Physics*. Translated by R. P. Hardie and R. K. Gaye. classics.mit.edu.
———. *Politics*. Translated by Benjamin Jowett. Oxford: Clarendon Press. Archive.org.
———. *Rhetoric*. Translated by W. Rhys Roberts. ebooks.adelaide.edu.au.
———. *The Nicomachean Ethics*. Translated by H. A. Rackham. Cambridge, MA: Harvard University Press, 1956.
Benhabib, Seyla. *The Reluctant Modernism of Hannah Arendt*. Lanham: Rowman & Littlefield, 2003.
Benner, Dietrich. *Wilhelm von Humboldts Bildungstheorie. Eine problemgeschichtliche Studie zum Begründungszusammenhang neuzeitlicher Bildungsreform*. Weinheim und München: Juventa Verlag, 1990.
Bernstein, Richard. "Provocation and Appropriation: Hannah Arendt's Response to Martin Heidegger." *Constellations* 2, no. 4 (1997): 153–71.
Blumenberg, Hans. *The Legitimacy of the Modern Age*. Translated by Robert M. Wallace. Cambridge, MA: The MIT Press, 1983.
Cavarero, Adriana. "Regarding the Cave." Translated by Paul Kottman. *Qui Parle* 1, no. 10 (1996): 1–20.
Diels, Hermann H. *Die Fragmente der Vorsokratiker*. Dublin-Zürich: Weidmann, 1966.
Duarte, Eduardo. "The Eclipse of Thinking: An Arendtian Critique of Cooperative Learning." In *Hannah Arendt and Education: Renewing Our Common World*, edited by Mordechai Gordon, 201–24. Boulder, CO: Westview Press, 2001.

Elon, Amos. *The Pity of It All: A Portrait of the German-Jewish Epoch, 1743–1933*. New York: Picador, 2002.
Euben, Peter. "Politicizing the University and Other Clichés." In *Hannah Arendt and Education: Renewing Our Common World*, edited by Mordechai Gordon, 175–200. Boulder, CO: Westview Press, 2001.
Farias, Victor. *Heidegger and Nazism*. Edited by Joseph Margolis and Tom Rockmore. Philadelphia: Temple University Press, 1989.
Fichte, Johann Gottlieb. "Deduzierter Plan einer zu Berlin zu errichtenden höheren Lehranstalt, die in der gehöriger Verbindung mit einer Akademie der Wissenschaften stehe." In *Die Idee der deutschen Universität. Die fünf Grundschriften aus der Zeit ihrer Neubegründung durch klassischen Idealismus und romantischen Realismus*, edited by Ernst Anrich, 127–217. Darmstadt: Wissenschaftliche Buchgesellschaft, 1956.

———. *Addresses to the German Nation*. Translated by R. F. Jones and G. H. Turnbull. Chicago: The Open Court Publishing, 1922. Archive.org.
Foucault, Michel. "La philosophie analytique du povoir." In *Dits et écrits*, edited by Daniel Defert and François Ewald, vol. 3. Paris: Gallimard, 1994.

———. *Omnes et Singulatium: Towards a Criticism of 'Political Reason'*. https://tannerlectures.utah.edu/_documents/a-to-z/f/foucault81.pdf.

———. *Security, Territory, Population*. Lectures at the Collège de France, 1977–1978. Translated by Graham Burchell. New York: Palgrave Macmillan, 2007.

———. *Society Must Be Defended*. Lectures at the Collège de France, 1975–1976. Translated by David Macey. New York: Picador, 2003.

———. *The Birth of Biopolitics*. Lectures at the Collège de France, 1978–1979. Translated by Graham Burchell. New York: Picador, 2008.

———. *The History of Sexuality*, vol. 1. Translated by Robert Hurley. New York: Pantheon Books, 1978.
Giroux, Henry A. "What Might Education Mean after Abu Ghraib: Revisiting Adorno's Politics of Education." *Comparative Studies of South Asia, Africa and the Middle East* 24 (2004): 5–24.

———. *Neoliberalism's War on Higher Education*. Chicago: Haymarket Books, 2014.
Grunenberg, Antonia. *Martin Heidegger and Hannah Arendt: History of a Love*. Translated by Peg Birmingham, Kristina Lebedeva, and Elisabeth von Witzke Birmingham. Bloomington: Indiana University Press, 2017.
Habermas, Jürgen. "Die Idee der Universität—Lernprozesse." In *Die Idee der Universität. Versuch einer Standortbestimmung*, 139–73. Berlin-Heidelberg: Springer Verlag, 1988.

———. *The Philosophical Discourse of Modernity: Twelve Lectures*. Translated by Frederick Lawrence. Oxford: Blackwell Publishers 1998.
Heidegger, Martin. *Towards the Definition of Philosophy*. Translated by Ted Sadler. New York: Continuum, 2008.

———. *Plato's Sophist*. Translated by Richard Rojcewicz and André Schuwer. Bloomington: Indiana University Press, 1997.

———. "Arbeitsdienst und Universität." In *Reden und andere Zeugnisse eines Lebensweges 1910–1976*. Gesamtausgabe I Abt., Band 16. Frankfurt am Main: Vittorio Klostermann, 2000.

———. "German Students (November 3, 1933)." Translated by William S. Lewis. In *The Heidegger Controversy: A Critical Reader*, edited by Richard Wolin, 46–47. Cambridge, MA: The MIT Press, 1998.

———. "Labor Service and the Univerity (June 20, 1933)." In *The Heidegger Controversy: A Critical Reader*, edited by Richard Wolin, 42–43. Cambridge, MA: The MIT Press, 1998.

———. "The Rectorate 1933/34: Facts and Thoughts." Translated by Karsten Harris. *Review of Metaphysics* 38, no. 3 (1985): 481–502.

———. "The Self-Assertion of the German University." Translated by William S. Lewis. In *The Heidegger Controversy: A Critical Reader*, edited by Richard Wolin, 29–39. Cambridge, MA: The MIT Press, 1998.

———. "The Self-Assertion of the German University." Translated by Karsten Harris. *Review of Metaphysics* 38, no. 3 (1985): 470–80.

———. "Zum Semesterbeginn (3.11.1933)." In *Reden und andere Zeugnisse eines Lebensweges 1910–1976*. Gesamtausgabe I Abt., Band 16. Frankfurt am Main: Vittorio Klostermann, 2000.

———. "Zur philosophischen Orientierung für Akademiker." In *Reden und andere Zeugnisse eines Lebensweges 1910–1976*. Gesamtausgabe I Abt., Band 16. Frankfurt am Main: Vittorio Klostermann, 2000.

———. *Basic Writings*. Edited by David Farell Krell. Auckland: HarperCollins, 2008.

———. *Being and Time: A Translation of Sein und Zeit*. Translated by Joan Stambaugh. Albany: State University of New York Press, 1996.

———. *Der deutsche Idealismus (Fichte, Schelling, Hegel) und die philosophische Problemlage der Gegenwart*. Gesamtausgabe II Abt., Band 28. Frankfurt am Main: Vittorio Klostermann, 1997.

———. *Die Grundbegriffe der Metaphysik. Welt-Endlichkeit-Einsamkeit*. Gesamtausgabe II Abt., Band 29/30. Frankfurt am Main: Vittorio Klostermann, 1983.

———. *Die Grundprobleme der Phänomenologie*, II Abt., Band 24. Frankfurt am Main: Vittorio Klostermann, 1997.

———. *Die Metaphysik des deutschen Idealismus. Zur erneuten Auslegung von Schelling: Philosophische Untersuchungen über das Wesen der menschlichen Freiheit und die damit zusammenhängenden Gegenstände (1809)*. Gesamtausgabe II. Abt., Band 49. Frankfurt am Main: Vittorio Klostermann, 1991.

———. *Discourse on Thinking: A Translation of Gelassenheit*. Translated by John M. Anderson and E. Hans Freund. New York: Harper & Row Publishers, 1966.

———. *Einleitung in die Philosophie*. Gesamtausgabe Abt. II, Band 27. Frankfurt am Main: Vittorio Klostermann, 1996.

———. *History ot the Concept of Time*. Translated by Theodore Kisiel. Bloomington: Indiana University Press, 1985.

———. *Hölderlins Hymnen "Germanien" und "Der Rhein"*. Gesamtausgabe II Abt., Band 39. Frankfurt am Main: Vittorio Klostermann, 1999.

———. *Introduction to Metaphysics*. Translated by Gregory Fried and Richard Polt. New Haven, CT: Yale University Press, 2000.

---. *Logic and the Question Concerning the Essence of Language*. Translated by Wanda T. Gregory and Yvonne Unna. Albany: State University of New York Press, 2009.

---. *Logic. The Question of Truth*. Translated by Thomas Sheehan. Bloomington: Indiana University Press, 2010.

---. *Logik und die Frage nach der Sprache*. Gesamtausgabe II Abt., Band 38. Frankfurt am Main Vittorio Klostermann, 1998.

---. *Logik. Die Frage nach der Wahrheit*. Gesamtausgabe II Abt., Band 21. Frankfurt am Main: Vittorio Klostermann, 1976.

---. *Metaphysische Anfangsgründe der Logik im Ausgang von Leibniz*. Gesamtausgabe II Abt., Band 26. Frankfurt am Main: Vittorio Klostermann, 1978.

---. *Nietzsche, Volume I: Will to Power as Art*. Translated by David F. Krell. San Francisco: HarperCollins, 1991.

---. *Nietzsche, Volume III: Will to Power as Knowledge and as Metaphysics*. Translated by Joan Stambaugh, David F. Krell, and Frank A. Capuzzi. San Francisco: HarperCollins, 1991.

---. *Off the Beaten Track*. Translated by Julian Young and Kenneth Haynes. New York: Cambridge University Press, 2002.

---. *Pathmarks*. Edited by William McNeill. Translated by John van Buren et al. New York: Cambridge University Press, 1998.

---. *Philosophical and Political Writings*. Edited by Manfred Stassen. Translated by Manfred Stassen et al. New York: Continuum, 2003.

---. *Platon: Sophistes*. Gesamtausgabe, II abt., Band 19. Frankfurt am Main: Vittorio Klostermann, 1992.

---. *Ponderings II–VI (Black Notebooks 1931–1938)*. Translated by Richard Rojcewicz. Bloomington: Indiana University Press, 2016.

---. *Ponderings XII–XV (Black Notebooks 1939–1941)*. Translated by Richard Rojcewicz. Bloomington: Indiana University Press, 2017.

---. *Prolegomena zur Geschichte des Zeitbegriffs*. Gesamtausgabe II Abt., Band 20. Frankfurt am Main: Vittorio Klostermann, 1994.

---. *Question Concerning Technology and Other Essays*. Translated by William Lovitt. New York: Garland Publishing, 1977.

---. *Sein und Wahrheit*. Gesamtausgabe II Abt., Band 36/37. Frankfurt am Main: Vittorio Klostermann, 1978.

---. *Sein und Zeit*. Tübingen: Max Niemeyer Verlag, 2001.

---. *The Basic Problems of Phenomenology*. Translated by Albert Hofstadter. Bloomington: Indiana University Press, 1982.

---. *The Essence of Truth: On Plato's Cave Allegory and Theaetetus*. Translated by Ted Sadler. New York: Continuum, 2002.

---. *The Fundamental Concepts of Metaphysics: World, Finitude, Solitude*. Translated by William McNeill and Nicholas Walker. Bloomington: Indiana University Press, 1995.

---. *The Metaphysical Foundations of Logic*. Translated by Michael Heim. Bloomington: Indiana University Press, 1992.

———. *Überlegungen II–IV (Schwarze Hefte 1931–1938)*. Gesamtausgabe IV. Abt., Band 94. Frankfurt am Main: Vittorio Klostermann, 2014.

———. *Überlegungen XII–XV (Schwarze Hefte 1939–1941)*. Gesamtausgabe IV. Abt., Band 96. Frankfurt am Main: Vittorio Klostermann, 2014.

———. *Vom Wesen der Wahrheit. Zu Platons Höhlengleichnis und Theätet*. Gesamtausgabe II Abt., Band 34. Frankfurt am Main: Vittorio Klostermann, 1997.

———. *What Is Called Thinking?: A Translation of Was heisst Denken?* Translated by J. G. Gray. New York: Harper Perennial, 2004.

———. *Zur Bestimmung der Philosophie*. Gesamtausgabe II Abt., Band 56/57. Frankfurt am Main: Vittorio Klostermann, 1999.

Heidegger, Martin, and Elisabeth Blochmann. *Briefwechsel 1918–1969*. Marbach am Neckar: Deutsche Schillergesellschaft, 1990.

Heidegger, Martin, and Karl Jaspers. *The Heidegger-Jaspers Correspondence (1920–1963)*. Edited by Walter Biemel and Hans Saner. Translated by Gary E. Aylesworth. New York: Humanity Books, 2003.

Herder, Johann Gottfried. *Herders sämmtliche Werke* (Suphan), Band 6, 8, 24. Berlin: Weidmannsche Buchhandlung, 1883.

———. *Outlines of the Philosophy of the History of Man*. Translated by T. Churchill. New York: Bergman Publishers, 1800.

———. *Philosophical Writings*. Translated by Michael N. Forster. New York: Cambridge University Press, 2002.

———. *Another Philosophy of History and Selected Political Writings*. Translated by Ioannis D. Evrigenis and Daniel Pellerin. Indianapolis: Hackett Publishing Company, 2004.

———. *Werke in fünf Bänden*, Band 5. Berlin und Weimar: Aufbau Verlag, 1959.

Herodotus. *The History of Herodotus*. Translated by George Rawlinson. New York: The Tandy-Thomas Company, 1909. Archive.org.

Hinchmann, L. P., and S. K. Hinchmann. "In Heidegger's Shadow: Hannah Arendt's Phenomenological Humanism." *The Review of Politics* 2, no. 46 (1984): 183–211.

Hohendorf, Gerd. *Wilhelm von Humboldt (1767–1835)*, "Prospects: The Quarterly Review of Comparative Education" (Paris, Unesco: International Bureau of Education), XXIII, nos. 3–4 (1993): 613–23.

Homer. *The Odyssey*. Translated by Samuel Butler. classics.mit.edu.

Humboldt, Wilhelm. *The Sphere and Duties of Government (The Limits of State Action)*. Translated by Joseph Coulthard, A Project of Liberty Fund. http://oll.libertyfund.org/title/589.

———. *Werke in 5 Bänden,* Band I, *Schriften zur Anthropologie und Geschichte*. Darmstadt: Wissenschaftliche Buchgesellschaft, 1960.

———. *Werke in 5 Bänden, t*Band IV, *Schriften zur Politik und Bildungswesen*. Darmstadt: Wissenschaftliche Buchgesellschaft, 1964.

Jaeger, Werner. *Paideia: The Ideals of Greek Culture*, vol. 2. Translated by Gilbert Highet. Oxford: Blackwell, 1946.

Jones, Michael T. "Heidegger the Fox: Hannah Arendt's Hidden Dialogue." *New German Critique* 73 (1998): 164–92.

Kant, Immanuel. *Answer the Question: What Is Enlightenment?* Translated by Daniel F. Ferrer. Archive.org.
———. *Kritik of Judgment*. Translated by J. H. Bernard. New York: Macmillan, 1892. Archive.org.
Kisiel, Theodore. "The Demise of Being and Time: 1927–1930." Translated by Richard Polt. In *Heidegger's Being and Time: Critical Essays*, edited by Richard Polt. Oxford: Rowman & Littlefield, 2005.
Knoll, Joachim, and Horst Siebert. *Wilhelm von Humboldt. Politik und Bildung*. Heidelberg: Quelle & Meyer, 1969.
Koller, Hans-Christoph. *Bildung und Widerstreit. Zur Struktur biographischer Bildungsprozesse in der Postmoderne*. München: Wilhelm Fink Verlag, 1999.
Koopman, Colin. *Three Intellectual Histories of Modernity: Arendt, Blumenberg, Dewey*. Presented at the Canadian Political Science Association, June 2006, York, Ontario.
Kristeva, Julia. *Hannah Arendt*. Translated by Ross Guberman. New York: Columbia University Press, 2001.
Künzel, Reiner. "Politische Kontrolle und Finanzierung—die Zukunft staatlicher Steuerung." In *Mythos Humboldt—Vergangenheit und Zukunft der deutschen Universitäten*, edited by Mitchell Ash, 181–94. Wien: Böhlau, 1999.
Laertius, Diogenes. *Lives of Eminent Philosophers*, Greek and English. Translated by R. D. Hicks. London: Heinemann, 1972.
Lessing, Gotthold Ephraim. *Nathan the Wise*. Translated by Ellen Frothingham. New York: Leypold & Hold, 1871.
Lilla, Mark. *The Reckless Mind: Intellectuals in Politics*. New York: The New York Review of Books, 2001.
Lipman, Matthew, Ann Margaret Sharp, and Frederick S. Oscanyan. *Philosophy in the Classroom*. Philadelphia: Temple University Press, 1980.
Löwith, Karl. "Heidegger: Problem and Background of Existentialism." *Social Research* 15, no. 3 (1948): 345–69.
———. "My Last Meeting with Heidegger in Rome, 1936." In *The Heidegger Controversy: A Critical Reader*, edited by Richard Wolin, 140–43. Cambridge, MA: The MIT Press, 1998.
———. "The Political Implications of Heidegger's Existentialism." Translated by Richard Wolin and Melissa J. Cox. *New German Critique* 45 (1988): 117–34.
———. *My Life in Germany Before and After 1933: A Report*. Translated by Elisabeth King. Champaign: University of Illinois Press, 1994.
Lundgreen, Peter. "Mythos Humboldt in der Gegenwart: Lehre—Forschung—Selbstverwaltung." In *Mythos Humboldt—Vergangenheit und Zukunft der deutschen Universitäten*, edited by Mitchell Ash, 145–69. Wien: Böhlau, 1999.
MacIntyre, Alasdair. *After Virtue: A Study in Moral Theory*. Notre Dame, IN: University of Notre Dame Press, 2007.
Meyer-Abich, Hans-Joachim. "Die Universitäten und die deutsche politische Kultur der Gegenwart." In *Mythos Humboldt—Vergangenheit und Zukunft der deutschen Universitäten*, edited by Mitchell Ash, 23–40. Wien: Böhlau, 1999.

Newell, R. "Heidegger on Freedom and Community: Some Political Implications of His Early Thought." *The American Political Science Review* 78, no. 3 (1984): 775–84.

Nietzsche, Friedrich Wilhelm. *On the Future of Our Educational Institutions*. Translated by John McFarland. Archive.org.

Ott, Hugo. *Martin Heidegger. A Political Life*. Translated by Allan Blunden. New York: Basic Books, 1993.

Plato. *Plato's Complete Works*. Edited by J. M. Cooper. Translated by G. M. A. Grube et al. Indianapolis: Hackett, 1997.

———. *The Republic of Plato*. Translated by Francis Macdonald Cornford. Oxford: Clarendon Press, 1944.

———. *Werke in Acht Bänden. Griechisch und Deutsch*, Band 4, Πολτεία. Der Staat. Translated by Friedrich Schleieremacher. Darmstadt: Wissenschaftliche Buchgesellschaft, 1971.

Richter, Wilhelm. *Der Wandel des Bildungsgedankes. Die Bruder Humboldt, das Zeitalter der Bildung und die Gegenwart*. Berlin: Colloquium Verlag, 1971.

Rockmore, Tom. "Heidegger after Farias." *History of Philosophy Quarterly* 8, no. 1 (1991): 81–102.

Safranski, Rüdiger. *Ein Meister aus Deutschland. Heidegger und seine Zeit*. Frankfurt am Main: Fischer Verlag, 2006.

———. *Martin Heidegger: Between Good and Evil*. Translated by Ewald Osers. Cambridge, MA: Harvard University Press, 1998.

Schäfer, Alfred. *Das Bildungsproblem nach der humanistischen Illusion*. Weinheim: Deutscher Studien Verlag, 1996.

Schelling, Friedrich Wilhelm Joseph. "Vorlesungen über die Methode des akademischen Studiums." In *Die Idee der deutschen Universität. Die fünf Grundschriften aus der Zeit ihrer Neubegründung durch klassischen Idealismus und romantischen Realismus*, edited by Ernst Anrich, 3–123. Darmstadt: Wissenschaftliche Buchgesellschaft, 1956.

Schleiermacher, Friedrich Daniel. "Gelegentliche Gedanken über Universitäten in deutschem Sinn." In *Die Idee der deutschen Universität. Die fünf Grundschriften aus der Zeit ihrer Neubegründung durch klassischen Idealismus und romantischen Realismus*, edited by Ernst Anrich, 221–308. Darmstadt: Wissenschaftliche Buchgesellschaft, 1956.

Schmitt, Carl. *Political Theology: Four Chapters on the Concept of Sovereignty*. Translated by George Schwah. Chicago: The University of Chicago Press, 2005.

Schutz, Aaron. "Theory as Performative Pedagogy: Three Masks of Hannah Arendt." *Educational Theory* 2, no. 51 (2001): 127–50.

Senellart, Michael. "Course Context." Translated by Graham Burchell. In *Security, Territory, Population*, edited by Michel Foucault, 477–507. Lectures at the Collège de France, 1977–1978. New York: Palgrave Macmillan, 2007.

Sophocles. *Oedipus in Colonus*. Translated by Robin Bond. https://ir.canterbury.ac.nz/bitstream/handle.

Spengler, Oswald. *The Decline of the West: Form and Actuality*. Translated by Charles Francis Atkinson. New York: Alfred A. Knopf, 1926.

Spranger, Eduard. *Wilhelm von Humboldt und die Humanitätsidee*. Berlin: Reuther & Reichard, 1909.

———. *Wilhelm von Humboldt und die Reform des Bildungswesens*. Tübingen: Max Niemeyer Verlag, 1965.

Steiner, George. "Heidegger, Again." *Salmagundi* 82/83 (1989): 31–55.

Stern, Peter, and Jean Yarbrough. "Teaching: Hannah Arendt." *The American Scholar* 3, no. 47 (1978): 371–81.

Taminiaux, Jacques. *The Thracian Maid and the Professional Thinker: Arendt and Heidegger*. Translated by Michael Gendre. Albany: State University of New York Press, 1997.

Taubes, Jacob. *From Cult to Culture: Fragments toward a Critique of Historical Reason*. Palo Alto, CA: Stanford University Press, 2009.

Villa, Dana R. "The Banality of Philosophy." In *Hannah Arendt Twenty Years Later*, edited by Larry May and Jerome Kohn, 179–219. Cambridge, MA: The MIT Press, 1997.

———. *Arendt and Heidegger: The Fate of the Political*. Princeton, NJ: Princeton University Press, 1996.

Voegelin, Eric. *The Collected Works, v. 16, Order and History, v. III*. Columbia: University of Missouri Press, 2000.

Vollrath, Ernst. "Hannah Arendt und Martin Heidegger." In *Heidegger und die praktische Philosophie*, edited by Annemarie Gethmann-Siefert and Otto Pöggeler, 357–72. Frankfurt am Main: Suhrkamp, 1998.

Wagner, Hans-Josef. *Die Aktualität der strukturalen Bildungstheorie Humboldts*. Weinheim: Deutscher Studien Verlag, 1995.

Weber, Max. *Essays in Sociology*. Translated by H. H. Gert and C. Wright Mills. New York: Oxford University Press, 1946.

Weil, Hans. *Die Entstehung des deutschen Bildungsprinzips*. Bonn: H. Bouvier u. C. Verlag, 1967.

Wolin, Richard. *Heidegger's Children: Hannah Arendt, Karl Löwith, Hans Jonas and Herbert Marcuse*. Princeton, NJ: Princeton University Press, 2001.

———. *The Politics of Being: The Political Thought of Martin Heidegger*. New York: Columbia University Press, 1990.

Young-Bruehl, Elisabeth. *Hannah Arendt: For Love of the World*. New Haven, CT: Yale University Press, 2004.

Index

Abensour, Miguel, 27n76
academic freedom, 37, 38, 40, 41, 95, 203
action, 11, 12, 16, 17, 20, 21, 22, 31, 36, 37, 64, 73, 83, 86, 98, 101, 103, 104, 109, 111, 112, 114, 117, 118, 120, 121, 122, 123, 124, 125, 126, 132, 139, 142, 145, 147, 149, 150, 199, 201
Adorno, Theodor Wiesengrund, 82
Aeschylus, 41
Agamben, Giorgio, 155, 163–78, 179, 180
Alcibiades, 14, 195
aletheia, 5, 8, 9, 23, 96, 116, 191
alienation, 33, 35, 137, 138, 141, 142, 143, 144, 147, 148
Anaxagoras, 140
Anderson, John M., 207n19
Angst (*Angst*, Heidegger), 65, 66, 67, 68, 88, 89, 90, 94, 126, 146
animal laborans, 139, 168, 178
Anrich, Ernst, 52n35
anthropology, 23, 32, 34, 35, 68, 71, 85, 117, 156, 157, 158, 160, 167
anti-Semitism, 47, 97, 188
appearance, 5, 61, 64, 65, 116, 126, 131, 132, 139, 140, 142, 148, 151n2, 164, 191, 194, 196, 199, 201, 202

arche, 111, 112
archein, 125
Archimedes, 141
Aristotle, 59, 82, 90, 103, 109–29, 197
Ash, Mitchell, 52n29
assimilation, 29, 42–50, 51, 82
Atkinson, Charles Francis, 74n2
Attell, Kevin, 183n72
attunement (Heidegger), 66, 88, 89, 90, 94, 95, 112, 145
Augenblick, moment-of-vision (Heidegger), 71, 88, 91, 93, 114, 150
Augustine of Hippo
authenticity, xi, 10, 55–77, 79, 83, 91, 102, 112, 115, 121, 146, 153
authoritarianism, 99, 100
authoritarian rule, 20, 99, 100
authority, 19, 20, 24n5, 26n49, 26n61, 39, 60, 79, 82, 99, 100, 103, 104, 156, 157, 172, 177, 190
Aylesworth, Gary E., 105n20

Beiner, Ronald, 152n30
being-in-the-world, viii, 23, 62, 63, 64, 89, 133, 134
being thrown (*Geworfenheit*), 67, 70, 87, 145

225

being-towards-death (Heidegger), 66, 67, 70, 71, 88, 115, 126, 146, 156
being-with (*Mitsein*, Heidegger), 6, 63, 64, 67, 115, 144, 156
Benhabib, Seyla, x, xiiin13, 72, 76n58, 77n72, 126, 148
Benjamin, Walter, 69, 148
Benner, Dietrich, 53n58
Bernard, J. H., 209n60
Bernstein, Richard, xiiin14
Biemel, Walter, 105n20
Bildung, x, xi, 1, 4, 22–23, 24n17, 29–54, 55, 58, 83, 84, 95, 150, 153, 162, 203
biopolitics, 168, 175, 179
biopower, 168, 171, 172, 173, 176, 177, 178
bios theoretikos, 17, 113, 118
Birmingham, Peg, xiin12
Bismarck, Otto, 40
Blochmann, Elisabeth, 85, 105n18
Blücher, Heinrich, 151n11
Blumenberg, Hans, 152n40
Bond, Robin, 152n30
boredom (Heidegger), 88, 89, 90, 94
bourgeoisie, 44, 45, 46, 48, 49, 50, 171
Breaugh, Martin, 27n76
Burchell, Graham, 182n54, 210n85
Buren, John van
Bush, George W., 176
Butler, Samuel, 26n57

Capuzzi, Frank A., 104n11, 105n17
Cassirer, Ernst, 85
Cavarero, Adriana, 26n55
cave (Plato), 3–27, 53n47, 59, 65, 66, 73, 92, 93, 98, 133, 150, 160, 198
Chiesa, Lorenzo, 183n73
Christianity, 100, 173, 177
Churchill, T., 180n8
Clausewitz, Carl von, 169, 170
concentration camp, 165, 166, 174, 175
conscience, 48, 67, 68, 70, 72, 91, 92, 112, 187, 188, 196, 201

conscience (Heidegger), 67, 68, 70, 72, 91, 92, 112
Constantine, Peter, 151n11
contemplation, 8, 11, 13, 15, 20, 21, 68, 73, 92, 95, 102, 113, 114, 115, 116, 119, 120, 121, 122, 123, 124, 138, 139, 140, 141, 142, 147, 150, 151, 185, 190, 193, 194
Cooper, John Madison, 25n17
Copernicus, Nicolaus
Cornford, Francis Macdonald, 24n14
Coulthard, Joseph, 51n10
Cox, Melissa J., 76n65
Critias, 14, 195

Dante, Alighieri, 54n134
Dasein, 10, 23, 61, 62, 63, 66, 67, 68, 70, 75n12, 85, 87, 88, 89, 90, 91, 93, 94, 97, 98, 103, 112, 113, 114, 115, 116, 117, 120, 133, 134, 135, 145, 146, 155, 156, 157, 193
deconstruction, 5, 22, 58, 59, 60, 61, 67, 85, 90, 104, 115, 122, 123, 143, 146, 157, 191, 192
Defert, Daniel, 182n62
Descartes, 63, 101, 132–37, 142, 152n35
destiny (*Geschick*, Heidegger), 70, 71, 72, 93, 98
Dewey, John, 152n41
dialectics, 9, 13, 14, 15, 19, 35, 135, 170, 175, 194, 212
Diels, Hermann, 25n37
Dilthey, Wilhelm, 59, 72
Diogenes Laertios, 128n57
Dohm, Christian Wilhelm, 42, 46, 47
Dostoyevsky, Fiodor, 197
doxa, 13, 17, 116, 117
Duarte, Eduardo, 209n76

economy, political, 48, 173, 177
education, viii, x, xi, xii, 3, 4, 8, 13, 14, 15, 16, 20, 23, 25n17, 26n51, 29, 30, 31, 32, 33, 35, 36, 37, 38, 39, 40, 43, 44, 45, 46, 48, 49, 50,

55, 58, 59, 73, 79, 81, 83, 95, 96, 103, 104, 131, 132, 145, 150, 153, 154, 155–83, 202, 203, 204, 206, 209n77, 211, 212, 213
Eichmann, Adolf, 164, 176, 177, 187, 188, 189, 190, 196, 197, 200, 204, 205, 209n77, 210n79
Elisabeth, von Witzke Birmingham, xiin12
Elon, Amos, 53n48
energeia, 121
Engel, Amir
enlarged mentality, 149, 198, 199, 200, 205
Enlightenment, 30, 35, 36, 42, 43, 44, 46, 47, 82, 157, 161, 162, 163
episteme, 13, 111, 112, 114, 182
Erhardt, Ludwig, 205, 206
Euben, Peter, 209n76
eudaimonia, 115
everydayness (Heidegger), 10, 59, 61, 62, 63, 67, 70, 194
Evrigenis, Ioannis D., 181n11
Ewald, François, 182n62
existential philosophy, viii, ix, 77n65, 86

fabrication, 19, 20, 22, 64, 111, 122, 124, 125, 126, 138, 142, 147, 150, 157, 167, 168
falling prey (*Verfallen*, Heidegger), 67, 119
Farias, Victor, 57, 71, 72, 77n68
fate (*Schicksal*, Heidegger), 9, 70, 71, 98, 186
fear (*Furcht*, Heidegger), 14, 41, 46, 65, 66, 206
Feldman, Ron H., 53n54
Ferrer, Daniel F., 208n57
Fest, Joachim, 185
Fichte, Johann Gottlieb, 34, 37, 38, 39, 41, 54n69, 95
The First World War (WWI), 55, 71
Fornobert, Charlotte Elisheva, 54n79
Forster, Michael N., 181n10

Foucault, Michel, 155, 161, 163–78, 179, 182n60, 205, 206, 211
fourfold (Heidegger), 136, 137
Frederic the Great, 42
freedom, 1, 5, 21, 31, 32, 33, 34, 35, 36, 37, 38, 39, 40, 41, 50, 57, 66, 67, 68, 69, 79, 95, 125, 126, 131–52, 153, 157, 158, 177, 180, 198, 199, 200, 203, 205, 206
freedom, academic, 37, 38, 40, 41, 95, 203
Freund, E. Hans, 207n19
Fried, Gregory, 107n91
Frothingham, Ellen, 53n49
fundamental ontology, 1, 4, 70, 83, 85, 86, 89, 91, 92, 110, 114, 115, 118, 153

Gadamer, Hans-Georg, 72, 143
Galilei, Galileo, 141, 144
Gaus, Günter, 185
Gaye, R. K., 128n70
Gendre, Michael, 75n22
George, Stefan
Gert, H. H., 54n81
Gethmann-Siefert, Annemarie, xiiin14
Giroux, Henry A., 206, 210n89, 211
Goethe, Johann Wolfgang, 29, 42, 43
Gordon, Mordechai, 209n76
Gotthold, Ephraim Lessing, 42, 69
Gregory, Wanda T., 107n89
Gregory of Nazianzus, 173
Grimme, Adolf, 86
Grube, George Maximilian Antony, 25n17
Grunenberg, Antonia, xiin12, 79, 153, 154, 179, 212
Guberman, Ross, 180n4
guilt (Heidegger), 67, 91, 188, 202

Habermas, Jürgen, 40, 53n40, 91
Hardenberg, Karl August
Hardie, Robert Purves, 128n70
Hausner, Gideon, 187
Haynes, Kenneth, 151n13

228   *Index*

Heim, Michael, 105n24
Heller-Roazen, Daniel, 182n65, 183n76
Heraclitus, 94
Herder, Johann Gottfried, 29, 30, 31, 34, 42, 43, 51n5, 51n7, 53n50, 150, 155, 159–63, 179, 180, 180n7, 180n8, 181n10, 181n11
Herz, Henriette, 43
Heydrich, Reinhardt, 188, 210n79
Hicks, Robert Drew, 128n57
Highet, Gilbert, 24n1
Himmler, Heinrich, 188, 189, 210n79
Hinchman, Lewis P., xiiin14
Hinchman, Sandra K., xiiin14
Hitlerism, 71
Hobbes, Thomas, ix
Hofstadter, Albert, 24n15
Hohendorf, Gerd, 52n31
Hölderlin, Johann Christian Friedrich, 98, 191, 192
Homer, 16, 18, 26n57
homo sacer, 174, 175, 178
humanism, 23, 30, 31–35, 45, 46, 54n69
Humboldt, Wilhelm von, 29, 30, 31–42, 43, 44, 47, 51n9, 95, 203
Hurley, Robert, 181n43
Husserl, Edmund, 61, 86, 87, 110, 133, 134

the idea of, xi, 1, 3, 7, 15, 19, 20, 23, 27n66, 29–54, 55, 56, 57, 59, 61, 67, 68, 73, 82, 83, 84, 86, 90, 92–98, 120, 122, 134, 137, 140, 141, 142, 144, 156, 160, 161, 162, 163, 174, 190, 199, 203
ideology, 47, 57, 82, 97, 98, 165, 172, 187, 211
idle talk (Gerede, Heidegger), 64, 65, 66, 87, 116, 117, 118
inauthenticity, 10, 63, 64, 65, 66, 70, 71, 72, 92, 112, 116, 119, 120, 126
individuality, 31, 32, 34, 39, 70, 72, 79, 132, 153, 163
instrumental categories, 20, 65, 132, 147, 168

Jaeger, Werner, 3, 4, 23, 24n1, 26n49
Jaspers, Karl, ix, xiin5, 25n24, 58, 76n51, 86, 204
Jay, Martin, x, xiiin13
Jonas, Hans, 72
Jones, Michael, xiiin13
Jones, R. F., 54n69
Jowett, Benjamin, 128n67
judgement of taste, 198, 199, 200
judging (Arendt), 162, 186, 189, 190, 199, 200, 201
Judith, Ch. Stark, 76n51

Kant, Immanuel, 27n71, 33, 34, 38, 42, 60, 90, 149, 150, 157, 158, 190, 192, 194, 197, 198, 199, 200, 201
Kierkegaard, Søren, 101
Kimber, Rita, xiin5
Kimber, Robert, xiin5
King, Elisabeth, 74n7
Kisiel, Theodore, 74n11, 105n14
Kleist, Heinrich von, 47
Knoll, Joachim, 52n30
Kohler, Lotte, xiin5, 151n11
Kohn, Jerome, 53n54, 207n18
Koller, Hans-Christoph, 54n64
Koopman, Colin, 152n41
Kottman, Paul, 26n55
Krell, David Farell, 104n10, 104n11, 106n72, 152n24
Krieck, Ernst, 74n5, 100
Kristeva, Julia, 157, 180n4
Künzel, Rainer, 52n29

labor (Arendt), 138, 139, 147, 167, 168
Lawrence, Frederick, 106n54
Lebedeva, Kristina, xiin12
Leibniz, Gottfried Wilhelm, 34
Less, Avner
Lewis, William S., 53n44, 107n77, 107n81
liberalism, 31–35, 38, 40, 54n69
life, bare (Agamben), 174, 175, 176, 206
Lilla, Mark, xiin3

Lindley, Denver, 210n83
Lipman, Mathew, 209n76
Livy (Titus Livius Patavinus), 169
logos, 119
Lovitt, William, 208n29
Löwith, Karl, 56, 71, 74n7, 76–77n65, 91, 96
Ludz, Ursula, xiin1
Lundgreen, Peter, 52n33
Luxemburg, Rosa, 69

Macey, David, 182n44
Machiavelli, Niccolo, 126, 150, 159
MacIntyre, Alasdair, 126, 129n86
Mandarini, Matteo, 183n73
Marcuse, Herbert, 72
Margolis, Joseph, 77n68
Marx, Karl, 82, 101, 102, 138
masses, 17, 49, 50, 100, 143, 147, 164, 165, 166, 167, 168, 171, 172, 173, 189, 204
mass society, 143, 164, 165, 168
May, Larry, 207n18
McNeill, William, 75n12, 151n7
Mendelssohn, Moses, 42, 43, 47, 49
metaphysics, Western, 9, 11, 18, 58, 60, 84, 145, 157, 213
Meyer-Abich, Hans-Joachim, 53n42
Mills, C. Wright, 54n81
modern age, 97, 141, 147, 148, 150
modernity, 97, 141, 147, 148, 150
Montesquieu, Charles de, 150, 159
multispectrality, 137, 139, 140

Napoleon Bonaparte, 31, 36, 40, 44, 55
natality (Arendt), 72, 145, 156
nation, 32, 37, 38, 40, 41, 42, 43, 46, 49, 51, 54n69, 55, 57, 161, 169, 170, 171, 175, 176
nationalism, 46, 47, 91, 95
National Socialism, 71, 93, 97, 98
Nazism, ix, xii, 50, 77n65, 84, 91, 172, 173
neohumanism, 31–35, 36
neoliberalism, 206, 211

Newell, Waller R., 76n64
Newton, Isaac, 141
Nietzsche, Friedrich Wilhelm, ix, 18, 45, 84, 89, 100, 101, 102, 136, 158, 191
nihilism, 15, 71, 77n65, 195
Nordmann, Ingeborg
nothingness (Heidegger), 66, 67, 71, 85, 95, 116
nous, 111, 112, 119

oikos, 173, 177
ontic, 61, 68, 86, 134, 145
ontological difference, 7, 8, 10, 11, 16, 85, 86, 87, 93, 192
ontology, 1, 4, 57, 58, 59, 60, 61, 67, 70, 71, 73, 79, 83, 85, 86, 89, 91, 92, 99, 110, 114, 115, 116, 117, 118, 134, 153, 157, 177
ontotheology, 60
Oscanyan, Frederick S., 209n76
Osers, Oswald, 54n60
Ott, Hugo, 99, 106n69

paideia, xi, 1, 3–27, 42, 50, 55, 58, 83, 150, 153
parias
Parmenides of Elea, 116
parvenu, 48, 49
Pellerin, Daniel, 181n11
Pericles, 118, 126
persuasion, 13, 14, 19, 20, 165
Pestalozzi, Johann Heinrich, 44
phenomenology, 61, 65, 68, 86, 89, 157, 193
phenomenon, 5, 14, 15, 23, 29, 61, 66, 67, 69, 83, 85, 88, 89, 90, 100, 122, 125, 133, 147, 148, 151n2, 157, 160, 162, 182n60, 189, 192, 193, 194, 197
phronesis, 26n49, 111, 112, 113, 114, 115, 118, 119, 124
physis, 5, 135
Pickford, Henry W., 213n1

Plato, 1, 3–27, 50, 53n47, 55, 58, 59,
60, 65, 66, 68, 69, 73, 79, 80, 83,
84, 90, 92–98, 99, 101, 103, 110,
113, 115, 116, 118, 120, 121–26,
147, 150, 159, 190, 191, 192, 193,
194, 195, 196, 197
plurality of people, human, 17, 20, 68,
144, 147, 150, 153, 163, 168, 199
Pöggeler, Otto, xiiin14
poiesis, 20, 111, 112, 122, 123, 124,
125, 126, 192
polis, 11, 16, 18, 20, 64, 69, 116, 117,
118, 121, 123, 124, 148, 175, 177,
191, 194, 195, 197, 203
political philosophy, 11, 16, 20, 21, 22,
64, 69–73, 92, 103, 122, 123, 126,
159
Polt, Richard, 105n14, 107n91
Pontius, Pilate (Pilatus), 188
Popper, Karl Ramund
Power:
 administrative, 178;
 disciplinary, 168, 171;
 pastoral, 173, 177;
 sovereign, 159, 169, 171, 172, 174,
 177, 206
power of judgement, 139, 197
praxis, 16, 20, 111, 112, 113, 114, 115,
117, 119, 122, 123, 124, 125, 126,
147
presence-at-hand (*Vorhandenheit*,
Heidegger), 60
private sphere, 19, 21, 102, 131, 143,
167, 173
public opinion, 64, 65, 68, 70, 71, 89,
120
public sphere, 17, 64, 65, 67, 68, 69, 73,
98, 100, 102, 103, 126, 131, 139,
143, 144, 146, 147, 148, 149, 150,
156, 164, 167, 173, 177, 185

racism, 168, 169, 172
Rackham, H. A., 127n8
Rauscher, William
Rawlinson, George, 128n56

ready-to-hand (*Zuhandenheit*,
Heidegger), 62
Reeve,C. D. C., 25n17
Reif, Adalbert, 210n83
religion, 43, 82, 99, 101, 103, 104
resoluteness, 1, 67, 68, 71, 76n65, 97,
120, 126, 150
rhetoric, 13, 17, 20, 84, 91, 97, 100,
116, 118, 146, 204
Rhys, Roberts William, 128n40
Richard III, 196
Richter, Wilhelm, 53n57
rights, civil, 176
rights, human, 176, 211
Robert, M. Wallace, 128n40, 152n40
Rockmore, Tom, 77n68
Rojcewicz, Richard, 104n3, 105n22,
107n88
Ross, William David, 127n4
Rousseau, Jean Jacques, 30, 32

SA (*Sturmabteilung*), 96
Sadler, Ted, 24n3, 24n14, 74n8
Saner, Hans, 105n20, xiin5
Sartre, Jean-Paul, 72
Schäfer, Alfred, 52n22, 52n28
Schelling, Friedrich Wilhelm Joseph
von, 37, 38, 39, 52n36
Schleiermacher, Friedrich Daniel,
24n17, 37, 38, 39, 47, 52n38, 66,
96, 107n78
Schmitt, Carl, x, 77n65, 94, 100, 177,
182n63
Schraig, Calvin, xiin12
Schutz, Aaron, 158, 180n5
Schuwer, André, 104n3
Schwah, George, 182n63
Scott, Johanna V., 76n51
self-education, 20, 43
Senellart, Michael, 182n62
sensus communis, 199
Shakespeare, William, 197
Sharp, Margaret Ann, 209n76
Sheehan, Thomas, 24n4, 75n19
Shields, Andrew, xiin1

Siebert, Horst, 52n30
significance (*Bedeutsamkeit*, Heidegger), 62
Socrates, 11, 12, 13, 14, 15, 16, 21, 118, 122, 190, 192, 194, 195, 196, 197, 198, 200, 201, 202, 203
sophia, 111, 112, 113, 114, 115, 119
sophistic, 17, 118
sophistry, 65, 116, 118
Sophocles, 140
sovereignty, 37, 169, 170, 171, 172, 176, 177, 178, 206
Spengler, Oswald, 56, 57, 70, 89
Spinoza, Baruch, 197
Spranger, Eduard, 29, 51n2, 52n30
SS (*Schutzstaffel*), 187
Stambaugh, Joan, 75n23, 104n11, 127n5, 208n20
Stassen, Manfred
Steffens, Henrich
Stein, Heinrich Friedrich Karl
Stern, Peter, 210n77
Strauss, Leo, 72, 143

Taminiaux, Jacques, x, 75n22, 128n45
Taubes, Jacob, 54n79
techne, 111, 112, 114, 119, 122
telos, 66, 111, 112, 125
temporality (Heidegger), 66, 70, 71, 88, 115, 193
terror, 82, 165, 166, 167, 172
theology, 39, 59, 146, 156, 160, 177
the they (Heidegger), 63, 67, 69, 92, 103, 147, 190
thinking (Arendt), 22, 79, 98–103, 109, 119, 124, 158, 160, 163, 180, 185, 187, 189, 193, 194, 195, 198, 199, 202
thinking (Heidegger), 22, 84, 85, 122, 134, 190, 191, 193, 194
thinking, calculative, 97, 190–91
The Third Reich, 92, 98, 164, 187, 200
Tillich, Paul, xiin12
tool (*Zeug*, Heidegger), 62

totalitarianism, xii, 22, 79, 82, 99, 100, 103, 153, 154, 157, 164, 165, 166, 167, 168, 175, 201, 212
total relevance (*Bewandtnisganzheit*, Heidegger), 62
tradition (general), 82, 83, 102
tradition of political philosophy, 11, 22, 122
tradition of political thought, 11, 16, 19, 59, 82, 92, 101, 102, 104, 123, 147
tradition philosophical, viii, 1, 11, 22, 57, 58, 59, 73, 82, 90, 102, 126, 146, 147, 150, 158, 190, 193
transcendentalism, 85, 193
truth, 5, 6, 8, 9, 11, 13, 14, 16, 19, 21, 23, 25n24, 39, 57, 59, 64, 94, 96, 100, 101, 102, 111, 112, 114, 115, 116, 117, 118, 119, 120, 135, 136, 139, 141, 142, 144, 160, 161, 162, 169, 185, 186, 191, 197, 205
Turnbull, G. H., 54n69
tyranny, 14, 99, 100, 157, 169

unhiddennes, 5, 6, 7, 8, 9, 135, 139
university, 10, 29, 31, 35–42, 44, 45, 50, 51, 55, 56, 57, 83, 87, 88, 92–98, 170, 186, 201-7
Unna, Yvonne, 107n89

values, 6, 12, 22, 23, 26n49, 50, 84, 96, 101, 124, 134, 158, 209
Varnhagen, Rahel, 47, 148, 159
Villa, Dana Richard, x, 122, 123, 190
violence, 6, 14, 18, 19, 20, 118, 174, 210n89
vita activa, vii, 21, 65, 102, 142
vita contemplativa, 21, 65, 102, 140, 142
Voegelin, Eric, 27, 82
Volk, 41, 71, 92, 93, 97
Vollrath, Ernst, xiiin14
Voltaire (François-Marie Arouet), 161

Wagner, Hans-Josef, 52n25

Walker, Nicholas, 75
Weber, Max, 50, 54n81, 56, 57, 70, 74n12
Weil, Hans, 51n1, 180n7
White, P. Nicholas, 127n29, 128n38
willing (Arendt), 186
Wolff, Christian
Wolin, Richard, x, xiiin13, 57, 71, 75n13, 76n65, 210n79
work (Arendt), ix, 58, 99, 134, 138, 149, 155, 158, 159, 167
work of art, 135, 137, 138, 139
The world (Arendt), 17, 63, 79, 121, 125, 126, 132, 137–43, 144, 146, 202

worldliness (Heidegger), 132, 134, 136, 137, 139
world-view, 57
World War II (WWII), 99, 209n67

Yarbrough, Jean, 210n77
Yorck von Wartenburg, Paul
Young, Julian, 151n13
Young-ah, Gottlieb Susannah, 180n7
Young-Bruehl, Elisabeth, 58, 159

zoon logon echon, 117, 161
zoon politicon, 117

About the Author

Paulina Sosnowska, PhD, is assistant professor at the University of Warsaw, Faculty of Education. Her research interests include philosophy of politics, with a focus on the problems of power and totalitarianism, philosophy of education, and German philosophy, especially phenomenology and hermeneutics. She is also an academic translator from German and English to Polish, with published works ranging from Immanuel Kant to Hans-Georg Gadamer, Karl Löwith, and Leo Strauss. Her recent relevant publications include the articles "Between the Continuity and the Break-up: What's Left of *Bildung*," *Modern Culture* 1, no. 99 (2018); "'Still the Same: The Omission of People': Hannah Arendt and Carl Schmitt," *Kronos* 3, no. 42 (2017); "Academic Freedom and the Ethical Value of Thinking," *Pedagogical Quarterly* 2, no. 244 (2017) (in English); and books *The Philosophy of Education in the Perspective of Heideggerian Ontological Difference* (Warsaw, 2009); *Arendt and Heidegger: The Pedagogical Promise of Philosophy* (Cracow, 2015).

www.ingramcontent.com/pod-product-compliance
Lightning Source LLC
Chambersburg PA
CBHW050902300426
44111CB00010B/1346